# Essential
# DATES

# Essential
# DATES

## *A TIMELINE OF NEW ZEALAND HISTORY*

## Alison Dench

RANDOM HOUSE
NEW ZEALAND

National Library of New Zealand Cataloguing-in-Publication Data

Dench, Alison.
Essential dates : milestones in New Zealand history / Alison
Dench.
Includes index.
ISBN 1-86941-689-9
1. New Zealand—History. I. Title.
993—dc 22

A RANDOM HOUSE BOOK
published by
Random House New Zealand
18 Poland Road, Glenfield, Auckland, New Zealand

www.randomhouse.co.nz

First published 2005

ISBN: 1 86941 689 9

Design: Grace Design, Auckland
Index : Diane Lowther
Cover illustration: Top: Mt Egmont, 1873. John Barr Clarke, neg no. B.041107,
Te Papa Tongarewa. Bottom: Rainbow Warrior, 1985. Gil Hanly
Internal illustrations: Alexander Turnbull Library, Wellington
Cover design: Grace Design, Auckland
Printed in China by Bookbuilders

# Contents

Compiling a chronology of a country's history is a daunting, some might say foolhardy, task to embark upon. There is such a strong emphasis on verifiable facts, rather than analysis, that traps for the researcher await in every dark corner of the library.

*Essential Dates* examines New Zealand's human history as a simple sequence of events, including firsts and lasts of every description, as well as political, cultural, sporting and technological turning points. It cannot possibly be comprehensive because, apart from the prehistory section, the only happenings included are those for which a precise date down to the day can be found. Unfortunately this means great swathes of Maori history, including the wars and mass migrations of the early 19th century, are not fully covered just because no one wrote down exactly when they took place.

Some of the dates given in this book are different from those commonly accepted. Even our finest historians have occasionally recorded incorrect details or have fallen victim to typographical errors, and I have found that if an incorrect date is repeated often enough it eventually becomes established as 'right'. In *Essential Dates* I have looked at the work of historians and other experts and matched it with contemporary sources where possible to clean up mistakes that have been perpetuated.

I have not tried to interpret events or determine their relative importance. *Essential Dates* is unabashedly about the who, when, what and where but not necessarily the how or the why. I hope it's a useful reference work but I also hope it's a fun read.

Alison Dench
May 13, 2005

7

# New Zealand's story begins
# Prehistory to 1813

**The human history** of the Pacific region began as many as 5000 years ago when Asian seafarers explored the area. Over the millennia, as great civilisations came and went in the Middle East, China, Europe and the Americas, the way of life of these early Polynesians changed little as they criss-crossed the ocean in search of islands on which to settle. While Maori were making New Zealand their home in the 13th century, the Mongol empire stretched all the way to Egypt. When the first Europeans arrived in New Zealand in 1642 the Renaissance was over and the first English civil war had just begun. By the time James Cook embarked on his first expedition to the Pacific, Catherine the Great was ruling Russia, the industrial revolution was under way and life was about to be turned upside down for the indigenous people of New Zealand.

| | |
|---|---|
| 6000 to 4000 years ago | A seafaring people leaves south-east Asia to start to settle islands in the Pacific Ocean. They are the distant ancestors of today's Polynesian people. |
| 3000 years ago | Early Polynesians reach Tonga and Samoa, where they will spend a thousand years consolidating the culture and developing the Austronesian language that is the predecessor of New Zealand Maori. They have brought with them pigs, dogs, rats, fowls, taro, yam, gourds, bananas, breadfruit, pandanus, sugar cane and paper mulberry, and possibly coconut palm. |
| 2200 years ago | Polynesians migrate from central Polynesia to east Polynesia, including the Society Islands and the Marquesas. They most likely also make return trips to South America, where they discover the kumara and possibly leave behind the coconut palm. |
| 2000 years ago | The kiore may have become established in New Zealand, according to radiocarbon dating of bones. This Polynesian rat may have come with an early human landing, either visitors or migrants who did not survive long in New Zealand's more challenging environment. |
| 1250 | New Zealand's founding population, including at least 70 women, has arrived from east Polynesia. They have come in outrigger canoes with sails, using deliberate navigation. Within 250 years some descendants will move on to the Chatham Islands. |
| 1400 | Moa and other big game birds have become extinct through over-hunting, and seals and sea lions are severely depleted. |
| 1595 | Pukapuka (in the island group later named the Cook Islands) is found by Spanish explorer Alvaro de Mendaña and named *San Bernardo*. |
| 1600 | The cultivation of karaka, cabbage tree and ferns has probably begun. |

# 1642

| | |
|---|---|
| August 1 | The governor-general and council of the Dutch East India Company resolve to send an expedition into the Pacific. |
| August 14 | Dutch navigator Abel Tasman sails from Batavia (present-day Jakarta) with the *Heemskerck* and the *Zeehaen*. He has instructions from the Dutch East India Company to explore the South Pacific for trading opportunities. |
| December 13 | Having visited Mauritius and found Tasmania (which he has called Van Diemen's Land), Tasman sights the west coast of Te Wai Pounamu (the South Island). |
| December 18 | The *Heemskerck* and the *Zeehaen* anchor in Taitapu (now called Golden Bay) and are approached by two canoes of curious Ngati Tumata people. |
| December 19 | A Ngati Tumata canoe rams the *Zeehaen's* cockboat and its occupants set upon the crew, killing four of them and taking one of the bodies ashore. The Dutch ships depart in haste, and the bay is named Murderers' Bay. |

**Ngati Tumata prepare to attack the *Zeehaen's* cockboat on December 19, 1642.**
**This depiction is by Isaac Gilsemans, who accompanied Abel Tasman.**

| | |
|---|---|
| December 26 | The Dutch vessels leave their anchorage off the island now called D'Urville and head north. |
| December 27 | The Dutch ships pass Cape Egmont, which Tasman names Cape Peter Boreel. Mt Taranaki, concealed by mist, remains unseen. |
| December 28 | Mt Karioi, on the Waikato coast, is sighted. |

## 1643

| | |
|---|---|
| January 4 | Tasman names Cape Maria van Diemen, at the northern tip of the North Island, after the wife of the governor-general of the Dutch East India Company. |
| January 5 | A pinnace and cockboat investigate Manawa Tawhi (which Tasman has named Three Kings) looking for water, but stay away when the islands are found to be inhabited by what appear to be giants. |
| January 6 | Tasman's expedition leaves New Zealand waters without having set foot on land. Tasman has called his discovery Staten Landt, but it will soon be renamed Nieuw Zeeland or Zeelandia Nova. Tasman's negative reports of New Zealand will deter explorers and traders for more than a century. |
| June 15 | The *Heemskerck* and the *Zeehaen* arrive back in Batavia. Tasman has found Tasmania, New Zealand and some of the islands of the Tonga and Fiji groups. |

## 1765

| | |
|---|---|
| June 24 | Commodore John Byron of HMS *Dolphin* becomes the first known European to find one of the Tokelau atolls — Atafu, which he names Duke of York's Island. |

## 1768

| | |
|---|---|
| August 26 | HMS *Endeavour*, commanded by Lieutenant James Cook RN, departs Plymouth for the Pacific Ocean to observe the transit of Venus in 1769. Among those on board are |

astronomer Charles Green and botanists Joseph Banks and
Daniel Solander.

## 1769

| | |
|---|---|
| June 2 | Jean-François-Marie de Surville leaves Pondicherry in India with the French-Indian vessel *St Jean-Baptiste*. He is on a trading expedition looking for rich lands in the Pacific. |
| June 3 | James Cook, Daniel Solander and Charles Green of the *Endeavour* observe the transit of Venus from Tahiti. |
| September 24 | Seaweed is seen from the *Endeavour*, giving the promise of land. |
| October 6 | Nicholas Young, the surgeon's boy on the *Endeavour,* is the first to sight the North Island of New Zealand. Cook will later name Young Nicks Head in his honour. |
| October 8 | The Rongowhakaata people get their first sight of the *Endeavour*, some believing it to be an island, others a giant bird. Cook, Solander and Banks go ashore on the banks of the Turanganui River, where a crew member shoots dead Te Maro of Ngati Oneone. It is the first of many encounters between Cook's men and the people of the east coast of the North Island. |
| October 9 | The crew of the *Endeavour* kill more Maori and take three prisoner. Despite their reluctance to go, the captives will be put ashore the next day. |
| October 11 | The *Endeavour* sails south from what Cook has named Poverty Bay 'because it afforded us no one thing we wanted'. |
| October 15 | Maori attempt to kidnap Tupaia, a Tahitian servant from the *Endeavour*. The incident inspires Cook to name Cape Kidnappers. |
| October 16 | Cook turns the *Endeavour* northwards at Cape Turnagain (Poroporo). |

| | |
|---|---|
| November 9 | Cook and Green observe the transit of Mercury at what will later be named Cooks Beach. Te Whanganui-a-Hei will be named Mercury Bay to mark the event. |
| November 15 | At Mercury Bay the British colours are flown for the first time in New Zealand, and Cook claims the place in the name of the king. |
| November 20 | Cook, Banks, Solander and Tupaia row about 20 km up the Waihou River (which Cook calls the Thames) as far as Hikutaia. It is the farthest inland Cook will go on any of his visits to New Zealand. |
| November 26 | The *Endeavour* passes Cape Brett (Rakaumangamanga) and enters the Bay of Islands. Cook finds the bay to be heavily populated. |
| December 12 | Surville sees the west coast of the North Island from the *St Jean-Baptiste*. |
| December 15 | The *Endeavour* sights the northernmost part of New Zealand. During his exploration of the east coast of the North Island, Cook has had many dealings with Maori, some violent and some more encouraging. |
| December 16 | The *Endeavour* and the *St Jean-Baptiste* pass in a gale off North Cape, each unaware of the other's presence. |
| December 17 | Eight days after the *Endeavour* has passed there, the *St Jean-Baptiste* limps into Doubtless Bay (Tokerau), which Surville names Lauriston Bay. The ship has been damaged and the crew is diseased, emaciated and dispirited. |
| December 18 | Maori visit the *St Jean-Baptiste* in canoes, then Surville goes ashore for the first time. Over the following days, relations between crew and Maori will be marked by misunderstandings and tension. |
| December 25 | The *Endeavour* spends Christmas off Three Kings Islands. |
| December 25 | Probable date of the first Christian service in New Zealand |

waters. It is likely that on this day chaplain Paul-Antoine Léonard de Villefeix celebrates a Christmas mass on the *St Jean-Baptiste*, and it is also possible he led a service the night before, on Christmas Eve.

| | |
|---|---|
| December 27 | More than 30 visiting sailors are marooned onshore overnight when a gale strikes. The *St Jean-Baptiste* loses three anchors and a yawl. |
| December 30 | Cook sights Cape Maria van Diemen. |
| December 31 | After Surville discovers a lost yawl has been taken by Maori, he obtains revenge by destroying a canoe and fishing nets, setting fire to food stores and dozens of buildings — and kidnapping a man, Ranginui of Te Patupo. The *St Jean-Baptiste* leaves New Zealand the same day. |

## 1770

| | |
|---|---|
| January 10 | Mt Taranaki is first sighted by Cook. He will later name it Mt Egmont. |
| January 15 | The *Endeavour* enters Totaranui, which Cook calls Queen Charlotte Sound, and anchors in the 'very snug' Ship Cove (Meretoto). Cook has completed his exploration of the west coast of the North Island, but because of dangerous onshore winds he has never come very close to land. |
| January 16 | Maori in Queen Charlotte Sound confirm to Cook that they eat human flesh, trading a human bone with tooth marks on it. Cook is shocked by this first convincing evidence of cannibalism. |
| January 22 | Cook Strait, previously thought to be a bay, is identified when Cook climbs to a viewpoint on the island of Arapaoa. It becomes apparent to the expedition's leader, if not his officers, that the North Island is unlikely to be part of a great southern continent. |
| January 31 | The Union Jack is flown high on Motuara, in Queen Charlotte Sound, and the land nearby claimed as a British possession. |

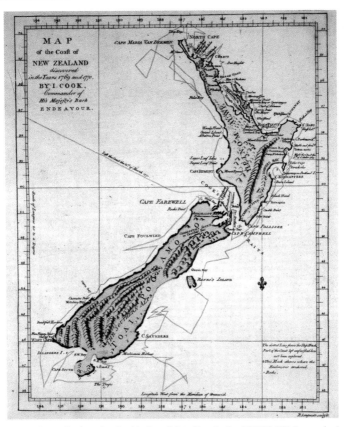

The map James Cook made after his first visit to New Zealand (1769–70) is amazingly accurate, even if Banks Peninsula is shown as an island and Stewart Island as part of the mainland.

| February 5 | Having been replenished with wood, water and food, the *Endeavour* leaves Ship Cove and heads north again. |
| --- | --- |
| February 9 | The *Endeavour* comes to Cape Turnagain. Having proved that the ship has circumnavigated the North Island, the captain turns it southwards again to explore the land south of Cook Strait. |
| February 17 | Mistaking Banks Peninsula for an island, Cook names it Banks Island. |

| March 9 | South Cape, the southernmost point of Rakiura (later named Stewart Island), is sighted. |
| March 13 | After trying and failing to enter Tamatea at twilight, Cook names it Dusky Bay. |
| March 24 | Ranginui dies of scurvy on board the *St Jean-Baptiste*. After nearly three months at sea the vessel is within sight of the Juan Fernandez Islands, off Chile. |
| March 26 | Having sailed around the South Island and Rakiura (Stewart Island) without the crew going ashore, the *Endeavour* puts in at Admiralty Bay in the Marlborough Sounds. |
| March 31 | Restocked with water and wood, the *Endeavour* leaves Admiralty Bay and heads west, home to England. Those on board have established mutual respect with the indigenous people, albeit based on bravado and intimidation. They have mapped the coastline with amazing accuracy and found many new species of plants and animals. |

## 1771

| July 13 | The *Endeavour* anchors off Kent at the conclusion of Cook's first great voyage. |

## 1772

| March 25 | Captain Marc-Joseph Marion du Fresne, in command of the *Mascarin* and the *Marquis de Castries*, sights the west coast of the North Island. The French vessels, searching for the great southern continent Binot de Gonneville claimed to have found more than 250 years earlier, need supplies. |
| April 12 | The *Mascarin* and the *Marquis de Castries* explore Three Kings Islands. |
| April 16 | Marion du Fresne's vessels anchor in Kapowairua (Spirits Bay), only to be driven out again by squalls the following day, leaving behind five anchors. |

| | |
|---|---|
| May 3 | Off Rakaumangamanga (Cape Brett or, as the French call it, Cap Quarré), more than 350 Maori, including chief Te Kuri, board the *Mascarin* and the *Marquis de Castries* over the course of a day. Their gifts of fish and kumara are reciprocated with small items and ships' biscuits. |
| May 4 | The French vessels enter the Bay of Islands. |
| May 12 | Marion du Fresne orders a camp to be made on Moturua (Ile Marion) for use as a hospital for scurvied crew members. The establishment of three onshore camps will result in the first extended contact between Maori and Pakeha. |
| June 7 | Despite attempts by Ngati Pou to stop him, Marion du Fresne fishes in Opunga Bay. This is deeply offensive to Te Kuri, who has placed a tapu because of earlier drownings there. |
| June 8 | High on Moturua, Marion du Fresne is fêted in a Maori ceremony. Later, Ngati Pou take items from a guardhouse, and in revenge the French will burn a recently abandoned village and tie a Ngati Pou chief to a stake. These events mark the end of a period of peaceful interaction between Maori and Pakeha. |
| June 12 | Marion du Fresne and 15 of his men leave the *Mascarin* in the company of Te Kuri to go fishing. The men will not be seen alive again by their compatriots. |
| June 13 | Twelve members of a French woodcutting party are attacked at Orokawa Bay, and only one escapes alive. Later, Te Kuri is shot by French marksmen after at least 1000 warriors surround the hospital camp. |
| June 14 | Twenty-seven Frenchmen launch an assault on Paeroa pa on Moturua. They will claim to have killed more than 200 Maori as they fight or attempt to flee. The pa is burnt to the ground. |
| July 12 | Officers of the *Mascarin* and the *Marquis de Castries* claim possession of New Zealand in the name of Louis XV and bury documentation of the claim on Moturua. |

| | |
|---|---|
| July 13 | As soon as repair work is complete the *Mascarin* and the *Marquis de Castries* depart the Bay of Islands for Mauritius via Manila. The last five weeks of their stay have been tense and frequently violent. |
| July 13 | A year to the day after returning from his first voyage, Captain James Cook leaves Plymouth to circumnavigate the globe in the high southern latitudes and explore the Pacific Ocean. He is in command of HMS *Resolution*, and sails with Tobias Furneaux in command of HMS *Adventure*. |

# 1773

| | |
|---|---|
| January 17 | The *Resolution* and the *Adventure* become the first ships to cross the Antarctic Circle. |
| February 8 | The *Resolution* and the *Adventure* lose sight of each other in fog and become separated. |
| March 25 | Cook and the *Resolution* sight New Zealand after four months at sea without touching — or even seeing — land. |
| March 26 | The *Resolution* puts in to Dusky Sound. |
| March 27 | Cook's crew begins brewing New Zealand's first batch of beer, from rimu branches, molasses, 'inspissated juice of wort' and yeast. |
| March 28 | Maori in canoes approach the *Resolution* in Dusky Sound. |
| April 2 | Having explored the coast of Tasmania, Furneaux and the *Adventure* catch a first glimpse of the west coast of the South Island. |
| April 6 | Cook first spends time with one of the Maori families of Dusky Sound. |
| April 7 | The *Adventure* anchors at Ship Cove in Queen Charlotte Sound to await a planned rendezvous with the *Resolution*. |

**An engraving of an image by expedition artist William Hodges shows the Maori family Cook met in Dusky Sound on April 6, 1773.**

| | |
|---|---|
| April 9 | Local people make their first contact with the *Adventure* in Queen Charlotte Sound. |
| May 11 | After more than a month spent exploring the sound and making contact with local Maori, Cook and the *Resolution* leave Dusky Sound and head north. |
| May 18 | The *Resolution* meets up with the *Adventure* at Ship Cove. |
| May 20 | Cook releases a ram and a ewe, the first sheep in New Zealand, but they will die within three days. |
| June 7 | The *Resolution* and the *Adventure* depart Queen Charlotte Sound for the Society Islands. |
| September 23 | Cook finds and names the Hervey Islands in the Cook group. |
| October 21 | On their return from an exploration of the South Pacific, Cook and Furneaux sight Table Cape on the Mahia Peninsula. |
| November 3 | Having earlier lost sight of the *Adventure* in a storm, the *Resolution* anchors in Ship Cove, the designated meeting place in case of separation. |

| | |
|---|---|
| November 9 | The *Adventure* anchors in Tolaga Bay (Uawa) after being driven off the coast. |
| November 25 | Giving up hope of meeting the *Adventure*, Cook and the *Resolution* leave Ship Cove to explore the high southern latitudes of the Pacific Ocean. |
| November 30 | The *Adventure* reaches Queen Charlotte Sound. |
| December 17 | Ten of the crew of the *Adventure* are killed in a dispute with Maori at Grass Cove, Queen Charlotte Sound. They are then dismembered and eaten. |
| December 23 | The *Adventure* leaves New Zealand for England via Cape Horn and the Cape of Good Hope. |

## 1774

| | |
|---|---|
| June 16 | Palmerston Island in the Cook group is found by Cook and the *Resolution*. |
| June 20 | Cook finds Niue, which he calls Savage Island after he is met with a particularly spirited challenge by the inhabitants. |
| July 14 | Furneaux and the *Adventure* arrive back in England at Spithead. |
| October 17 | Returning to New Zealand once more, Cook sights Mt Egmont (Taranaki). |
| October 19 | The *Resolution* is moored in Ship Cove, Queen Charlotte Sound. Evidence is discovered that the *Adventure* has visited. |
| November 10 | The *Resolution* leaves Queen Charlotte Sound to complete the circumnavigation of the globe. |

## 1775

| | |
|---|---|
| July 30 | Cook arrives at Spithead at the conclusion of his second voyage. The *Resolution* has been away for more than three |

years, and Cook has demonstrated there is no great southern continent.

## 1776

| | |
|---|---|
| July 12 | The *Resolution* departs Plymouth on Cook's third Pacific voyage. HMS *Discovery* (Captain Charles Clerke) will follow later. |

## 1777

| | |
|---|---|
| February 12 | The *Resolution* and the *Discovery* anchor in Ship Cove, Queen Charlotte Sound, to get supplies. |
| February 26 | Cook makes his final departure from Queen Charlotte Sound. With him on board the *Resolution* are local man Te Weherua and the boy Koa, who have agreed to travel as the Tahitian interpreter Omai's companions. |
| March 29 | Cook finds Mangaia in the Cook Islands. |
| March 31 | The British explorers find Atiu and Takutea in the Cook Islands. |
| November 2 | Cook leaves Te Weherua and Koa — against their wishes — in the Society Islands. They are the first New Zealanders to return to island Polynesia in perhaps 400 years. |

## 1779

| | |
|---|---|
| February 14 | Captain James Cook is killed at Kealakekua Bay, Hawaii. He is 50 years old. |

## 1788

| | |
|---|---|
| January 26 | The 'First Fleet' of convict transports drops anchor in Port Jackson (now Sydney, Australia), bringing the Pakeha world very much closer. New Zealand has been rejected as a location for the penal colony since the incident at Grass Cove in 1773. |

| March 6 | At Norfolk Island, newly appointed superintendent Philip Gidley King lands with convicts from the armed tender *Supply* to establish a penal colony. The island will become a staging post between Australia and New Zealand. |
| September 19 | The Bounty Islands, south-east of New Zealand, are found and named by Captain William Bligh of HMS *Bounty*. |

## 1791

| June 12 | Nukunonu in the Tokelau Islands is found by Captain Edward Edwards of HMS *Pandora*. He names it Duke of Clarence's Island. |
| November 2 | The *Discovery* (Captain George Vancouver) and the *Chatham* (Lieutenant William Broughton) put in at Dusky Sound for supplies. |
| November 22 | The *Discovery* and the *Chatham* leave Dusky Sound, having stocked up with wood for fuel, timber for spars, salted fish and spruce beer. |
| November 29 | Lieutenant Broughton finds Rekohu (Chatham Island). He goes ashore and tries to barter with a group of Moriori men. After a misunderstanding, local man Tamakaroro is shot and killed. A later council of all Moriori will decide that in future visitors shall be greeted with an emblem of peace, and conflict is to be resolved without violence. |

## 1792

| November 6 | The *Britannia* (Captain William Raven) anchors in Facile Harbour, Dusky Sound. |
| November 14 | In Dusky Sound, construction begins on the first European-style house in New Zealand. Built to accommodate a sealing gang, it will be completed by the end of the month. |
| December 1 | The *Britannia* departs Dusky Sound. Left behind is a party of men with supplies for 12 months and the materials to build a small vessel. Under the command of William Leith, they |

will operate New Zealand's first commercial sealing operation.

## 1793

| | |
|---|---|
| February 25 | The Italian explorer Alessandro Malaspina, with the Spanish corvettes *Descubierta* and *Atrevida,* arrives at Doubtful Sound. During a brief visit an armed boat is sent to chart the sound. |
| March 11 | Antoine-Raymond-Joseph de Bruni d'Entrecasteaux, with the *Recherche* and the *Espérance*, comes to Three Kings Islands. He is searching the Pacific for the missing French navigator La Pérouse. |
| March 15 | Admiral d'Entrecasteaux finds Espérance Rock in the Kermadec Islands. Over the next few days he will also find and name Raoul Island and Recherche Island (now Sunday Island). |
| April 24 | Tuki and Huru arrive in Norfolk Island on the *Shah Hormuzear*, having been kidnapped from Northland by Lieutenant Hanson of HMS *Daedalus.* At the request of lieutenant-governor Philip King, they have been brought to the penal colony (via a brief stop in Sydney) to teach flax dressing to convicts. However, they are able to pass on all they know very quickly — being high-born men they know little of this women's work. |
| September 27 | Captain Raven in the *Britannia* returns to Dusky Sound. All except one of the sealing party landed 10 months earlier are in good health but they have collected only about 4500 seal skins. Fearing they will never be picked up, the sealers have nearly finished building a boat. |
| November 8 | The *Britannia* leaves Norfolk Island for New Zealand having been commandeered by the lieutenant-governor, Philip King. Travelling with King and the Rev. James Bain are Tuki and Huru, who have formed a friendship with the lieutenant-governor's family. |

| | |
|---|---|
| November 13 | Tuki and Huru leave the *Britannia* at North Cape. They take with them livestock, seed, food and hardware, and among the items King receives in return are two pounamu mere. |

## 1794

| | |
|---|---|
| November 20 | The snow *Fancy* (Captain Thomas Dell) sails into Hauraki, to a friendly reception from Maori. |

## 1795

| | |
|---|---|
| March 15 | The *Fancy* returns to Sydney. During a stay in the Waihou of over a month, the crew has felled more than 200 trees — and killed three Maori. |
| September 18 | The *Endeavour* (Captain William Wright Bampton) sets sail from Sydney for India via Dusky Sound. There are 50 freed convicts and at least 41 stowaways (runaway convicts and deserters) on board. Also sailing for New Zealand this day is the *Fancy*. |
| October 11 | Approximate date the *Endeavour* and the *Fancy* arrive at Dusky Sound. Between them they carry more than 240 people, including at least two women. The *Endeavour* is in desperately poor condition after encountering gales in the Tasman Sea. |
| November 1 | The crippled *Endeavour*, having been stripped of all supplies, is hauled onto a beach. The passengers and crew now occupy a shipwreck colony built on shore. |

## 1796

| | |
|---|---|
| January 7 | The *Providence* and the *Fancy* depart Dusky Sound for Norfolk Island, leaving behind about 90 men. The *Providence* is the partly built vessel abandoned by the *Britannia*'s sealing party in 1793, and is the first European-style vessel to be launched in New Zealand. |
| March 17 | The *Assistance* (a converted longboat from the *Endeavour*) arrives at Sydney, out of water and food. The last 35 men |

stranded in Dusky Sound will be picked up, half starved, more than a year later by the *Mercury*.

## 1798

| August 20 | The 300-ton snow *Hunter* (Captain James Fearn) departs Sydney for New Zealand. In the Waihou, it will take on board spars for sale in China. |

## 1799

| October 7 | The prize ship *Hunter* (Captain William Hingston) leaves Sydney for Bengal via New Zealand. While the vessel is in the Waihou to cut timber, four crewmen will run away and become 'Pakeha Maori'. They are the first Europeans known to have lived with Maori for any length of time. |

## 1801

| March 2 | The Spanish prize *El Plumier* (Captain William Reid) arrives at Hauraki looking for supplies. The vessel will stay for nearly six months, some of that time spent stranded on a sand bank. |
| April 20 | The *Royal Admiral* (Captain William Wilson) arrives at Hauraki to collect timber. During the vessel's two-month stay, a group of London Missionary Society brothers become the first missionaries to investigate the possibility of establishing a station in New Zealand. |
| August 20 | After being repaired, *El Plumier* leaves the Firth of Thames for Sydney. |
| October 19 | The *Britannia* (Captain Robert Turnbull) returns to Sydney from the New Zealand fishery. It has as cargo 550 barrels of sperm oil. The whale rush has begun. |

## 1803

| June 1 | Teina, a young man from the Bay of Islands, arrives at Sydney having joined the *Alexander* (Captain Robert Rhodes) as a sailor. During his 15-week stay he will live with the governor, Philip King. |

| September 19 | Teina leaves for New Zealand with the *Alexander*. He is weighed down with gifts, including pigs. |
| --- | --- |
| October 7 | The small schooner *Endeavour* (Captain Oliphant) puts in at Sydney with about 2000 seal skins taken from the rookeries of the southern South Island and offshore islands. The sealing voyage is one of more than 30 in southern New Zealand waters by a number of vessels over more than a decade. |

**Whalers cut blubber from their catch. Whaling vessels frequented the waters around New Zealand in the early 19th century.**

# 1804

| June 6 | The *Lady Nelson* (Lieutenant James Symons) puts in at the Bay of Islands to take on wood and water. The bay is becoming a popular haven for whalers and traders. |
| --- | --- |
| June 12 | A prisoner, James Cavanagh, escapes from the *Lady Nelson* to become the first Pakeha to live in Northland. |

# 1805

| April 23 | The *Independence* (Captain Isaiah Townsend) returns |
| --- | --- |

to Sydney after landing sealing gangs at the Antipodes Islands. The rookeries at Dusky Sound are in decline and the Antipodes Islands seal rush has begun. Within a year at least seven vessels will visit, and over the next decade more than a quarter of a million skins will be taken.

| May 26 | Governor King of New South Wales issues an order prohibiting the removal of Maori from New Zealand without his permission. |
|---|---|
| June 9 | The *Ferret* (Captain Philip Skelton) arrives at Sydney. On board is Matara, son of the Bay of Islands chief Te Pahi. |
| July 5 | Maori living in Sydney attend a meeting at which Philip King promises them redress for any ill-treatment. He also offers passage home to those who want it, or training in European trades to those who don't. The governor is making moves to extend the rights of British subjects to Maori. |
| July 28 | Matara leaves Sydney on the *Venus* (Captain William Stewart) to return to the Bay of Islands. |
| September 20 | John Savage, a Sydney surgeon, arrives at the Bay of Islands as a passenger on the *Ferret*. His *Some account of New Zealand* will be the first book devoted completely to New Zealand. Local man Te Mahanga (Te Moehanga) will travel on to London with Savage. |
| November 27 | Te Pahi and several of his sons arrive at Sydney on HMS *Buffalo*. The chief is the first influential Maori leader to visit New South Wales, and he is taken to meet the governor. |

# 1806

| February 25 | Te Pahi leaves Sydney on the *Lady Nelson*. His meeting with the Rev. Samuel Marsden has encouraged the missionary to believe that it will be possible to set up a Church Missionary Society (CMS) station under Te Pahi's protection in New Zealand. |
|---|---|
| March 10 | The *Favorite* (Captain Jon Paddock), an American vessel, |

| | |
|---|---|
| | arrives at Sydney. On board are a record 60,000 seal skins, most of them probably taken in the Antipodes Islands. |
| April 22 | In the far north, George Bruce deserts the *Lady Nelson*, having a week earlier been flogged for 'theft, disobedience and embezzlement'. He will become one of New Zealand's best-known 'Pakeha Maori'. |
| April 27 | Te Mahanga arrives in London as the first Maori known to have visited England. He will later make extravagant claims to have, during a six-week stay, performed a haka for the king and queen and conceived a child with a woman named Nancy. |
| May 7 | The *Lady Nelson* departs the Bay of Islands for Norfolk Island. Te Pahi has been dropped off at Te Puna and a prefabricated house has been erected for the use of future European officials and missionaries. |
| June 17 | Convicts and crew mutiny on the brig *Venus* at Port Dalrymple, New South Wales, and set sail for the Bay of Islands. Among them is Charlotte Badger, who will become one of the first European women to settle in New Zealand, at Rangihoua. The mutineers will kidnap several local women, then abandon them on the east coast. Here they will be killed and probably eaten by Ngai Te Rangi and Ngati Porou, providing a cause for devastating Nga Puhi campaigns in 1818. |
| June 26 | Teina and Maki arrive with the *Alexander* at Gravesend near London, where they are abandoned without pay. Teina will die in London and Maki will be kidnapped and forced to go back to sea on another vessel. |
| August 18 | Captain Abraham Bristow of the whaler *Ocean* finds the Auckland Islands. The seal rush to this area will begin the following year. |
| September 20 | The *Argo* (Captain John Bader) puts in at Sydney. Ruatara, a young Nga Puhi rangatira who has been working on the vessel, is discharged without pay. While in Sydney he will meet Samuel Marsden for the first time. |

# 1807

| April 14 | Matara reaches London on the *Richard and Mary*, sent by his father, Te Pahi, to see the king and obtain hardware and muskets. |
| April 24 | The *General Wellesley* (Captain David Dalrymple) leaves Sydney for Penang via the South Pacific. While the vessel is in New Zealand, George Bruce and his wife, Te Atahoe (Te Pahi's daughter), will be trapped on board and taken to Fiji and Malaya. Bruce will be stranded in Malacca while Dalrymple takes Te Atahoe to Penang and sells her as a slave. |

# 1808

| April 14 | The *Parramatta* (Captain John Glenn) leaves Sydney for New Zealand. In the Bay of Islands, the vessel will be wrecked and all the crew killed after a dispute with Maori traders. The relationship between visitors and locals is rapidly deteriorating. |
| July 10 | Te Pahi arrives with three of his sons in Sydney on the *Commerce* (Captain James Ceroni). In poor health, he at first stays at Government House but will eventually be forced out onto the street. |
| August 8 | The *Perseverance* departs Sydney on a sealing expedition to New Zealand. It is one of the first vessels to work the productive seal rookeries in Foveaux Strait. |
| September 26 | The *Commerce* leaves Sydney with Te Pahi and his sons. Te Pahi has been frustrated in his attempt to obtain redress for the offences against his people by visiting Europeans. |

# 1809

| March 1 | The *City of Edinburgh* (Captain Simeon Pattison) arrives at the Bay of Islands. Among the passengers is Matara, returning from his trip to London. During a three-month stay at Kororareka, the ship will be completely refitted. |

| | |
|---|---|
| August 28 | The convict ship *Ann* departs Cowes for Australia. On board are the Rev. Samuel Marsden, William Hall and John King of the CMS. Ruatara is also on the vessel, having failed during a short stay in England to achieve his goal of meeting King George III. |
| November 8 | The *Boyd* (Captain John Thompson) departs Sydney for the Cape of Good Hope via New Zealand with about 70 people on board. About six weeks later, the vessel will be overwhelmed and burnt in Whangaroa Harbour by Ngati Uru. |
| December 31 | Possible date Alexander Berry of the *City of Edinburgh* and Matengaro, a Bay of Islands chief, set out from Kororareka for Whangaroa with armed volunteers to investigate rumours a European vessel has been attacked. They rescue a woman and three children, the only survivors of the burning of the *Boyd* about two weeks earlier. The remainder of the passengers and crew have been killed and eaten by Ngati Uru. |

## 1810

| | |
|---|---|
| January 4 | Campbell Island is found by Captain Frederick Hasselburg and the *Perseverance*. |
| January 6 | Alexander Berry and two officers of the *City of Edinburgh* write a letter to be delivered to the governor of New South Wales blaming Te Pahi — probably incorrectly — for the burning of the *Boyd*. |
| January 10 | The *Sydney Cove* (Captain Charles McLaren) lands a sealing gang on Stewart Island. Three of them will be killed and eaten by Honekai's people on the other side of Foveaux Strait, but one young man, James Caddell, will stay living among Maori for several years. Two more sealing gangs will be murdered within a year. |
| February 27 | CMS missionaries Marsden, Hall and King arrive with Ruatara at Sydney on the *Ann*. During the voyage, Marsden has nursed Ruatara back to health, and in return Ruatara has taught Marsden much about Maori language and customs. |

| | |
|---|---|
| March 9 | News of the *Boyd* massacre reaches Sydney with the sealer *King George*. Subsequently, it will become almost impossible to find a captain prepared to go to the Bay of Islands, and CMS plans to start a mission there under Te Pahi's patronage will be ruined. |
| March 26 | Te Puna, Te Pahi's island pa between Rangihoua Bay and Moturoa, is attacked by whalers who blame the chief for the killing of the passengers and crew of the *Boyd*. Within weeks Te Pahi will be killed while fighting over the Boyd affair with Whangaroa Maori. |
| April 5 | William Leith and his party arrive at the Bay of Islands on the *Experiment*. They have been sent to investigate setting up a flax-gathering settlement but will leave 10 days later with only 4 lb of the stuff. They will also try unsuccessfully to find more survivors of the *Boyd* massacre. |
| September 1 | A new account of the *Boyd* massacre is published in the *Sydney Gazette*. It exonerates Te Pahi, noting that he had tried to intervene to save some of the sailors. |

# 1812

| | |
|---|---|
| September 19 | Ruatara departs Sydney for New Zealand on the whaler *Ann*. Five months later, he will at last be returned to the Bay of Islands, where he discovers he has been chosen to succeed chief Te Pahi. During an 18-month stay at Parramatta he has learnt European agricultural methods, which he will use to grow the first full wheat crop in New Zealand. |

# 1813

| | |
|---|---|
| November 27 | A sealing gang abandoned by the *Active* at the Open Bay Islands, off the west coast of the South Island, nearly four years earlier is rescued by the *Governor Bligh*. |
| December 1 | The governor of New South Wales, Lachlan Macquarie, issues a proclamation affirming native rights and requiring ships' captains to stop their mistreatment of New Zealanders and South Sea Islanders. |

# The early European impact
# 1814 – 1839

**Hard on the heels** of European sealers, whalers and traders, the first missionaries came to live in New Zealand from 1814. As they were settling in to their new lives, and Maori were learning to accommodate their presence, the defeat of Napoleon at Waterloo saw the establishment of a new order in Europe. Hongi Hika's brutal attempt to dominate the North Island tribes was mirrored in Africa, where Shaka was expanding his Zulu kingdom. An outbreak of cholera in Europe in the 1830s had its own trans-global echo in New Zealand as European diseases swept through the vulnerable Maori population.

# 1814

| | |
|---|---|
| June 10 | Lay missionaries Thomas Kendall and William Hall arrive at the Bay of Islands on the CMS brig *Active* (Captain Peter Dillon) to investigate the possibility of starting a mission. |
| June 12 | William Hall reads a Sunday service to a few Maori on board the *Active*. |
| June 13 | Ruatara is given a steel handmill by the missionaries to allow him to make the first New Zealand flour — once his wheat crop is fully grown. |
| July 25 | The *Active* departs the Bay of Islands for Sydney with a cargo of timber and flax. Kendall and Hall are joined by Ruatara and his uncle Hongi Hika, and several other local men. The missionaries have had meetings with chiefs Kaingaroa, Hongi Hika, Tara and Korokoro who, with an eye to trading opportunities, have encouraged them to start a mission. |
| November 9 | Governor Lachlan Macquarie issues an order protecting the 'just rights and privileges' of the natives of New Zealand and the Bay of Islands. |
| November 12 | Governor Macquarie appoints Thomas Kendall as justice of the peace in New Zealand. |
| November 28 | Rev. Samuel Marsden leaves Sydney on the *Active* (Captain Thomas Hansen) on his first visit to New Zealand. Among the CMS entourage are the King, Kendall and Hall families, and Ruatara and Hongi Hika. |
| December 17 | The *Active* anchors off North Cape. |
| December 20 | On board the *Active*, a peace is concluded between Nga Puhi and Ngati Uru after long negotiations. They have been in conflict since the *Boyd* massacre. |
| December 22 | The *Active* anchors at Rangihoua in the Bay of Islands. Ruatara takes Marsden's party up to his village for a formal reception. |

| December 23 | Livestock, including horses and cattle, is landed from the *Active*, causing great amazement among Maori, who have not seen such creatures before. |
| --- | --- |
| December 25 | Marsden conducts the first full Christian service on New Zealand soil. At Oihi Beach, he preaches in English to a largely Maori congregation. |
| December 26 | Work on constructing a mission station begins, with the help of Ruatara's men, at Rangihoua. A large shed will be built to accommodate the missionary families. |

# 1815

| January 9 | Hongi Hika takes Marsden to Kerikeri and inland from there. Over the next three days they will visit Okuratope pa and travel as far west as Lake Omapere. It is the first significant inland exploration by a Pakeha. |
| --- | --- |
| February 21 | Thomas Holloway King, son of John and Hannah King, is born at Rangihoua. It is the first recorded Pakeha birth in New Zealand. Thomas will not survive early childhood. |
| February 24 | Samuel Marsden negotiates with Te Uri o Kanae the first effective land purchase, for the mission station land at Rangihoua. On the same day he baptises Thomas King. |
| February 26 | Marsden departs the Bay of Islands for Sydney at the end of his first visit. Travelling with Te Morenga, he has with him on the *Active* a cargo of flax and timber gathered in the Waihou. Left behind are Kendall, Hall and King, the first resident missionaries in New Zealand, and their families. They have been told not to participate in private trade with Maori, an instruction that will be largely ignored. |
| March 3 | Ruatara dies after a short illness. His death is a blow to the hopes of the missionaries, but his role as their patron and protector will be taken over by Hongi Hika. |
| July 11 | The *Active* departs the Bay of Islands with a cargo of flax and timber as well as several chiefs going to stay with Marsden. |

Also on board is the manuscript of Kendall's *A korao no New Zealand; or, the New Zealander's first book; being an attempt to compose some lessons for the instruction of the natives.* It will be the first book to be published in Maori.

**Nga Puhi chief Te Morenga's drawing of his own moko, made on board the *Active* on March 9, 1815.**

August 20 — The *Trial* and the *Brothers* are attacked by Maori at what will later become known as Kennedy Bay, Coromandel. Several crew members are killed, but dozens of Maori are shot dead and their village burnt in retribution. After a five-year break when few vessels called by, the difficult and often violent relations hip between Maori and the crews of visiting ships has picked up where it left off.

## 1816

February 23 — The surviving crew of the wrecked *Betsey*, captured and held by Maori in the far north for four months, is rescued by the *Active*.

August 12 — At Rangihoua, Thomas Kendall starts the first European-style school in New Zealand with an opening roll of 33 pupils. It will close two years later.

# 1818

| February 7 | Hongi Hika leaves the Bay of Islands with a fighting force to avenge the deaths of his relatives at the hands of East Coast tribes. He will return 11 months later with as many as 2000 prisoners, and claiming to have burnt 500 villages in the Bay of Plenty and East Cape. |
| November 12 | At Rangihoua, Thomas King dies of 'a consumption' aged 3 years 9 months. |

# 1819

| August 12 | Samuel Marsden, James Kemp and the Rev. John Butler arrive at the Bay of Islands on the sealing vessel *General Gates*. Butler will be the mission's first resident clergyman and superintendent. |
| August 17 | Kerikeri is chosen by Marsden as the site of a second CMS mission station, and Hongi Hika gives his approval. |
| September 25 | Marsden records that 100 grape vines are being planted at Kerikeri. They are the first grapes to be grown in New Zealand. |
| October 9 | Marsden visits Patuone inland at Te Papa. Within weeks of this visit Patuone will set off with his brother Nene on a great journey of conquest. On its way south from Hokianga to Cook Strait, the taua will be joined by Te Rauparaha and his warriors, and major battles will be fought in Taranaki. |
| November 4 | Hongi Hika's grant of land at Kerikeri is made official. |
| November 9 | Marsden departs Rangihoua at the end of his second visit. |

# 1820

| March 2 | Thomas Kendall leaves on the *New Zealander* on an unauthorised trip to England with Hongi Hika and Waikato. The idealistic layman has been at odds with his fellow missionaries and the CMS for some time. |

| April 13 | In the first British military action under orders in New Zealand, the captain of HMS *Dromedary* seizes the US vessel *General Gates* for smuggling convicts out of Sydney. The vessel is sent from the Bay of Islands back to Sydney with a British naval crew. |
| May 3 | A European-style plough, drawn by six bullocks, is used for the first time in New Zealand, by John Butler at Kerikeri. He will later write in his diary, 'I trust that this auspicious day will be remembered with gratitude and its anniversary kept by ages yet unborn.' |

**Waikato, Hongi Hika and Thomas Kendall, as painted by James Barry during their visit to London in 1820.**

| August 8 | Kendall, Hongi Hika and Waikato reach England. Kendall plans to be ordained and work on a Maori grammar book with Professor Lee at Cambridge, while Hongi aims to enhance his mana — and acquire muskets for his tribe. |

# 1821

| | |
|---|---|
| July 11 | Hongi Hika arrives at the Bay of Islands with Thomas Kendall on the *Westmoreland* after their trip to Europe. Hongi has with him a suit of armour presented by King George IV and perhaps 500 firearms. The arrival of such a large number of muskets sparks an arms race between tribes. |
| September 5 | Hongi Hika leaves the Bay of Islands with the final contingents of a combined taua of Nga Puhi, Te Ngare Raumati, Ngai Tawake, Ngati Manu and others. In raids on pa at Mauinaina and Te Totara at Tamaki, about 500 Ngati Paoa and Ngati Maru men, women and children will be killed. |
| September 27 | Thomas Kendall writes a letter, endorsed by other Pakeha, to the CMS defending the settlers' participation in the gun trade and explaining they are at the mercy of Maori. |
| December 21 | Hongi Hika returns to Kerikeri after a successful campaign in the Auckland district. He has with him 2000 captives. |

# 1822

| | |
|---|---|
| January 22 | Rev. Samuel Leigh arrives at the Bay of Islands with his wife to set up a Wesleyan (Methodist) mission. They will stay with the CMS missionaries until they are settled. |
| February 21 | The Butlers host other missionaries at the first meal eaten in their newly completed house at Kerikeri. The house, later renamed Kemp House, is now the oldest building still standing in New Zealand. |
| July 28 | The first canoes return from Hongi Hika's latest, five-month taua. Three thousand of his men have taken on the Waikato tribes, and during the assault on Matakitaki in the Waikato 2000 from both sides have died. |
| September 6 | The CMS writes a letter of dismissal to Thomas Kendall. He has defiantly continued to trade in muskets, and has had a relationship with a young Maori woman called Tungaroa. He will not receive the letter until nearly a year has passed. |

# 1823

| | |
|---|---|
| March 4 | The first Maori baptism, that of Maria Ringa, is performed by Thomas Kendall so that she can wed a European in a Christian marriage. However, Maori will not start to offer themselves for baptism in significant numbers until later in the decade. |
| May 16 | The Rev. William White disembarks from the *St Michael* at the Bay of Islands. Before long, he will replace the ill Samuel Leigh as the leader of the Wesleyan mission. |
| June 6 | Samuel Leigh, accompanied by Butler, Hall and White, arrives at Whangaroa on the *St Michael*. They will establish Wesleydale, a Wesleyan mission station at Kaeo, despite memories of the attack made on the *Boyd* 15 years earlier. |
| June 22 | Mission services at Whangaroa begin when John Butler of the CMS preaches in the morning and Wesleyan Samuel Leigh in the evening. |
| June 23 | Phillip Tapsell (Hans Falk) and Maria Ringa marry at the Bay of Islands. The ceremony, conducted by Thomas Kendall, is the first known Anglican marriage in New Zealand. Tapsell, a Danish whaler, will be deserted by his wife very quickly after the wedding. |
| August 3 | Samuel Marsden arrives at the Bay of Islands for his fourth visit. He is accompanied by CMS missionaries Henry Williams and William Fairburn, and Wesleyans Nathaniel Turner and John Hobbs, and their families. The arrival of Williams heralds a change in Pakeha relations with Maori, and the end of missionary involvement in the musket trade. |
| August 7 | Marsden and Henry Williams choose a site at Paihia for a new CMS mission station. |
| November 14 | Marsden leaves the Bay of Islands on the *Dragon* with John Butler, who has been suspended for 'falling into sin'. Despite being dismissed, Kendall has refused to leave New Zealand with Marsden. |

# 1824

| | |
|---|---|
| February 26 | The *Urania* (Captain Reynolds) is becalmed in Cook Strait. Chief Te Peehi Kupe of Ngati Toa boards the vessel and demands to be taken to England. Four years later he will return to New Zealand with muskets. |
| April 3 | The exploration vessel *Coquille*, with Captain Louis Duperry in command and Jules Sébastien César Dumont d'Urville second in command, enters the Bay of Islands. On board are Taiwhanga, who has been living in Australia since 1822 learning farming methods, and lay missionary George Clarke. |
| April 17 | The *Coquille* leaves the Bay of Islands for the Caroline Islands. Before long, a stowaway named Burns is found. |
| June 13 | A school/chapel is opened at Wesleydale. It is the first Methodist church to be consecrated in New Zealand. |

# 1825

| | |
|---|---|
| September 14 | Rangi, the first Maori chief to be converted to Christianity, is baptised on his deathbed as Christian Rangi. |

# 1826

| | |
|---|---|
| January 24 | The CMS schooner *Herald* is launched at Paihia. Having taken five months to build, it will make the missionaries less reliant on Maori co-operation. |
| March 7 | E. G. Wakefield, the future mastermind of organised colonisation in New Zealand, abducts 15-year-old heiress Ellen Turner from her home in England. They will be married the following day in Gretna Green, Scotland. |
| March 25 | The New Zealand Company (1825) vessel *Rosanna*, commanded by Captain James Herd, arrives at Stewart Island. The vessel, which is travelling in company with the *Lambton*, has come to New Zealand to buy land for settlement. |

| October 26 | The *Rosanna* anchors in the Bay of Islands. The visitors are not welcomed by the missionaries, who are against European settlement. Despite the purchase of land for them at Hokianga, Manukau and Paeroa, almost all of the would-be settlers are intimidated by Maori hostility and will decline to stay. |
| December 29 | Chief Patuone and his son arrive in Sydney on the *Elizabeth*. To secure further trade in the Hokianga Harbour, he will offer to leave his son in Sydney as a guarantee that Pakeha traders will be safe. |

# 1827

| January 10 | The Wesleydale mission at Whangaroa is plundered and burnt by a taua led by Hongi Hika. Under the protection of Patuone, the missionary families flee to Kerikeri. |
| January 10 | Explorer Dumont d'Urville, in command of the *Astrolabe* (originally the *Coquille*), sights the west coast of the South Island. |
| January 11 | The Wesleyan missionaries are received by the CMS missionaries after their flight from Whangaroa. |
| January 15 | The brig *Glory* is wrecked off Pitt Island, in the Chatham Islands. Six stranded crew members will eventually sail a longboat to the Bay of Islands. |
| January 28 | After several aborted attempts, Dumont d'Urville sails through French Pass in the *Astrolabe* and enters Admiralty Bay in the Marlborough Sounds. It is a feat of great navigational daring. |
| March 18 | The *Astrolabe* leaves New Zealand waters. Dumont d'Urville has collected extensive notes on Maori life, language and customs, and has charted parts of Nelson, the Marlborough Sounds and the Waitemata Harbour. |
| March 23 | The trial of E. G. Wakefield for the abduction of Ellen Turner takes place. He will be convicted and sentenced to three years in jail. |

**Louis Auguste de Sainson's depiction of the *Astrolabe* negotiating French Pass on January 28, 1827.**

# 1828

| February 26 | The first trial by a jury — of sorts — takes place at Paihia. A group of Maori is encouraged by missionaries to formally determine the guilt of a slave accused of cheating, and, having found him guilty, decide his punishment. |

| March 9 | Missionaries hear 'official' news of Hongi Hika's death. The chief had been wounded at Hokianga. The death, an uncertain number of days previously, of the Nga Puhi warrior chief is the end of an era of bloody taua — and the beginning of a time of insecurity for the missionaries who have been protected by him. |

| May 26 | The mission schooner *Herald* is wrecked on the Hokianga bar. |

# 1830

| February 7 | Taiwhanga of Nga Puhi is baptised with the name Rawiri. The conversion of this man of mana will be influential in the conversion of others. |

| | |
|---|---|
| March 5 | Ururoa, Hongi's kinsman, lands with a taua at Kororareka, which now has a Pakeha settlement of traders and whalers. He has heard that Te Urumihia has cursed him and his Ngai Tawake people after a fight between girls on the beach at Korerareka. In the fighting that follows his arrival about 30 people will die. |
| March 17 | The 'Girls' War' is brought to an end by a peace meeting facilitated by missionaries. A large-scale war has been narrowly avoided. |
| March 29 | Marsden and the missionaries resolve to establish New Zealand's first farm based on European principles at Waimate, in Northland. Maori at the settlement there have already proved the richness of the land by cultivating extensive crops of maize, kumara and potatoes. |
| April 21 | Phillip Tapsell is married for the second time, to Karuhi, sister of the chief Wharepoaka of Rangihoua. |
| July 31 | The *Active* arrives in the Bay of Islands with Rev. William Yate and a small hand press for printing. The first publication printed in New Zealand, a Maori catechism entitled *Ko te Katikihama III*, will be completed by the end of the year. |
| October 29 | Ngati Toa war leader Te Rauparaha sets sail from Kapiti in the brig *Elizabeth* with perhaps 100 warriors hidden on board. To avenge the death of Te Peehi Kupe, they will go to Akaroa and, with the collusion of Captain John Stewart, capture chief Te Maiharanui, his wife, Te Whe, and his daughter. Te Maiharanui will, it is claimed, kill his daughter to save her from slavery, and back at Kapiti he will be given to Ngati Toa war widows to torture and kill. |

# 1831

| | |
|---|---|
| January 5 | Phillip Tapsell buys land at Maketu in exchange for weapons, pipes and tobacco. He has been invited to settle there by Te Arawa chiefs, and will set up a trading station. Pakeha traders and shore-based whalers are gradually becoming established in permanent settlements around the country. |

| August 27 | Chief Wharetutu, in the Bay of Islands, asks for missionaries to be sent to Rotorua. The CMS will expand its activities southwards as a result. |
| October 1 | Elizabeth Guard gives birth to a son at her husband's Te Awaiti whaling station. John Guard is the first European child to be born in the South Island. |
| October 3 | The *Favorite*, an armed French vessel, arrives at the Bay of Islands. Its appearance in the bay sparks rumours and feeds fears about French colonial ambitions in New Zealand, but during the week-long stay the crew's intentions will turn out to be benign. |
| October 11 | William G. Puckey marries Matilda Davis at the Bay of Islands. It is the first wedding of two Pakeha in New Zealand. |
| October 18 | Henry Williams, Thomas Chapman and Rawiri Taiwhanga leave the Bay of Islands on the *Karere* to investigate extending the work of the CMS to Rotorua and Tauranga. |
| October 26 | Te Rauparaha and Ngati Toa capture the great Ngai Tahu pa of Kaiapohia (Kaiapoi). |

# 1832

| January 3 | Henry Williams leaves the Bay of Islands, accompanying — as a hopeful peacemaker — an 800-strong taua bound for Tauranga. As many as 200 people will die before the taua ends. |
| May 9 | The foundations are laid for the Stone Store in Kerikeri, which is today New Zealand's oldest surviving commercial building. It will not be completed until 1836. |
| December 20 | Henry Williams plays cricket with the boys of the school at Paihia. In the first recorded game of cricket in New Zealand, the boys turn out to be 'expert bowlers'. |

NEW-ZEALAND WAR EXPEDITION.

**An engraving based on Henry Williams's drawing of one of the many taua of the intertribal wars of the 1820s and 1830s.**

# 1833

| | |
|---|---|
| May 17 | At Paihia, viticulturist James Busby is officially welcomed as the newly appointed British resident by contingents coming from as far afield as Kororareka, Waikari and Kawakawa. His brief is to look after 'well disposed settlers and traders' and apprehend escaped convicts — but mostly it is to prevent the mistreatment of Maori by Pakeha. |
| July 3 | Richard Davis makes the first documented reference to the emergence among Nga Puhi of the cult of the prophet Papahurihia (later called Te Atua Wera). It is the first of many syncretic movements that will combine elements of Maori and Judaeo-Christian religious thought. |

# 1834

| | |
|---|---|
| March 20 | At Waitangi, chiefs from the far north meet with James Busby to choose a flag to represent New Zealand. The flag of the United Tribes of New Zealand will be recognised by the admiralty, and Busby will grant certificates of registration to New Zealand-built ships. |
| April 29 | The barque *Harriet* is driven ashore at Cape Egmont. All the |

| | passengers and crew make it to land safely, including whaler Jacky Guard, his wife, Betty, and their family. |
|---|---|
| April 30 | Ngati Tautahi attack James Busby's house and the British resident is slightly injured. |
| May 10 | Ngati Ruanui attack the survivors of the *Harriet* and Betty Guard and her two children are taken hostage. Twelve sailors captured at the same time will be killed and eaten. |
| September 21 | HMS *Alligator*, escorted by the *Isabella*, arrives to rescue the survivors of the wreck of the *Harriet*. The actions of the next several weeks are the first time British troops have seen armed combat against Maori. It is an ugly affair in which Maori under a flag of truce will be killed. |

## 1835

| February 17 | Missionary William Colenso begins printing his first pamphlet, the Epistles to the Philippians and Ephesians in Maori. |
|---|---|
| September 21 | A public meeting attended by chiefs of the Hokianga district and chaired by the additional British resident, Thomas McDonnell, prohibits the importation and sale of liquor in the area. The measure will prove to be ineffective. |
| October 28 | At Waitangi, James Busby persuades 34 chiefs to sign a declaration of independence that asks for the crown's protection. Busby is anxious about the intentions of the Baron de Thierry, who claims to have bought 40,000 acres of land in the Hokianga through Thomas Kendall. The chiefs' declaration will later be found to have no constitutional status. |
| November 14 | The *Lord Rodney* (Captain John Harewood) leaves Port Nicholson crammed with 500 Te Ati Awa, the first contingent of a heke to the Chatham Islands. |
| November 17 | The *Lord Rodney* arrives at the Chatham Islands after a dreadful journey in which the passengers have been barely able to move. They invade the islands and overwhelm the Moriori people, who have outlawed warfare and greet all |

| | visitors with peace in mind. More than 200 Moriori will die in the initial onslaught, and the rest are enslaved. Within a couple of years almost all the survivors will have died. |
|---|---|
| December 16 | Richard Davis writes that Rawiri Taiwhanga has a thriving farm and is offering butter for sale in the Bay of Islands, making him the first commercial dairy farmer in New Zealand. |
| December 21 | Naturalist Charles Darwin puts in at the Bay of Islands on the *Beagle*. He will not be overly impressed with what New Zealand has to offer. |
| December 25 | Te Hunga, an influential chief of Ngati Haua, is murdered by Haerehuka at Rotorua. The tribal warfare that follows will last until 1840. |

## 1836

| | |
|---|---|
| January 22 | At Puriri, William Fairburn negotiates the purchase of a huge tract of land at Tamaki in exchange for blankets, tobacco and hardware. Although it is initially estimated to be 10,000 acres (4000 ha), when surveyed it will turn out to be 83,000 acres (34,000 ha). One of many large land sales to missionaries, this sale will later be validated by the land claims commission. |
| March 29 | Maketu pa in the Bay of Plenty succumbs to a combined attack by Waikato, Ngai Te Rangi and Ngati Haua. |
| May 7 | Te Tumu pa in the Bay of Plenty falls. The assault, in which Ngai Te Rangi suffer great losses, provides a Rotorua and Ngati Raukawa taua with utu for destruction of the pa at Maketu. |
| August 6 | The Te Arawa pa at Ohinemutu, Rotorua, is attacked by Ngati Haua but 2000 defenders stand firm. Afterwards, the mission station at nearby Te Koutu is sacked by both sides. |

## 1837

| | |
|---|---|
| February 23 | Marsden arrives at Hokianga with his daughter Martha on the *Pyramus*. On what will turn out to be his last visit to New |

| | |
|---|---|
| | Zealand, he will be fêted wherever he goes. |
| February 24 | The CMS resolves to dismiss William Yate after allegations of liaisons with a large number of Pakeha and Maori men. |
| March 20 | Captain Hempleman lands at Peraki, Banks Peninsula, from the *Dublin Packet* to start a whaling station. He and his wife are thought to be New Zealand's first German settlers, and Peraki the first permanent settlement in Canterbury. |
| April 1 | Travelling with Henry Williams, Marsden visits Kaitaia, where many parties of Maori come to pay their respects. |
| May 22 | The New Zealand Association holds its first public meeting in London. The forerunner of the New Zealand Company has been formed to pursue E. G. Wakefield's plan for the 'systematic' colonisation of New Zealand. |
| May 27 | Captain William Hobson RN and HMS *Rattlesnake* arrive at the Bay of Islands. Hobson is under orders from governor Richard Bourke of New South Wales to report on the situation in New Zealand. |
| July 4 | Hobson and the *Rattlesnake* leave the Bay of Islands for Sydney, with Samuel and Martha Marsden as passengers. While in New Zealand, Hobson has interviewed missionaries and tribal chiefs and tried to reconcile warring factions. |
| November 4 | Baron de Thierry, self-proclaimed 'Sovereign Chief of New Zealand and King of Nukuhiva' arrives at Hokianga on the *Nimrod* with a party of would-be colonists. He claims to have bought, through Thomas Kendall, 40,000 acres (16,187 ha) in the Hokianga for 36 axes. He will be unable to substantiate his claim, and the settlers will riot and scatter. |
| December 30 | William Colenso completes the printing of 5000 copies of a 356-page New Testament translated into Maori by William Williams. He will do much of the massive job of binding them himself. |

# 1838

| | |
|---|---|
| January 10 | Bishop Jean-Baptiste Pompallier arrives at Hokianga with a Roman Catholic priest and brother. He is the first bishop of any denomination to come to New Zealand, and will establish the first Roman Catholic mission station at Papakawau. |
| January 13 | At Totara Point, Pompallier performs the first recorded Roman Catholic mass on New Zealand soil. He then performs the first Catholic baptism, of Catherine Poynton. |
| May 23 | The Kororareka Association is formed by settlers, who take on legislative and judicial powers for themselves. The association, essentially a group of vigilantes, is responding to increasing lawlessness in Kororareka. |
| August 2 | French whaler Captain Jean Langlois negotiates with Maori at Port Cooper to buy almost all of Banks Peninsula for 1000 francs. He will return to France to set up a colonisation company that will use the newly acquired land. |

**The US flag of consul James Clendon flies over the Bay of Islands.**

| | |
|---|---|
| August 29 | The New Zealand Colonisation Company is founded at a meeting in Covent Garden, London. It supersedes the New Zealand Association, which has failed to obtain a government charter for the settlement of New Zealand under E. G. Wakefield's plan. |
| October 12 | James Clendon is empowered to act as the first US consul in New Zealand, protecting the interests of US citizens. The versatile Englishman will, at various times, serve as a justice of the peace, police inspector and collector of customs. |
| December 12 | Lord Glenelg, secretary of state for the colonies, asks the foreign office to appoint a British consul to New Zealand. |

## 1839

| | |
|---|---|
| January 6 | At the first ordination in New Zealand, Octavius Hadfield becomes an Anglican priest, at Paihia. Later in the year he will go to the Kapiti district to begin mission services. |
| March 19 | Mary Bumby arrives in the Hokianga with her brother, John Bumby, and other Wesleyan missionaries. She brings with her the first honey bees in New Zealand. |
| May 2 | The first prospectus of the New Zealand Company (aka New Zealand Land Company) is published in London. The new company will seek to profit by settling British people in New Zealand under E. G. Wakefield's scheme. |
| May 12 | The New Zealand Company ship *Tory* (Captain Edward Chaffers) departs English waters — without government approval for the new settlement. Colonel William Wakefield has instructions to purchase land from Maori with the £5000 worth of goods carried in the hold. |
| June 15 | Letters patent are issued making Sir George Gipps governor-in-chief of the enlarged territory of New South Wales, which now includes New Zealand. |
| July 6 | Bishop Pompallier buys a parcel of waterfront land at Kororareka for the exorbitant sum of £370. The station |

| | built here will serve as the Roman Catholic mission's new headquarters. |
|---|---|
| August 13 | William Hobson's appointment as British consul to New Zealand is confirmed. Lord Normanby will issue him with lengthy instructions to take the measures necessary to establish New Zealand as a British colony. Among these measures is the negotiation to buy land from Maori, 'by fair and equal contracts', to be resold to settlers. |
| August 17 | The New Zealand Company's *Tory* anchors in Ship Cove, Queen Charlotte Sound. |
| August 21 | The first edition of the *New Zealand Gazette*, the country's first newspaper, is published in London. It has been produced for the New Zealand Company settlers about to depart. |
| August 25 | On HMS *Druid*, William Hobson and his family depart Plymouth for his posting in New Zealand. On the way they will stop at Sydney, where Hobson will have meetings with the governor and select his own staff. |
| September 9 | An official farewell dinner is held in London to mark the imminent departure of the first New Zealand Company immigrant ships. Over the next month the *Oriental*, the *Aurora*, the *Adelaide*, the *Duke of Roxburgh* and the *Bengal Merchant* will leave Great Britain — without the 856 paid-up settlers knowing if any land has been obtained for them. |
| September 20 | The *Tory*, piloted by Dicky Barrett, arrives at Port Nicholson and is met by canoes carrying Te Ati Awa chiefs Te Wharepouri and Te Puni. |
| September 27 | Four days after negotiations began, Te Wharepouri, Te Puni and other chiefs agree to sign over land in the Hutt Valley to the New Zealand Company. William Wakefield begins the distribution of goods, including jew's harps and nightcaps, as well as 120 new muskets, in payment for 11,000 acres (44,500 ha). |
| September 30 | Wakefield takes formal possession of Port Nicholson on behalf |

| | |
|---|---|
| | of the New Zealand Company. The occasion is marked by a hakari (feast) and a 21-gun salute. |
| October 16 | Ngati Raukawa, despite being supported by Te Rauparaha's warriors, suffer a severe defeat at the hands of Te Ati Awa in the battle of Te Kuititanga at Waikanae. Later the same day, medics from the *Tory* tend the wounded. |
| October 25 | In exchange for guns, blankets and other goods, Te Rauparaha and other chiefs sign over huge blocks of land in both the North and South Islands to the New Zealand Company. Later, Te Rauparaha will say he understood he was selling only Whakatu and Taitapu, in the Nelson and Golden Bay areas. |
| November 8 | The New Zealand Company buys the land around Cook Strait for a third time, when William Wakefield persuades minor Te Ati Awa chiefs in Cloudy Bay to confirm the sale. |
| December 13 | At Hokianga, William Wakefield purchases from Mrs Blenkin-sop, for £100, the deed to the Wairau. Her late husband claimed to have bought the land from Te Rauparaha. |
| December 19 | The *Tory* runs aground on a sandbank in the Kaipara Harbour and is nearly lost. |
| December 25 | Ernst Dieffenbach and James 'Worser' Heberley, left at Ngamotu (New Plymouth) by the *Tory*, reach the summit of Mt Taranaki on their second attempt. They are the first Europeans known to have climbed the volcano. |

# Coming to terms
# 1840–1851

**The most significant event** in New Zealand's modern history, the signing of the Treaty of Waitangi, brought about an influx of British migrants to the country. During the 1840s some great international migrations took place – notably the millions who fled Ireland following the famine that began in 1845, and the 85,000 hopefuls who were drawn to California from all around the world in search of gold in 1848 and 1849. Many prospectors moved on to Australia in 1851, and then to New Zealand a decade later. Away from the free market opportunities of the gold fields, Karl Marx and Friedrich Engels were publishing the *Communist Manifesto* in Europe in 1848. The seminal work of communism would have little effect on New Zealand life compared to another innovation of the 1840s — galvanised corrugated iron.

# 1840

| | |
|---|---|
| January 3 | The New Zealand Company survey ship *Cuba* reaches Port Nicholson. The surveyors, led by Captain William Mein Smith, will lay out the town of Britannia behind Petone beach (Pito-one) — contrary to the instructions left behind by William Wakefield. |
| January 14 | Governor Gipps prepares three proclamations extending his jurisdiction to New Zealand, appointing Captain William Hobson as lieutenant-governor and stating that land sales will not be recognised unless derived from the crown. |
| January 18 | William Wakefield returns to Port Nicholson and is horrified to discover the settlement is not being laid out at Lambton Harbour. Smith refuses to back down and continues to work at Petone. |
| January 22 | The New Zealand Company ship *Aurora* enters Port Nicholson and anchors off Somes (Matiu) Island, only to find the shelters promised to the settlers have not been built. The first five immigrant ships will all have arrived by March 7, bringing with them a hundred times more Pakeha settlers than local Maori are expecting. |
| January 29 | Captain Hobson arrives at the Bay of Islands in HMS *Herald*. |
| January 30 | At Kororareka, Hobson reads his commission as lieutenant-governor, somewhat prematurely given New Zealand sovereignty has not been ceded. He also reads Gipps's proclamation concerning land sales. |
| February 4 | Henry Williams begins translating the draft of the Treaty of Waitangi, which has been prepared by James Busby. Work will continue overnight. |
| February 5 | Hobson explains the terms of the treaty to a meeting of chiefs at Waitangi. Debate begins and will last throughout the day. |

| February 6 | The Maori translation of the Treaty of Waitangi is signed by William Hobson and 43 chiefs at Waitangi. Signature gathering will continue around the country for eight months. |
|---|---|
| February 8 | Samuel Parnell lands at Petone beach from the *Duke of Roxburgh*. Taking advantage of the shortage of tradesmen at Port Nicholson, he will soon negotiate an eight-hour working day for himself and other workers. In doing so, he forms New Zealand's first union of labour. |
| February 12 | Lieutenant-Governor Hobson meets 1000 or more Maori at Hokianga. After being assured the queen does not want the land, only sovereignty, 64 more chiefs sign the treaty. |
| February 17 | William Colenso prints 200 copies of the Maori text of the Treaty of Waitangi. |
| February 21 | Lieutenant-Governor Hobson sails in HMS *Herald* to the Waitemata Harbour to investigate a site for a more salubrious capital than the rough and lawless Kororareka, and to get more treaty signatures. |
| February 23 | John Macfarlane leads the first Sunday service of the Church of Scotland (Presbyterian) on New Zealand soil, on the banks of the Hutt River at Petone. |
| March 1 | William Hobson has a stroke on board the *Herald* in Waitemata Harbour. His right side is paralysed and his speech impaired. It will later be concluded that his illness was caused by 'violent mental excitement'. |
| March 2 | Floods at Britannia (Petone) raise questions over whether the new settlement should be relocated to Wakefield's chosen site on the other side of the harbour. The survey of a new site at Thorndon, beside Lambton Harbour, will begin a month later. |
| March 6 | Hobson returns to the Bay of Islands on the *Herald*. He will be cared for at the CMS station at Waimate North and make a steady recovery. |

| March 17 | The first official post office in New Zealand is established at Kororareka, with Clayton Hayes as postmaster. Hayes will soon be dismissed for 'inebriety and other misconduct', including destroying mail and keeping the postage money. |
| March 24 | The Union Bank of Australia commences New Zealand's first successful banking business, from a tin shed at Petone. It is a forerunner of today's ANZ bank. |
| April 12 | A small party of settlers lands at Goashore on Banks Peninsula from the *Sarah and Elizabeth*. They are the first farmer-settlers in Canterbury — although their farm will be abandoned within 18 months. |
| April 16 | Major Thomas Bunbury arrives at the Bay of Islands on HMS *Buffalo* with Hobson's family and a detachment of soldiers. |
| April 18 | The second issue of the *New Zealand Gazette* — the first newspaper published in New Zealand — is issued at Port Nicholson by Samuel Revans. Among the items in the four-page newspaper is a provisional constitution for the settlement. |
| April 19 | Henry Williams arrives at Port Nicholson with the Treaty of Waitangi to collect signatures. He will find William Wakefield strongly opposes the treaty and believes the Port Nicholson settlement should not be affected by it because the land was bought before it was signed. |
| April 29 | Thirty-one chiefs, including Te Wharepouri, sign the Treaty of Waitangi at Port Nicholson. |
| May 1 | Lieutenant-Governor Hobson formally takes possession of land at Okiato, a few kilometres from Kororareka, for use as the first capital, Russell. |
| May 5 | A meeting of the directors of the New Zealand Company resolves to change the name of its Port Nicholson settlement from Britannia to Wellington. |
| May 14 | Te Rauparaha is among a group of chiefs who sign the Treaty |

| | of Waitangi at Kapiti, believing it will guarantee him possession of all the territories he has gained by conquest. He will sign another copy of the treaty on June 19 at the insistence of Major Thomas Bunbury. |
|---|---|
| May 21 | Lieutenant-Governor Hobson proclaims the sovereignty of Queen Victoria over the North Island by virtue of the Treaty of Waitangi — despite the fact that the gathering of signatures has not been completed. He also proclaims sovereignty over the South Island on the ground of discovery. |
| May 25 | Hobson sends Willoughby Shortland with troops to Port Nicholson to subdue rebellious New Zealand Company settlers. |
| May 25 | A street of new cottages in Cornish Row, Britannia (Petone), is destroyed by fire. The new settlers are unhurt but lose all their possessions. |
| May 26 | An earthquake shakes Port Nicholson. It is the first of a number of tremors that will alarm the recent arrivals. |
| May 27 | Jerningham Wakefield negotiates the purchase of land at Wanganui. |
| June 5 | Major Thomas Bunbury raises the British flag at Stewart Island and, having found no Maori there, claims sovereignty over it and the islands in Foveaux Strait. |
| June 17 | At Port Underwood, Major Bunbury proclaims British sovereignty over the South Island for a second time, this time on the ground of the cession by 'several independent chiefs'. |
| July 11 | Captain Charles Lavaud arrives at the Bay of Islands on the French naval corvette *Aube*. The king's agent is on his way to Akaroa to oversee the establishment of the Nanto-Bordelaise Company settlement of Port Louis-Philippe on land bought by Jean Langlois. It is only now that Lavaud discovers Hobson has proclaimed British sovereignty over the whole of New Zealand. |

| July 14 | The first liquor licence in New Zealand is granted to the Duke of Marlborough hotel in Kororareka, legitimising a business that has been running since 1828. The licence issued by Hobson gives the hotel the right to operate as an ale house, common inn and victualling house. |
| --- | --- |
| July 23 | HMS *Britomart* (Captain Stanley) leaves the Bay of Islands with two magistrates on board. They have been sent by Hobson to hold court at Akaroa as a sign of 'effective occupation' by British subjects. |
| July 27 | Captain Lavaud sets sail for Akaroa with the *Aube*. |
| August 11 | The magistrates and ship's officers from the *Britomart* hoist the British flag at Akaroa to confirm sovereignty over the South Island. |
| August 13 | Land speculators John Logan Campbell and William Brown settle at Motukorea (Browns Island) in the Waitemata Harbour, anticipating that the capital will soon be moved to the area. |
| August 15 | The *Aube* is towed into Akaroa Harbour by boats from HMS *Britomart*. |
| August 19 | French settlers on the Nanto-Bordelaise ship *Comte de Paris* land at Akaroa. Forced to accept they have come to a British, not French, outpost, they will reach an accommodation with British settlers there and live alongside them. |
| September 1 | The New Zealand Banking Company, the first bank founded in this country, opens at Kororareka. |
| September 3 | The final signature is added to the Treaty of Waitangi, at Kawhia. |
| September 18 | Having purchased the site from Ngati Whatua, Lieutenant-Governor Hobson proclaims Auckland as a government settlement. The British flag is hoisted at what will later be called Point Britomart, and the event is celebrated with a regatta on the harbour. By February 1841 the transfer of the seat of government from Russell will be complete. |

| November 16 | Letters patent are issued making New Zealand a colony separate from New South Wales. The charter gives the names of New Ulster, New Munster and New Leinster to the three main islands and sets down a general system of government. |
|---|---|
| November 28 | The change of name from Britannia to Wellington is publicly made when the *New Zealand Gazette and Britannia Spectator* alters its title to the *New Zealand Gazette and Wellington Spectator.* |
| December 30 | At Paihia, William Colenso prints the first edition of the *New Zealand Government Gazette,* which will publish proclamations, orders-in-council, ordinances and other government announcements. |

## 1841

| January 22 | First anniversary celebrations begin in Wellington. Among the events are a subscription ball at Barrett's Hotel, a regatta — and on January 25 the first horse race in New Zealand, for a purse of 15 guineas, at Te Aro. |
|---|---|
| February 27 | The first organised settlers arrive at Wanganui on the *Elizabeth*. The New Zealand Company has called the place Petre, after one of its directors, but settlers will rarely use that name, and it will be officially confirmed as Wanganui in 1854. |

**The barracks built at New Plymouth in advance of the arrival of the first group of European settlers on March 31, 1841.**

| March 31 | Plymouth Company settlers from the *William Bryan* land at Ngamotu, the site of New Plymouth. |
| April 19 | The first sale of town allotments in Auckland begins. The announcement of the sale has led to an influx of settlers and land speculators. |
| April 27 | The *Whitby* and the *Will Watch* leave the quay at Gravesend to go to the New Zealand Company's Nelson settlement, even though no site has been decided. |
| May 3 | Captain William Hobson RN takes the oath as governor and commander-in-chief of the new colony of New Zealand. He will be advised by an executive council consisting of colonial secretary Willoughby Shortland, attorney-general Francis Fisher and colonial treasurer George Cooper. |
| May 17 | On the *Whitby*, part way through the voyage to New Zealand, the Nelson Literary and Scientific Institute is formed. |
| May 24 | At Auckland, the General Legislative Council (the Executive Council plus three justices of the peace and the governor) meets for the first time. The council has full power to enact laws and ordinances proposed by the governor. |
| July 1 | Duties become payable on imports and exports for the first time. |
| August 19 | Governor Hobson arrives at Port Nicholson on a long-awaited first visit to the troubled New Zealand Company settlement. |
| September 18 | The *Whitby* arrives at Wellington with Captain Arthur Wakefield of the New Zealand Company and Captain Francis Liardet of the Plymouth Company on board. The *Will Watch* has already arrived 10 days earlier. |
| September 28 | William Martin is officially appointed as chief justice and William Swainson as attorney-general. |
| October 9 | The *Will Watch* and the *Whitby*, and the store ship *Arrow*, anchor in the Astrolabe Roadstead in Tasman Bay so that |

|  | Arthur Wakefield and surveyors can look for a site for the new settlement of Nelson. |
|---|---|
| October 17 | At Lambeth in London, George Selwyn is consecrated as the first Anglican bishop of New Zealand. |
| October 28 | Twenty-seven settlers of the Manakou and Waitemata Company arrive in the Manukau Harbour on the *Brilliant*. Within three years their Cornwallis settlement will have been abandoned. |
| October 31 | The first known Jewish service in New Zealand is held at Russell. The occasion is the wedding of David Nathan, a pardoned convict who will found a huge business empire, and widow Rosetta Aarons. |
| November 1 | The *Arrow* enters Nelson Haven, and Arthur Wakefield decides this will be the site of the new settlement. |
| November 4 | The *Will Watch* and the *Whitby* arrive at Nelson Haven with the advance party of settlers. The *Whitby* becomes grounded on Arrow Rock at the entrance to the haven, but will be released the following day. They have three months to prepare for the arrival of the main contingent of settlers. |
| November 20 | Mrs Roberton, her family and servant are murdered by minor Nga Puhi chief Maketu at Motuarohia Island in the Bay of Islands. |
| November 22 | The *Columbine* anchors at Hicks Bay, East Cape. From here, William Colenso will return overland to the Bay of Islands on a long exploratory journey through the Urewera region. |
| December 24 | The first known public dramatic performance, of *The Lawyer Outwitted*, is put on at the 'Albert Theatre' — actually a room in Watson's Exchange Hotel, in Auckland. |
| December 24 | Land claims commissioner William Spain arrives at Auckland on the brig *Antilla* with a team of surveyors. His most important brief is to investigate the New Zealand Company's claim it has bought 20 million acres of land around Cook Strait. |

# 1842

| | |
|---|---|
| January 5 | A race meeting is held at Epsom Downs, Auckland, with the running of the Town Plate and Valparaiso Stakes. It is followed by a public banquet. |
| January 10 | William Martin takes the oaths of office as the first judge of the Supreme Court, and the first chief justice. |
| February 1 | The *Fifeshire* arrives at Nelson with the first of the main contingent of settlers. The *Mary Ann* and the *Lord Auckland* will follow before the end of the month. |
| February 15 | The *Lloyds* arrives at Nelson with the wives and children of the advance party of settlers. During the voyage, 65 children have died and the vessel has become a 'floating bawdy house' for the crew. |
| February 22 | Colenso arrives back in the Bay of Islands at the end of his three-month exploratory and botanising expedition. |
| February 28 | Maketu's trial for murder begins at the Supreme Court at Auckland, with William Martin presiding. |
| March 7 | Maketu is hanged in public at Auckland after being found guilty of the murder of six people including the Robertons, in the Bay of Islands. |
| April 11 | The distribution of town acres at Nelson begins. |
| May 1 | Government House and offices at Russell are destroyed by fire. It spells the end for the settlement at Okiato, with the last of the government functions moving to nearby Kororareka. The name of Russell will be transferred to Kororareka as well. |
| May 16 | At Wellington, land claims commissioner William Spain opens the first land court hearing. The first case concerns the New Zealand Company's land purchases and will examine whether the chiefs who sold it had the right to do so. |
| May 30 | Anglican bishop of New Zealand George Selwyn arrives |

| | at Auckland. |
|---|---|
| June 19 | Putiki Maori Church is opened at the Rev. John Mason's CMS mission at Wanganui. |
| July 20 | Governor Hobson issues a proclamation making Wellington a borough, allowing the election of the first borough council in New Zealand. |
| July 28 | George Selwyn begins a five-month survey of his episcopate. He will travel 2300 miles (3700 km), one-third of it on foot. |
| August 5 | Rev. Samuel Ironside opens a Maori church at the Cloudy Bay Wesleyan mission with the mass baptism of 190 adults and children and the marriage of 40 couples. |
| September 10 | Captain William Hobson, first governor of New Zealand, dies at Auckland at the age of 49 after a stroke. Lieutenant Willoughby Shortland will be administrator until December 1843. |
| October 9 | The first major influx of settlers — more than 500 — arrives at Auckland on the *Duchess of Argyle* and the *Jane Gifford*. Most of them are forced to wade through mud to reach the shore, to find the town offers little in the way of conveniences and comforts — just manuka waiting to be cleared from ridges and gullies. |
| October 20 | A fire in Wellington destroys dozens of buildings. |
| October 20 | At Petone, New Zealand's first formal race meeting is held and Figaro, the country's first thoroughbred horse, wins the 10-guinea sweepstake. |
| November 9 | Fire destroys nearly 40 houses and stores along Lambton Quay, Wellington. |
| December 18 | The *Victoria* arrives at Tauranga with troops led by Major Bunbury. They have come to act as a barrier between the warring people of Maketu and Tauranga. |

# 1843

| | |
|---|---|
| January 14 | Working men in Nelson submit a petition to Arthur Wakefield expressing a desire to 'live comfortably and decently'. Two days later, they will go on strike when their demand to be paid a guinea a week is refused. |
| March 11 | Te Rauparaha and Te Rangihaeata visit Arthur Wakefield to tell him not to stray into the Wairau, on the other side of the Richmond Range. Ngati Toa chief Nohorua has already warned the leader of the Nelson settlement that he should not take up the rich farming land there. |
| April 22 | The first edition of the *Southern Cross* newspaper is published in Auckland. |
| June 1 | Te Rauparaha and Te Rangihaeata land at the Wairau to stop the survey of the land. They send most of the surveyors off in boats and burn their huts. |
| June 13 | A party of settlers that includes almost all Nelson's leadership leaves Nelson for the Wairau. They plan to arrest Te Rauparaha and Te Rangihaeata. |
| June 14 | More than 100 German settlers arrive at Nelson on the *St Pauli* with the German Colonisation Company. Many will take up land at Moutere, although the settlement of St Paulidorf will later be abandoned. |
| June 17 | Te Rauparaha and Te Rangihaeata clash with Wakefield and his Nelson posse at Tuamarina. About 30 Pakeha and at least four Maori are killed. Among the dead is Te Rangihaeata's wife, Te Rongo, as well as Arthur Wakefield, whom Te Rangihaeata executes for killing his wife. |
| July 8 | At Wanganui, a 7.5 magnitude earthquake sends a large part of Shakespeare Cliff into the river. |
| September 12 | The Royal Victoria Theatre, the first purpose-built theatre, opens in Wellington with a gas-lit production of *Rover of the Seas*. |

| December 18 | The first A&P show is put on by the Auckland Agricultural and Pastoral Association at the Royal Exchange Hotel, with livestock at the Domain. Over the next 50 years A&P societies will be formed all over New Zealand with the aim of improving farming and the lot of country people. |
| --- | --- |
| December 26 | The probable swearing-in date of Captain Robert FitzRoy RN, newly arrived in the country, as the second governor of New Zealand. |
| December 26 | Henry Chapman is sworn in as the first puisne judge of the Supreme Court of New Zealand. |

# 1844

| January 26 | Robert FitzRoy arrives at Wellington and immediately goes on to Nelson to investigate the Wairau affair. At both places the new governor will reprimand Europeans for their part in the conflict. |
| --- | --- |
| February 12 | At Waikanae, FitzRoy hears Te Rauparaha's and Te Rangihaeata's version of events in the Wairau. While denouncing the murder of European prisoners, FitzRoy declares the settlers provoked the fighting and no further measures will be taken against Maori. |
| February 14 | William Colenso returns to Paihia after a four-month journey to investigate the condition of the Tuhoe people. |
| March 26 | Robert FitzRoy waives the crown's right of pre-emption, authorising the private purchase of land directly from Maori owners. The right will be restored the following year. |
| May 11 | FitzRoy attends a massive hakari at Remuera, Auckland. Thousands of Maori and Pakeha guests will enjoy the week-long open-air feast. |
| May 11 | Frederick Weld crosses Lake Wairarapa with the first sheep to enter the Wairarapa. At Wharekaka station he and his partner, Charles Clifford, will undertake the first large-scale wool growing in New Zealand. |

| July 8 | The flagstaff on Maiki Hill, Russell, is cut down and burnt by Te Haratua at the instigation of Hone Heke. Nga Puhi chief Heke is thought to be protesting the loss of the rangatiratanga (sovereignty) promised by the Treaty of Waitangi. |
| --- | --- |
| July 31 | At Koputai (Port Chalmers), the purchase of the Otago Block by the New Zealand Company from the depleted Ngai Tahu is completed. A Scottish colony is planned for the area. |
| August 24 | Governor FitzRoy arrives in the Bay of Islands with troops to quell the 'insurrection' of Hone Heke and others. |
| September 2 | At Waimate North, Robert FitzRoy tries to reassure Nga Puhi chiefs of the government's benevolent intentions. Tamati Waka Nene asks the governor to remove the troops, and FitzRoy complies. |
| December 13 | William Colenso and James Hamlin leave the Bay of Islands to found new mission stations, Hamlin at Wairoa and Colenso on the bank of the Waitangi Stream at Ahuriri, Hawke's Bay. |

## 1845

| January 10 | The flagstaff at Russell is felled for a second time on Hone Heke's instructions. |
| --- | --- |
| January 15 | The proclamation of a reward of £100 for the capture of Hone Heke is issued. |
| January 19 | Hone Heke cuts down the flagstaff for a third time, despite its being protected by Tamati Waka Nene's kupapa troops. |
| February 4 | William Colenso sets out for an arduous crossing of the Ruahine Range. He is accompanied by six baggage carriers. |
| March 11 | Six hundred warriors led by Kawiti and Hone Heke descend on Russell. The flagstaff is cut down for the fourth and last time, and the town is invaded. British troops and citizens are evacuated to the *Victoria* and the *Active*, then Russell is looted by forces from both sides. The flagstaff will not be re-erected until 1858. |

| | |
|---|---|
| March 25 | The Legislative Council signs an ordinance enabling militia units to be raised for temporary service. The units will be New Zealand's first local military force. |
| April 26 | Martial law is proclaimed at Russell, to allow military actions to suppress the rebellion. It will last until February 1 the following year. |
| April 28 | HMS *North Star* and other ships enter the Bay of Islands with more than 450 soldiers, marines and volunteers under the command of Lieutenant-Colonel William Hulme. They plan to engage the forces of Heke and Kawiti, and punish Pomare II for his alleged involvement in the rebellion. |
| April 30 | The white flag is flown from Pomare II's pa at Otuihu and the chief is arrested, then British troops destroy the pa. Pomare II will later be released without charge and compensated with a boat. |
| May 8 | An attack on Heke's pa at Puketutu by British troops, aided by Tamati Waka Nene's warriors, is repulsed. |
| June 7 | The first issue of the weekly *New Zealander* is published at Auckland. |

**The Royal Marines fire a rocket launcher during the battle of Puketutu on May 8, 1845. The artist is Cyprian Bridge, a senior British officer.**

| | |
|---|---|
| June 12 | At Te Ahuahu, Hone Heke suffers his only real defeat, by forces led by pro-government chiefs Te Taonui and Tamati Waka Nene. Heke is seriously wounded and his ally Te Kahakaha is killed. |
| June 24 | British forces under Lieutenant-Colonel Henry Despard begin an artillery bombardment of Ohaeawai pa, which is defended by Kawiti and Pene Taui. |
| July 1 | British forces storm the defences at Ohaeawai and are heavily repulsed with serious losses. Tamati Waka Nene, whose men are fighting alongside the British, will describe Despard as a 'very stupid person'. |
| July 11 | British forces enter Ohaeawai pa. Despard will claim a great victory, despite the fact the pa had been abandoned by its defenders during the night. |
| November 18 | Captain George Grey, until recently governor of South Australia, assumes office as governor of New Zealand. He is determined to win a peace with Maori and turn around the country's finances. |
| December 13 | Two companies of volunteer soldiers are formed at Auckland as the Auckland Rifle Volunteers. They will fail to re-register as required by the Volunteer Act 1865, thus missing out on being the country's senior army regiment. |

## 1846

| | |
|---|---|
| January 11 | Ruapekapeka pa, defended by followers of Heke and Kawiti, is occupied by British troops after two weeks of artillery bombardment. The action effectively brings to an end the war in the north, and the period of relative peace that follows will last for more than a decade. |
| February 12 | Governor Grey arrives at Wellington on HMS *Castor*. The *Castor* is accompanied by HMS *Driver*, which becomes the first steam vessel to enter the harbour. |
| February 27 | British troops, having forced Maori off land in the Hutt Valley |

| | |
|---|---|
| | considered sold, destroy Maraenuku pa and the surrounding cultivations. |
| March 3 | Martial law is proclaimed in the Wellington region as tensions rise over land ownership disputes. The Maori skirmishers are led by Te Rangihaeata and Te Mamaku. |
| April 2 | Te Pau of Ngati Rangatahi murders two members of the Gillespie family north of Boulcott's Farm in the Hutt Valley. |
| May 7 | The village of Te Rapa, on the shore of Lake Taupo, is buried by a landslide. Among the 61 dead is Te Heuheu Tukino II. |
| May 16 | Te Mamaku leads an attack on troops garrisoned at Boulcott's Farm in the Hutt Valley, and Bugler Allen is famously among those killed. The attack causes great alarm in Wellington. |
| July 23 | Governor Grey's men capture Te Rauparaha at Plimmerton. The neutral chief will be held prisoner on HMS *Calliope* for 10 months — and then under house arrest — but will never be charged with a crime. |
| July 29 | Te Rangihaeata evacuates Pauatahanui pa ahead of an attack by British troops. He will withdraw north to build a pa south of the Manawatu River. |
| December 11 | Thomas Brunner, with guides Kehu and Pikewati and their wives, leaves an outlying farm of Nelson. Brunner will not return from his exploratory journey to the West Coast for a year and a half. |
| December 23 | A royal charter is issued dividing New Zealand into two provinces and providing for responsible government. The new constitution will not be well received by Governor Grey, who finds it over-complex and racist. |

## 1847

| | |
|---|---|
| March 18 | George Grey buys the Wairau Valley and land in Marlborough and Canterbury as far south as Kaiapoi on behalf of the government, thus settling a long-running |

| | |
|---|---|
| | dispute. Further major purchases made throughout the country, the last of them the Waipounamu Purchase in August 1853, will effectively extinguish Maori land claims. |
| March 25 | At Wellington, a duel is fought between Colonel William Wakefield and Dr Isaac Featherston, after Featherston, editor of the *Wellington Independent*, has in an editorial indirectly accused Wakefield of being a thief. Neither man is hurt. |
| April 18 | Te Mamaku's men murder four members of the Gilfillan family near Wanganui. Four of the killers will be caught by lower Whanganui Maori and later hanged by the British. |
| May 19 | Te Mamaku raids the settlement at Wanganui, plundering shops and burning buildings. His forces will blockade the town for two months. |
| May 23 | Explorer Thomas Brunner, stranded and starving in the Buller Gorge, consents to the slaughter of his dog, Rover, for food. He finds the flesh 'very palatable'. |
| May 24 | Governor Grey, accompanied by Tamati Waka Nene and Te Wherowhero, arrives at Wanganui on HMS *Inflexible* to investigate the clashes there. |
| June 5 | The Auckland Savings Bank opens for business, although the first deposit will not be received until June 19. The first institution of its kind in New Zealand, the bank has been set up by John Logan Campbell, William Brown and other Auckland businessmen. |
| August 5 | The first detachment of the Royal New Zealand Fencible Corps arrives at Auckland on the *Ramillies*. The discharged British and Irish soldiers have been brought in to defend Auckland. In return they will be given a section and a two-bedroom cottage. |
| November 23 | The *Philip Laing* leaves Greenock with Scottish settlers for the Otago Association's site in New Zealand. The *John Wickliffe* will leave Gravesend the following day. |

| December 13 | A suspending bill is introduced into the imperial Parliament after Governor Grey has returned the 1846 constitution as unworkable. It will be passed in the following year, giving Grey great discretionary powers. |

## 1848

| January 1 | Sir George Grey, KCB, assumes office as governor-in-chief of New Zealand, and governor and commander-in-chief of the provinces of New Ulster (the North Island) and New Munster (the South Island). It is a partial implementation of the 1846 constitution but lacks any representative element. William Martin is temporarily appointed Grey's deputy in New Ulster, and Henry Chapman in New Munster. |
| January 26 | On the West Coast, Thomas Brunner discovers the coalfield that will be named after him. |
| January 28 | Edward Eyre becomes lieutenant-governor of New Munster. |
| February 14 | Major G. D. Pitt becomes lieutenant-governor of New Ulster. |
| March 10 | The part of New Ulster south of the Patea River is added to New Munster by proclamation. |
| March 23 | The *John Wickliffe*, the first of the Otago Association's immigrant ships, anchors at Port Chalmers. Many of the settlers are Scots escaping an economic depression as well as the traumatic split between the Church of Scotland and Free Church Presbyterians. |
| April 15 | The *Philip Laing* anchors at Port Chalmers. |
| June 23 | Government House in Auckland is destroyed by fire. |
| October 16 | An earthquake, the first in New Zealand to be documented in detail, causes extensive damage at Wellington. Centred in the Wairau Valley, it measures 7.1 on the Richter scale. Shocks will continue until October 24, the most violent being on October 19, and at least three people will die. |

| November 7 | HMSV *Acheron* (Captain John Lort Stokes) arrives at Auckland. The first survey vessel to work in New Zealand waters since the time of Captain Cook will spend four years charting the coastline. |
| December 13 | The first edition of the *Otago News* is published at Dunedin. |

# 1849

| February 1 | Governor Grey hosts the first government ball, at Wellington. There are more than 200 guests, including Te Puni and Tamihana Te Rauparaha, as well as the leading lights of Wellington society. |
| May 26 | A large public meeting in Dunedin protests against the proposed introduction of transported convicts to the settlement. |
| November 13 | A royal charter is granted to the Canterbury Association, the body that will organise the settlement of Christchurch. |
| November 27 | Great tribal leader Te Rauparaha dies at Otaki, at the age of about 85. |
| December 4 | About 60 Maori and Moriori settlers who have lived in the Auckland Islands since moving there from the Chatham Islands in 1842 are surprised to be joined by a group of European settlers. In a ceremony at Erebus Cove, the Auckland Islands are inaugurated as a British colony, and Charles Enderby assumes office as lieutenant-governor. The tiny whaling settlement will break up three years later. |
| December 13 | John Robert Godley, resident chief agent for the Canterbury Association, sails from Plymouth. |

# 1850

| May 25 | Rev. Henry Williams learns of his dismissal from the Church Missionary Society. He has refused Bishop Selwyn's demand that all missionaries give up large land claims. |

| | |
|---|---|
| July 4 | The New Zealand Company is authorised to surrender its charter. After being involved in the settlement of Wellington, Nelson, Wanganui and New Plymouth, as well as, to a lesser degree, Canterbury and Otago, E. G. Wakefield's company has succumbed to financial ill health. |
| August 6 | Hone Heke dies at Kaikohe from tuberculosis. He has made his peace with the crown, having presented his mere to Grey at Waimate in 1848. |
| September 7 | The *Charlotte Jane*, the *Randolph* and the *Cressy* leave Plymouth with passengers selected by the Canterbury Association. The *Sir George Seymour* will depart the following day. |
| December 16 | The *Charlotte Jane* arrives at Lyttelton, followed on the same day by the *Randolph* and a day later by the *Sir George Seymour*. The new settlers are faced with a demanding journey over the Port Hills and through a swamp to reach Christchurch, only to find that preparations for their arrival have been halted because the Canterbury Association's funds have run out. |
| December 27 | The *Cressy* arrives at Lyttelton, the last of the 'First Four Ships' to make port. John Godley will report the voyages to have been favourable — with only 12 deaths among the more than 750 passengers. |

## 1851

| | |
|---|---|
| January 11 | The first issue of the *Lyttelton Times* is published. |
| February 8 | The first edition of the fortnightly *Otago Witness* is published at Dunedin. |
| April 26 | Lieutenant-Colonel Robert Wynyard assumes office as lieutenant-governor of New Ulster. During his term he will oversee the inauguration of the first municipal corporation, Auckland. |

**Passengers from the *Cressy* alight at Lyttelton, having arrived in port on 27 December, 1850, to establish the Canterbury settlement.**

June 3    The French corvette *Alcmène* is wrecked at Baylys Beach, between the Kaipara and Hokianga harbours. Twelve lives are lost, and the survivors will live as castaways until rescued by Maori.

July 23    The barque *Maria* is wrecked off Cape Terawhiti with the loss of 26 lives, including the Canterbury pioneer William Deans, who was the first Pakeha to settle the Canterbury Plains, in 1843.

October 20    The foundation stone is laid for the first Baptist church in the country, at Nelson. Rev. Decimus Dolamore's church will not be completed for more than three years because the stone masons are needed for the more necessary task of building a brewery.

# War and peace
## 1852–1869

**As New Zealand made** its first attempts at responsible government in the 1850s, the United Kingdom was preoccupied with the 1854–1856 war in the Crimea. A bloody rebellion in India led the British crown to take over government of that country in 1858. The following year, righteous uproar followed the publication of Charles Darwin's theory on the origin of species. By the 1860s the USA was in turmoil with a civil war, the emancipation of the slaves and the assassination of Abraham Lincoln. Across the Pacific Ocean, the North Island suffered through a New Zealand civil war brought about by disputes over land. In contrast, the South Island was entering a time of prosperity with the success of sheep farming and the arrival of thousands of prospectors following the discovery of Otago gold in 1861.

# 1852

| | |
|---|---|
| January 19 | The *Governor Wynyard*, the first steamboat built in New Zealand, makes its first commercial trip, from Official Bay, Auckland, to Panmure. |
| April 26 | Christ's College, Christchurch, opens at St Michael's parsonage with five pupils. The school has moved from earlier premises at Lyttelton. |
| June 30 | A second New Zealand Constitution Act is passed by the imperial Parliament. The legislation establishes a system of responsible government for New Zealand, with a General Assembly consisting of a Legislative Council appointed by the crown and a House of Representatives elected every five years by male British subjects 21 years or over who own, lease or rent property of a certain value. The act also divides the country into six provinces with their own representative governments. |
| June 30 | Tamihana Te Rauparaha is presented to Queen Victoria. The son of the Ngati Toa war leader Te Rauparaha, he will try to unify his people by establishing a Maori monarchy. |
| October 15 | At Driving Creek in the Coromandel, Charles Ring makes the first find of payable gold in New Zealand — although traces of gold were first found at least 10 years earlier. When the news is published in the *New Zealander* at Auckland, New Zealand's first gold rush will be set in motion. However, only small amounts of gold will be found. |
| October 25 | The Auckland Museum — the forerunner to the Auckland Institute and Museum — opens in a disused government farm building in Grafton Road. The small collection includes mineral, animal and insect specimens. |
| November 9 | William Colenso's suspension as a deacon is formalised and he is dismissed from the mission at Ahuriri. He has fathered the child of Ripeka Meretene, a member of his household. He will be reinstated more than 40 years later. |

# 1853

| February 2 | E. G. Wakefield arrives with Henry Sewell at Lyttelton on the *Minerva*. He will be received with some hostility by disgruntled Canterbury settlers. |
| --- | --- |
| February 28 | The boundaries of the new provinces of Canterbury, Wellington, Nelson, Otago and New Plymouth (changed to Taranaki in 1858) are defined and constituted. |
| March 7 | Governor Grey assumes the powers vested in him by letters patent in accordance with the 1852 Constitution Act. |
| March 19 | A Wellington public meeting convened by Joseph Masters resolves to set up a working men's land association, which will become the Small Farm Association. Through this organisation, small farm owners will band together to buy large blocks of land. |
| July 14 | The first election for the House of Representatives begins, and Hugh Carleton becomes the first member of Parliament when he is returned unopposed. The elections for the remaining 36 members will continue for over 11 weeks. Only a small number of Maori will vote because most have been excluded under the property qualification as almost all Maori land is owned communally. |
| September 17 | The *Gazelle* arrives at Auckland bringing the first of Waipu's Scottish pioneers. Rev. Norman McLeod and his followers have travelled from Nova Scotia via Australia looking for somewhere to settle. Over the course of seven years nearly 900 people will make the long journey from Nova Scotia to Waipu, Northland. |
| October 1 | The election for the House of Representatives is completed. |
| December 31 | Governor Grey departs New Zealand on the *Commodore* at the conclusion of his term of office as governor. He has been sent to South Africa to become governor of Cape Colony. |

# 1854

| | |
|---|---|
| January 3 | Robert Wynyard assumes office as administrator until the arrival of the new governor. |
| May 24 | The first sitting of the first House of Representatives is opened at Auckland by Robert Wynyard. The parliamentarians are sworn in, then head off to a formal reception and a ball in the evening. |
| May 26 | Charles Clifford is elected unopposed as first speaker of the House of Representatives. |
| May 27 | The first state opening of the General Assembly takes place and Robert Wynyard delivers the opening address of the Legislative Council. |
| June 14 | James FitzGerald (as leader), Henry Sewell and Frederick Weld begin a short term as unofficial and temporary members of the Executive Council. |
| August 31 | Thomas Forsaith (as leader), Jerningham Wakefield, William Travers and James Macandrew begin a term as unofficial members of a new Executive Council (until September 2). |
| December 31 | The English Acts Act passes into law. This first act of the new New Zealand Parliament adopts statutes passed in the imperial Parliament. |

# 1855

| | |
|---|---|
| January 23 | A severe earthquake shakes Wellington and the Wairarapa. The death toll includes five Europeans and at least three Maori living outside the town. With a magnitude of 8 on the Richter scale, it lifts the southern end of the Rimutaka Range by 6.5 yds (6 m). Land raised in Wellington Harbour will later be drained and built upon. |
| March 4 | At the Levels, Canterbury, James Mackenzie is caught in the act of sheep stealing on a grand scale, but escapes. He will be captured again at Lyttelton on March 15. |

| April 12 | James Mackenzie is found guilty of sheep stealing. In a Lyttelton court, he is sentenced to five years' hard labour on the roads. |
|---|---|
| May 10 | Mackenzie escapes from custody at Lyttelton. A reward will be offered and he will be recaptured within days — before escaping and being captured for a third time the following month. |
| July 18 | New Zealand's first stamps for the prepayment of postage go on sale. The adhesive, imperforated stamps bear the image of Queen Victoria. |
| August 19 | British troops of the 58th Regiment arrive to protect New Plymouth after the escalation of skirmishes over land ownership, most of them Maori against Maori. |
| September 6 | Colonel Thomas Gore Browne assumes office as governor. The former soldier, although idealistic, will find it beyond him to understand Maori attitudes to land issues and authority. |

## 1856

| January 11 | James Mackenzie receives a free pardon. Henry Tancred, the resident magistrate at Christchurch, has found the folk hero's trial to have been flawed. The pastoral land where he was found in possession of stolen sheep will come to be called the Mackenzie Country. |
|---|---|
| January 24 | At the inaugural meeting of the Auckland Chamber of Commerce, merchants and traders join together to further their own interests. The Auckland group is the first of a nationwide network to get started. |
| May 7 | The first ministry under responsible government (formed by a majority in the house) is appointed, and Henry Sewell assumes office as the first premier. The ministry will last less than two weeks, Sewell quickly making himself unpopular by proposing to increase the powers of central government at the expense of the provinces. |

| May 20 | William Fox replaces Sewell as premier. His brief term is the first of four for the energetic former explorer and landscape painter. |

| June 2 | Edward Stafford assumes office as premier to lead the first stable responsible ministry. During his term, he will ensure that responsible government is a demonstrable success. |

## 1857

| February 9 | The first 7 ounces of gold from the Nelson diggings is put up for auction at Nelson. The discovery of gold and the ensuing rush will precipitate a name change from Massacre Bay to Golden Bay. |

| September 23 | A magic lantern show is held at the Oddfellows' Hall in Auckland. Accompanied by piano music and including 'dissolving views' of Mt Vesuvius in eruption, it is the first recorded public showing of magic lantern projections. |

| September 26 | A pass over the Southern Alps is found by Edward Dobson. It will later be named Harper Pass after Leonard Harper, the first Pakeha to use the pass to travel all the way to the West Coast. |

## 1858

| May 2 | Te Wherowhero is crowned as Potatau, the first Maori king, in elaborate ceremonies at Ngaruawahia. He has been chosen for his ancestry and personal mana, at a meeting at Pukawa in November 1856 called by Te Heuheu. |

| May 25 | The *Strathallan* sails from Otago for London with 800 bales of wool valued at £19,000, on the first direct voyage to England. |

| July 8 | In the early hours of the morning a fire takes hold at the Osprey Inn in central Auckland. It destroys an entire block of buildings, with only a change in wind direction and a downpour of rain preventing much worse damage. |

| | |
|---|---|
| November 1 | Hawke's Bay separates from the province of Wellington by order-in-council. |
| December 22 | Geologist Dr Ferdinand Hochstetter arrives at Auckland on the *Novara*. With Julius Haast, he will begin a survey of the Drury/Hunua coalfield a few days later. Afterwards, they will join up with Charles Heaphy to complete an extensive survey of the central North Island. |

## 1859

| | |
|---|---|
| January 1 | The first lighthouse built in New Zealand begins operation at Pencarrow Head. The lighthouse keeper is Mary Jane Bennett, the widow of the keeper of an earlier temporary beacon. |
| March 7 | Minor Te Ati Awa chief Teira offers to sell a block of land at Waitara to the government. Senior chief Wiremu Kingi immediately announces his intention to oppose the sale of the land, beginning a long and sometimes violent struggle over the Waitara Block. |
| May 21 | The New Zealand Insurance Company is established, with eight Auckland merchants pledging their savings to the venture. The formation of New Zealand's first insurance company has been prompted by the destructive fire in Auckland in 1858. |
| August 3 | Ferdinand Hochstetter arrives at Nelson to make a survey of the province. |
| November 1 | Marlborough separates from the province of Nelson by order-in-council. |
| November 8 | John Rochfort finds gold in the Buller River, but his discovery will not be followed up on immediately. |

## 1860

| | |
|---|---|
| March 1 | Governor Gore Browne, Colonel Charles Gold and military reinforcements arrive at New Plymouth, bringing the number of regular troops there to 450. |

| March 17 | Wiremu Kingi and his supporters build and occupy a pa on the disputed land at Waitara. Shots are exchanged and the Taranaki war erupts. |
| --- | --- |
| March 28 | The battle of Waireka is fought when British regulars and Taranaki volunteers go in to rescue settlers south of Omata and clash with Taranaki and Ngati Ruanui raiders. In the clash, the Taranaki Rifle Volunteers earn the colour 'New Zealand', the only New Zealand regiment to do so. |

**British soldiers attack the palisaded Waireka pa on March 28, 1860, during the Taranaki war.**

| April 20 | The governor orders Colonel Gold to suspend hostilities against Wiremu Kingi so that he does not gain wider Maori support. The ceasefire will last for more than two months. |
| --- | --- |
| May 20 | In the Grey River, Julius Haast finds the main bituminous coal seam of the Brunner field, leading to the coalfield's development. |

| | |
|---|---|
| June 25 | Potatau Te Wherowhero, the first Maori king, dies at Ngaruawahia. He is succeeded by his son Tawhiao (Potatau II). |
| June 27 | Elite British troops attack the pa at Puketakauere but are forced by Hapurona and his warriors to withdraw in chaos, abandoning the wounded. |
| July 10 | Governor Gore Browne convenes a meeting of Maori at Auckland. Known as the Kohimarama Conference, the gathering to discuss the welfare of the indigenous people of New Zealand will last until August 11. |
| November 6 | Imperial troops drive Ngati Haua out of an incomplete pa at Mahoetahi. It is a rare victory for the queen's forces in the continuing battle for control of the area around New Plymouth. |

# 1861

| | |
|---|---|
| March 18 | Hostilities in the Taranaki war are suspended. In a year, 3500 imperial troops stationed around New Plymouth have failed to make any significant progress. |
| March 25 | Southland is proclaimed as a province by order-in-council, to take effect from April 1. It will be reabsorbed into Otago in 1870. |
| April 8 | The Taranaki war officially ends when the government concludes an agreement with chief Hapurona of Te Ati Awa, although Wiremu Kingi declines to sign the articles of peace. |
| May 23 | Probable date Gabriel Read discovers gold at Gabriels Gully in the Tuapeka district. His find, which will eventually earn him £1000 in rewards, is the first of many major Otago gold discoveries that will see the province's population double within six months. |
| May 25 | The first issue of the *Press* is published in Christchurch. Founder James FitzGerald has produced the new newspaper on a hand-operated press in a cottage in Montreal Street. |

| July 12 | In a resolution of no confidence, William Fox's alliance defeats the government by 24 votes to 23. William Stafford resigns as premier and Fox assumes office for a second time. The new premier favours the greater involvement of Maori in government. |
| October 11 | Charles Cole's first Cobb & Co. coach service to the Otago goldfields runs between Dunedin and Gabriels Gully. The journey takes a single day, cutting the usual travelling time in half. |
| October 16 | The first offices of the privately owned Bank of New Zealand are opened in Auckland, with Alex Kennedy as general manager. Within six months there will be 10 branches scattered around the country. |
| November 15 | The first issue of the *Otago Daily Times* is published by W. H. Cullen and future prime minister Julius Vogel. Dunedin is the first centre to get a daily newspaper. |
| December 4 | Sir George Grey assumes office as governor for a second term. He has been recalled in the hope he will use his influence with Maori to resolve the land disputes. |

## 1862

| January 1 | Work begins on the Great South Road between Auckland and the Waikato. The construction of the military road will involve 2400 mostly British and Indian troops and allow a supply line to the anticipated conflict in the Waikato. |
| February 3 | The Dun Mountain Railway opens in Nelson. This first New Zealand railway line is 13.5 miles (22 km) long and uses gravity to transport chrome ore to Port Nelson, with horses pulling the empty wagons back up the hill. |
| May 7 | The country's first public tram service begins operation. The horse-drawn 'Dun Mountain bus' runs on the rails of the Dun Mountain Railway between Nelson and Port Nelson. |
| June 18 | The country's first telegraph line, between Christchurch and |

| | |
|---|---|
| | its port at Lyttelton, is completed. |
| July 8 | A prize fight is staged between George Barton and Harry Jones on the bank of the Waimakariri River, near Christchurch. Faced with a crowd of hundreds, police are unable to prevent the illegal fight, which is the first recorded professional boxing match in New Zealand. |
| July 30 | The rules of the Acclimatisation Society of Auckland are adopted. It is the first recorded organisation to devote itself to the introduction of exotic wildlife for hunting, pest control — and nostalgia. |
| August 6 | Alfred Domett assumes office as premier. A poet, linguist and newspaper editor, he has distinguished himself as the leader of the settlement of Nelson. |
| August 15 | Miners Horatio Hartley and Christopher Reilly deposit 1000 oz of gold at Dunedin. In return for a reward of £2000 they will divulge the location of a new goldfield at Dunstan on the Clutha River. |
| September 5 | Te Ua Haumene experiences a visitation by the Angel Gabriel, who tells him to cast off the yoke of the Pakeha. He will start Pai Marire (Hauhau), a religious fighting force to restore the birthright of the Maori people. |
| September 8 | The *Matilda Wattenbach* arrives at Auckland with the first migrants for the special settlement of Albertland on the Kaipara Harbour. They are the first of about 3000 Midlands non-conformist Protestants to arrive, although more than half will not end up in Albertland as intended. |
| September 29 | *The Daughter of the Regiment* is performed, in shortened form, at Dunedin's Royal Princess Theatre by the English Opera Troupe supplemented by local performers. It is the first time a fully staged professional opera production has been put on in New Zealand. |
| October 4 | Jack Tewa ('Maori Jack') begins gold-mining operations in the Arrow River, Central Otago. |

# 1863

| | |
|---|---|
| February 7 | HMS *Orpheus* founders on the Manukau Harbour bar after a navigation error. There are only 70 known survivors of the 259 on board, many of them British troops on their way to fight in the war in New Zealand, making it the most deadly of all New Zealand shipwrecks. |
| February 20 | Julius Haast stands in the Tasman surf to celebrate reaching the West Coast via the Haast River. His route uses a pass Charles Cameron has claimed, without proof, to have found a month earlier. The pass will become known as Haast Pass. |
| May 4 | Violence erupts again in Taranaki when Ngati Ruanui and Taranaki warriors ambush government troops at Tataraimaka, killing nine. |
| May 5 | The Colonial Defence Force Act 1862 comes into force, allowing New Zealand to raise troops for internal defence. This is the beginning of the country's regular army. |
| May 9 | In Dunedin, New Zealand's first gas street lights are lit by the Dunedin Gas Light and Coke Company. |
| May 11 | A proclamation is issued abandoning the crown's Waitara purchase, which has brought nothing but violence to Taranaki. |
| June 4 | Troops led by Lieutenant-General Duncan Cameron defeat a party of Maori at Katikara, south-west of New Plymouth. Subsequently, most of the imperial troops will be withdrawn to the Waikato. |
| June 8 | A law is passed by the imperial Parliament to extend New Zealand's territorial zone to include the Auckland, Campbell, Antipodes and Bounty islands. |
| June 28 | A group of 83 Bohemian settlers arrives at Auckland. The German-speaking immigrants from Staab, a district that is today part of the Czech Republic, will be taken by cutter to the mouth of the Puhoi River and then by canoe to the |

'special settlement' of Puhoi.

| | |
|---|---|
| July 9 | Governor Grey orders all Maori living between Auckland and the Waikato to swear an oath of allegiance to the crown — or retreat south of the Mangatawhiri River into Kingitanga (Maori King movement) territory. |
| July 12 | Lieutenant-General Cameron's force crosses the Mangatawhiri River. It is the first act of war in the Waikato campaign, which has been planned in part to gain land for European settlement. |
| July 17 | Cameron's troops defeat a Maori force at Koheroa. Meanwhile, behind the British line near Drury, a Ngati Paoa taua overwhelms a military convoy. A long series of Maori raids on settlers will follow, tying up British troops for months. |
| July 26 | A natural dam at Maori Point on the Shotover River breaks, drowning 13 men. By the end of winter hundreds of people will die in floods, landslides, blizzards and avalanches all over Otago. |
| August 8 | The locomotive *Lady Barkly* runs along wooden rails on the Invercargill jetty. The first steam locomotive in New Zealand spends the day impressing onlookers by shuttling backwards and forwards over the short track. |
| September 4 | Huria Matenga courageously swims with a line to save the crew of the stricken *Delaware* off Pepin Island, Nelson. She will become known as 'the Grace Darling of New Zealand'. |
| October 26 | Albert Victor Pomare is born in London. He is the son of Hare and Hariata Pomare, who are travelling with William Jenkins's party of Methodist converts performing and 'demonstrating good works'. The first Maori born in England will have Queen Victoria as a godmother. |
| October 30 | Solicitor and entrepreneur Frederick Whitaker assumes office as premier. He is representative of Auckland's 'war party', believing that to advance the colony it is necessary for settlers to gain access to Maori lands — by whatever means necessary. |

| November 1 | Meremere pa is strategically evacuated ahead of a British attack, allowing Cameron's troops to push further into the Waikato. |
| November 13 | The first issue of the *New Zealand Herald* is published in Auckland. |
| November 20 | British troops launch an assault on the Kingitanga position at Rangiriri, and there are heavy casualties on both sides. |

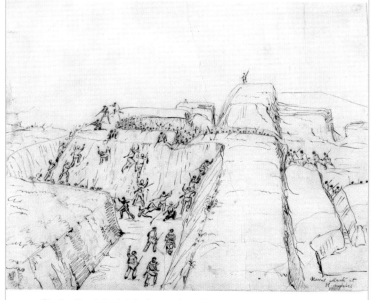

**Charles Heaphy's sketch of a naval attack on the earthworks at Rangiriri, November 20–21, 1863.**

| November 21 | The pa at Rangiriri is overrun by British troops after confusion over the meaning of a flag of truce. Most of the Kingitanga troops have been evacuated overnight, but 183 rearguard defenders are captured. |
| December 1 | A train excursion runs from Christchurch to Ferrymead at the official opening of the new railway line. The first locomotive-powered railway in the country will be closed four years later when the Lyttelton rail tunnel opens. |

| | |
|---|---|
| December 3 | The New Zealand Settlements Act (Confiscation Act) is passed. The new legislation allows the governor to confiscate land belonging to tribes any of whose members take part in the insurgency. |
| December 8 | Imperial troops occupy the deserted pa at Ngaruawahia and raise the British flag. |

# 1864

| | |
|---|---|
| January 21 | A British expedition lands at Tauranga to prevent neutral Bay of Plenty tribes from supplying Waikato troops with provisions and troops. |
| February 11 | In a skirmish at Waiari, not far from Te Awamutu, Major Charles Heaphy is involved in the daring rescue of an injured man. He will later be awarded the Victoria Cross for his actions, but only after persistent lobbying on his own behalf. It is the first time the British medal has been given to a soldier in a colonial army. |
| February 21 | Cameron's troops capture the unoccupied village of Rangiaowhia — a crucial part of the Kingitanga supply system — then withdraw to Te Awamutu to draw a counter-attack. |
| February 22 | The Paterangi Line, north-west of Te Awamutu, is evacuated by Kingitanga troops, preserving the lives of the men but sacrificing a good strategic position. |
| March 12 | Brothers Arthur, George and Edward Dobson become the first Pakeha to cross what will become known as Arthur's Pass. They are searching for the route between Christchurch and the West Coast that chief Tarapuhi has told them about. |
| March 31 | The siege of Orakau begins in the Waikato. Inside the partly completed pa, Rewi Maniapoto and a force of about 300 Kingitanga troops repel three attacks. |
| April 2 | The defenders of Orakau, having run out of water and ammunition, reject an invitation to surrender. Instead, they break out of the pa and cut through the cordon of imperial |

troops. They are ruthlessly pursued, and dozens, including women, are slaughtered.

April 6 — Members of prophet Te Ua Haumene's Pai Marire movement ambush a British patrol near Oakura, Taranaki. Captain Thomas Lloyd's head will be carried from village to village to gather support for the religious movement, whose name means 'good and peaceful'.

April 28 — The bombardment of Pukehinahina, or Gate Pa, begins. In the main action of the Tauranga campaign, Lieutenant-General Cameron has 17 pieces of artillery and more than 1700 troops at his disposal. The pa, deceptively well protected with trenches and bunkers, is defended by 230 Maori, most of them Ngai Te Rangi.

April 29 — After shelling Gate Pa for most of the day, imperial troops storm the fortifications. They are routed within 10 minutes and retreat, leaving behind more than 100 dead and wounded. The defenders will evacuate the pa during the night.

April 30 — Pai Marire attack the redoubt at Sentry Hill, Taranaki, and are repulsed with heavy casualties.

May 1 — The number of imperial troops in New Zealand is recorded at 11,355 men. By the end of the New Zealand Wars a total of about 18,000 will have served.

May 14 — Lower Whanganui Maori defeat 300 Pai Marire converts at Moutoa Island, Whanganui River, in a ritualised battle. Their success saves the grateful Pakeha residents of Wanganui from attack.

June 21 — Ngai Te Rangi, led by chief Rawiri Puhirake, are defeated in battle at Te Ranga, Tauranga. Puhirake is killed in action and, when he is buried the next day, British officers will gather to pay their respects.

June 29 — Ngai Tahu and Ngati Mamoe chiefs sell Stewart Island to the government for £6000. The initial distribution of payment will take place the following day.

| July 15 | Albert Hunt claims the reward for finding payable gold on the West Coast. His 'discovery' is at Greenstone Creek, a site shown to him by a Maori prospector named Simon. |
| July 19 | The first trees are planted in Christchurch's Hagley Park. They are English species, chosen to remind the settlers of 'Home'. |
| July 25 | At Tauranga, Maori troops surrender to Colonel H. H. Greer. As punishment for their rebelliousness, a quarter of their land will be confiscated and much of it transferred to military settlers. |
| November 24 | Pioneering sheep farmer Frederick Weld assumes office as premier. He has agreed to form a ministry on condition the seat of government be moved to the Cook Strait area and the British government be pushed to withdraw troops. |
| December 17 | A huge tract of Maori land in the Waikato is confiscated under the New Zealand Settlements Act. By 1867, nearly 5 million acres (2 million ha) will have been declared confiscated, including land in Taranaki, Bay of Plenty, East Coast and northern Hawke's Bay. However, the government will not take possession of the land straight away, leading to 'creeping confiscation' and future conflict. |

# 1865

| January 1 | Tiritiri lighthouse, the first built under the auspices of the Marine Board, begins operation. The tower has been built from cast-iron plates shipped from England in 279 packages. |
| January 5 | General Cameron is ordered by Governor Grey to engage in a campaign in Wanganui. The military commander is reluctant to take his troops there to secure land for settlement. He also doubts that a campaign in this district can be successful. |
| January 12 | The Dunedin International Exhibition begins. Despite the difficulties of travel, nearly 30,000 visitors from around the country will enjoy exhibits from all over the world. The only fly in the ointment is the absence from the official opening of |

| | |
|---|---|
| | the governor, who had been expected to grace this prestigious occasion. |
| January 24 | A British force of 1200 leaves Wanganui with General Cameron to crush the South Taranaki tribes. At Nukumaru, Ngati Ruanui spring a surprise attack, and the following day Pai Marire will do the same. |
| February 16 | The first sod of a railway line from Auckland to Drury is turned. Two years later the project will be abandoned when the money runs out. |
| March 2 | Missionary Carl Volkner is hanged and then beheaded by Kereopa Te Rau and other Pai Marire converts at Opotiki. The murderers will be pursued by colonial forces, and the deaths will lead to a virtual civil war between Pai Marire and factions of Ngati Porou. |
| March 13 | Ngati Ruanui attack Cameron's troops at Te Ngaio, near Patea, and are heavily defeated. |
| March 31 | The *Waitemata*, the first regular steam ferry on the Waitemata Harbour, begins the Flagstaff (Devonport) to Auckland run. An earlier steam service, on the *Emu*, ran for just six months in 1860. |
| April 15 | Auckland's business area is first lit by gas, with 42 of a promised 100 public lamps installed. |
| April 22 | Governor Grey issues a proclamation stating that Pai Marire practices 'repugnant to all humanity' will be suppressed — by force of arms if necessary. |
| April 30 | Captain Robert FitzRoy commits suicide in England. The former governor, who has been experiencing severe depression, will have his debts paid off by his friends after his death. |
| June 12 | American-born soldier Kimble Bent deserts from the 57th Regiment. He will end up in the hands of Ngati Ruanui, who will keep him as a slave initially, and will be immortalised in James Cowan's book *The Adventures of Kimble Bent*. |

July 20 — Without the recalcitrant General Cameron's approval or even knowledge, Governor Grey oversees the capture of a depot behind Wereroa pa, between Patea and Wanganui. The pa itself will be abandoned the next day, and Grey will claim a magnificent victory.

**Pai Marire prisoners ready for transportation to the Chatham Islands following their capture at Wereroa pa, July 20–21, 1865.**

July 26 — Parliament sits for the first time in its new home, the old Provincial Council chamber in the new capital, Wellington. The capital has been moved from Auckland to the more central Wellington at the recommendation of an Australian commission. Other sites, including Dunedin, Nelson, Havelock and Picton, have been considered and rejected.

September 2 — A proclamation of peace is issued, declaring an end to the war that began at Oakura.

September 12 — Parliament votes on the proposed political separation of the North and South Islands. The motion is defeated by 31 votes to 17.

October 16 — Edward Stafford somewhat reluctantly assumes office as premier for a second term.

| October 20 | At Te Teko in the Bay of Plenty, Pai Marire warriors surrender to Major William Mair. |
| October 30 | The Native Lands Act passes into law. It establishes the Native Land Court, to translate Maori land rights or customary titles into land titles recognisable under European law — thus enabling the sale of that land to Pakeha. Francis Fenton will be the first chief judge. |
| November 22 | Pai Marire forces surrender at Waerenga-a-hika in Poverty Bay, and 400 are taken prisoner. Many of them will later be transported to the Chatham Islands. |
| November 26 | The Native Rights Act passes into law, declaring Maori to be British subjects. |

## 1866

| January 1 | The Canterbury Rifles and the Christchurch City Guards re-register under the Volunteer Act 1865, entitling today's Canterbury Regiment to be recognised as the senior regiment of the New Zealand army. |
| January 14 | British troops take Otapawa pa, near Pipiriki. It is the last significant engagement by imperial troops in New Zealand. |
| January 18 | Prospectors digging on the beach at Port Taranaki strike oil and gas. The Moturoa field is New Zealand's — and Great Britain's — first oil field. The Alpha well will produce only three barrels of oil, and Taranaki's first oil rush will be over in a year. |
| January 27 | Five hundred weary British troops led by General Trevor Chute are fêted when they enter New Plymouth. They have taken nine days to cover 60 miles (96 km) on a rough inland route from Hawera to New Plymouth and have narrowly avoided starvation. The troops are part way through a six-week campaign that will see the area from Wanganui to New Plymouth cleared of Maori resistance, and dozens of pa and villages destroyed. |

| | |
|---|---|
| February 21 | The first 12 Chinese miners invited by the Dunedin Chamber of Commerce to work the goldfields arrive at Lawrence. They will be followed by many more of their countrymen (2000 within four years), inspiring moral hysteria over opium smoking and gambling — and legislation to make it harder for them to come. |
| March 23 | The coach road from Christchurch to Hokitika over Arthur's Pass is officially opened, although Cobb & Co. has already run its first service on the new route. Construction has taken less than a year, despite atrocious conditions. |
| May 14 | The *General Grant*, with 83 people and a cargo of gold on board, founders at Auckland Island. There are 15 survivors, four of whom will die going for help in a lifeboat and a fifth who will die of exhaustion. The remaining 10 will be picked up 18 months later by the *Amherst*. |
| June 5 | Te Kooti (Te Turuki of Ngati Maru) is deported with Pai Marire prisoners to a penal settlement at the Chatham Islands. He has been accused of spying for the enemy while fighting with government troops against Pai Marire. |
| June 12 | On the Maungatapu track between Canvastown and Nelson, a prospector is ambushed and murdered for money and gold dust. The next day four more men will be murdered there. |
| June 19 | Philip Levy is arrested in the Maungatapu murder case. The following day his accomplices Richard Burgess, Thomas Kelly and Joseph Sullivan will be arrested. |
| August 26 | A submarine telegraph cable across Cook Strait links the North and South Islands for the first time. The first message is sent between Lyall Bay, Wellington, and Whites Bay, near Blenheim. |
| September 12 | Burgess, Kelly, Levy and Sullivan go on trial at Nelson. |
| October 5 | Burgess, Kelly and Levy are hanged in Nelson for the Maungatapu murders. Sullivan has received a life sentence because he has turned queen's evidence. |

# 1867

| | |
|---|---|
| February 1 | Post office savings banks, authorised in 1864, begin operation at Auckland, Wellington, Christchurch, Dunedin and Hokitika. |
| February 5 | A railway line from Bluff to Invercargill is opened, despite political and practical difficulties during construction. |
| February 21 | Te Kooti, exiled in the Chatham Islands, writes in his diary of his first divine revelation. He will go on to establish the Ringatu movement. |
| June 10 | At Camp Waihi, Riwha Titokowaru leads off a great peace march seeking an end to the land disputes in Taranaki caused by 'creeping consfiscation'. The Ngati Ruanui leader, who has taken over the mantle of Te Ua Haumene since his death in late 1866, has declared 1867 to be the year of peace and instigated a series of peace meetings. |
| July 30 | The great Canterbury snowstorm begins. More than half a million sheep and cattle will die in the extreme winter weather. |
| August 1 | Thames is proclaimed a goldfield by negotiation with Ngati Maru. A week later, a rich reef will be found in the Kuranui Stream. |
| September 20 | The Native Schools Act is passed by the House of Representatives, enabling primary schools teaching in English to be established at the request of Maori communities. |
| October 10 | The Maori Representation Act institutes four Maori seats in Parliament, with only adult Maori males able to vote. Maori men are given universal suffrage — 12 years before Pakeha men — and become the first indigenous people to gain the vote in a neo-European country. |
| November 23 | Sparrows and starlings are imported by the Auckland Acclimatisation Society. |

| | |
|---|---|
| December 9 | The Lyttelton railway tunnel is officially opened. The new link between Christchurch and its port bypasses the arduous road trip over the Port Hills and renders the Christchurch–Ferrymead railway redundant. |

## 1868

| | |
|---|---|
| January 11 | The first cricket match is played at the Basin Reserve, Wellington, between Wellington Volunteers and a team from HMS *Falcon*. After the game, the umpire apologises to the players for the state of the ground, which has left the ball severely pockmarked. |
| February 5 | Sir George Bowen, a distinguished scholar, assumes office as governor. |
| April 15 | The first two Maori parliamentary representatives, Frederick Nene Russell and Tareha Te Moananui, are elected unopposed. Later polls for the other two new Maori seats will have disappointing turnouts. |
| June 9 | Titokowaru's war begins when settlers David Cahill, Thomas Squires and William Clark are murdered near Ketemarae, Wanganui, by Nga Ruahine warriors acting on the spiritual leader's orders. The deaths mark a change in strategy in the land disputes. |
| July 4 | Te Kooti captures the schooner *Rifleman* at the Chatham Islands. The prophet and 300 of his followers leave Waitangi for New Zealand, but head winds force them to return. They will eventually make land at Whareongaonga, near Gisborne, nearly a week later, when Te Kooti begins a bloody campaign of revenge, including defeats of the colonial militia at Paparatu, Te Konaki and Ruakituri. |
| August 21 | Lieutenant-Colonel Thomas McDonnell and Major Gustavus von Tempsky of the Forest Rangers launch an unsuccessful attack on Titokowaru's pa at Te Ngutu-o-te-manu. |
| September 7 | At Te Ngutu-o-te-manu, McDonnell's colonial troops are roundly defeated by Titokowaru's forces, and von Tempsky is killed. The |

dashing von Tempsky's death will shock fans around the country.

**An imaginative reconstruction of a Maori ambush at Te Ngutu-o-te-Manu in 1868.**

October 30    New Zealand mean time is officially adopted at eleven and a half hours ahead of Greenwich mean time, with government departments and offices operating according to the new time from November 2.

November 7    Colonel George Whitmore and Kepa Te Rangihiwinui (Major Kemp) launch a disastrous assault on Moturoa pa, near

Wanganui, recoiling under a counterattack from Titokowaru's troops. During this action, Constable Henare Kepa Te Ahururu climbs the palisades alone and is shot, earning with his 'gallant conduct' the later presentation of the first New Zealand Cross.

November 10    Te Kooti's Ringatu forces attack Matawhero and other Poverty Bay settlements simultaneously, and take control of the area.

November 14    Probable date Te Kooti seizes Oweta pa and executes six chiefs, including Paratene, who he believes betrayed him. Te Kooti now controls the whole Poverty Bay district but has gained many enemies. Five days later, he will begin a slow withdrawal through the Bay of Plenty to Te Urewera.

# 1869

January 4    Te Kooti is defeated at Ngatapa, but he escapes during the night by lowering himself on a rope down a precipice. On Ropata Whahawhaha's orders, Ngati Porou warriors and colonial regulars shoot 120 prisoners.

February 3    Titokowaru, at the height of his powers after a series of victories and secure in a formidable pa, inexplicably abandons Tauranga-ika, north of Wanganui. Subsequently, his troops will desert him and the land he has conquered will be reoccupied by colonial troops.

March 9    Te Kooti's warriors emerge from hiding to raid Whakatane. When militia and kupapa (Maori fighting on the British side) arrive, they will retreat again to Te Urewera, where the Ringatu guerrillas will continue to raid and skirmish, pursued by government troops, for several years.

March 10    The New Zealand Cross is instituted by order-in-council. The medal has been created because New Zealand local military are not eligible for the Victoria Cross. Only 23 will be awarded, making it one of the rarest military honours in the world.

| March 24 | Titokowaru is nearly captured at Te Ngaere and makes his final flight to Kawau pa, in the upper Waitara valley, Taranaki. |
| April 11 | Prince Alfred, Duke of Edinburgh, arrives at Wellington as captain of HMS *Galatea*. Queen Victoria's second son is the first royal visitor to New Zealand and will stay for six weeks. |
| May 17 | Auckland Grammar School is officially opened by the Duke of Edinburgh. |
| June 28 | William Fox again assumes office as premier, having displaced Stafford over the issue of the retention of British troops in New Zealand. |

# Depression looms
# 1870–1891

**The 1870s and 1880s** were marked by rampant colonialism as European nations joined a ruthless race for control of Africa, Asia and the Pacific. In Eastern Europe, Jews were being persecuted in pogroms and in Russia an attempted nihilist revolution failed in 1881. In New Zealand export prices fell and the land boom collapsed, throwing the country into a deep economic depression that would last into the 1890s. In the 1880s New Zealand was gripped by the fear of a Russian invasion. While the 1886 eruption of Mt Tarawera had a significant impact on New Zealand, it paled into insignificance when compared to the eruption of Krakatoa three years earlier. The world's inventors, meanwhile, were in a frenzy of innovation, and telephony, the phonograph, the incandescent lamp, the gasoline combustion engine and the motion picture camera would all sooner or later make their way to New Zealand.

# 1870

| | |
|---|---|
| January 8 | The first edition of the *Evening Star* is published in Auckland. The paper, later renamed the *Auckland Star*, will be a fixture for over a century. |
| February 24 | The final detachment of the 18th (Royal Irish) Regiment becomes the last of the imperial forces to leave New Zealand. The remaining two years of the New Zealand Wars will be conducted entirely between local forces. |
| May 14 | Nelson College and Nelson Rugby Club contest a game of rugby football. Since 1853, Christ's College pupils have played a form of the sport, but the Nelson match is the first officially documented rugby match in New Zealand. |
| June 28 | In his budget speech, treasurer Julius Vogel announces a massive public works and development programme. The expansionist scheme involves assisted migration, the construction of public buildings, roads, railways and telegraph lines. Over the next 10 years about 100,000 immigrants will arrive in New Zealand — and £20 million (twice Vogel's estimate) will have to be borrowed from overseas to pay for the ambitious scheme. |
| September 12 | An act is passed to establish the University of New Zealand and restrict the right to confer degrees. The news is greeted with displeasure in Dunedin, where the Otago Provincial Council has already taken steps to set up its own university. |
| September 30 | The new Canterbury Museum building is opened in the government domain at Christchurch. It is the culmination of a project begun by Julius Haast in 1861. |

# 1871

| | |
|---|---|
| January 14 | Voting begins in a general election under secret ballot for the first time. Before this, the elector was read the names of candidates, he stated his preference and a clerk wrote it down. |

| March 25 | Dr Isaac Featherston is appointed as New Zealand's first agent-general in London. |
| --- | --- |
| July 5 | The inaugural ceremony of the University of Otago takes place. To start with there are just three professors in this, New Zealand's first university. |
| August 8 | Otago University Council, having received a petition signed by 149 ladies of Dunedin, resolves to allow women to attend classes and sit examinations. Otago is the first university in the British Empire to open all its classes to women. |
| August 22 | A meeting is held at Springfield, Otago Peninsula, that establishes New Zealand's first dairy factory, to be called the Otago Peninsula Co-operative Cheese Factory Company Ltd. By the early 20th century most dairy factories will be owned by co-operatives. |
| September 20 | Mosgiel Woollen Mill teases its first wool, carding it the next day. The mill is the pioneer of the commercial production of wool cloth in New Zealand. |
| December 2 | The Grahamstown & Tararu Tramway Co. begins operating a steam tram in Thames. The new service, the first of its kind in New Zealand, carries both freight and passengers. |

## 1872

| February 14 | West of Lake Waikaremoana, Te Kooti is engaged by government forces, under the command of Captain George Preece, for the last time. It is the last engagement of the New Zealand Wars. Te Kooti's withdrawal will in May take him to sanctuary in the King Country. |
| --- | --- |
| April 12 | Telegraphic communication is established between Auckland, Wellington and the southern provinces with the completion of the Thames–Tauranga section of the main trunk telegraph. |
| August 5 | British novelist Anthony Trollope arrives at Bluff. He will form the impression that the New Zealander is 'more English than any Englishman at home' but 'very fond of getting drunk'. |

| | |
|---|---|
| September 10 | Edward Stafford assumes office as premier for a third time, having brought down the Fox ministry over Vogel's public works scheme. He will prove immediately unpopular. |
| October 11 | George Waterhouse assumes office as premier at the invitation of Vogel. He is the only man to head two British colonies: South Australia and New Zealand. On the same day, Wiremu (Wi) Tako Ngatata is called to the Legislative Council, the first Maori to be appointed. |
| November 4 | Wiremu Katene becomes the first Maori to be appointed to the Executive Council. |

## 1873

| | |
|---|---|
| February 17 | The *Southern Cross* publishes a hoax story of a visit to Auckland by a hostile Russian warship, fuelling fears of an imminent invasion. The penny drops for some when they read the name of the ship: *Kaskowiski* ('cask of whisky'). |
| March 3 | William Fox begins his third, caretaker term as premier after the sudden resignation of George Waterhouse. |
| April 8 | The ebullient, skilful but impatient Julius Vogel assumes office as premier on his return from overseas. |
| June 2 | The *Punjaub* departs London on the first charter sailing for the New Zealand Shipping Company, a locally controlled venture set up to provide competition for the British shipping companies. |
| June 14 | Sir James Fergusson, a Crimean War veteran, assumes office as governor. |
| June 16 | Canterbury College of the University of New Zealand is founded by ordinance of the provincial council. Housed in the buildings of today's arts centre, the college will control Christchurch secondary schools, the Canterbury Museum and the public library, as well as preparing students for degree examinations. |

| December 1 | Westland, a county separate from the province of Canterbury since 1868, gains full provincial status. |
| December 24 | The first scheduled train runs on the Auckland–Onehunga railway line. The first regular passenger rail service in New Zealand attracts little interest: the trip has only 15 passengers. |

## 1874

| January 9 | The Auckland Racing Club is formed at the Auckland Hotel with the amalgamation of the Auckland Jockey Club and the Auckland Turf Club. |
| November 18 | The immigrant ship *Cospatrick*, bound for Auckland with 473 on board, catches fire off South Africa in the early hours of the morning. The only survivors will be three crew members who drift for more than a week in a lifeboat without water. |
| December 3 | Sir James Fergusson retires as governor after Benjamin Disraeli regains office in Great Britain. |

## 1875

| January 9 | The Marquess of Normanby assumes office as governor. The relationship between the aristocratic military man and his ministers will be tense. |
| July 1 | The Union Steam Ship Company of New Zealand commences operations under managing director James Mills. Within a year it will have absorbed its main competitor, the New Zealand Steam Navigation Company of Wellington, and be on its way to becoming the 'Southern Octopus', New Zealand's largest private-sector employer. |
| July 6 | Daniel Pollen assumes office as premier when Julius Vogel is delayed on an overseas trip. |
| September 8 | The first party of settlers for Katikati arrives in Auckland from Belfast on the *Carisbrooke Castle*. They will go on to Vesey Stewart's special settlement in the next few days. |

September 22 — The first interprovincial rugby match, between Auckland Clubs and Otago Clubs, is played at Dunedin and won by Otago.

## 1876

February 15 — Sir Julius Vogel assumes office as premier after Daniel Pollen relinquishes the post.

February 18 — Work is completed on a new telegraph cable between Cable Bay, Nelson, and Australia. The link will allow telegraph communication with Great Britain.

September 1 — Harry Atkinson, a straight-talking farmer favouring the suppression and assimilation of Maori, assumes office as premier. Vogel has resigned in order to take up the post of agent-general in London, following Featherston's death.

September 13 — The Atkinson ministry is reconstituted.

November 1 — The Abolition of the Provinces Act 1875 comes into effect, leaving central government as the single legislative body. The non-legislative duties of the provincial governments are taken over by boroughs and counties.

December 25 — The national air 'God Defend New Zealand', with words by Thomas Bracken and competition-winning music by J. J. Woods, has its first public performance at the Queen's Theatre, Dunedin, by the Lydia Howard Burlesque & Opera Bouffe with the Dunedin Royal Artillery Band.

## 1877

July 11 — At the Choral Hall, Auckland, Kate Edger receives her Bachelor of Arts, becoming the first woman in the British Empire to gain an arts degree. She has been tutored by her father and attended classes at the otherwise all-male Auckland College and Grammar School.

October 15 — Sir George Grey assumes office as premier. He is the first — and for a century the only — person to hold office as both governor-general and premier, or prime minister.

| | |
|---|---|
| October 17 | Sir James Prendergast, the chief justice, delivers a reserved judgment in the case of *Wi Parata v. The Bishop of Wellington*, in which he declares that the Treaty of Waitangi is 'worthless' and 'a simple nullity'. The ruling will influence government decision-making on treaty issues for decades. |
| November 29 | The ground-breaking Education Act passes into law, providing for free, secular, compulsory primary school education. |

## 1878

| | |
|---|---|
| February 9 | There is panic in Wellington when a visiting British steamer is mistaken for a hostile Russian raider. Within months, in the grip of the First Russian Scare, the government will apply to Great Britain for heavy guns to bolster coastal defences. |
| March 28 | W. S. Furby of the Blenheim telegraph office gives a public demonstration of one of 'Professor Bell's speaking telephones', linking Blenheim and Nelson. Experimentation with the new technology has been taking place around the country for some months. |
| August 24 | Wellington becomes the first major centre to have steam passenger trams, with the Marquess of Normanby inaugurating the service. The trams will not prove popular, being noisy, dirty, frightening to horses, and prone to derailment. |
| September 7 | The newly completed Christchurch–Dunedin railway line opens. The governor and MPs are among the first passengers. |
| September 26 | The Clutha River and all its tributaries reach high flood after continuous rain and snow melt combine to raise the river levels. The settlement of Balclutha suffers the most serious damage. Over the next few days, Queenstown will be inundated, and the Clyde, Bannockburn, Roxburgh and Balclutha bridges all swept away. |
| November 15 | A bush fire begins at Waimate, South Canterbury, in which 70 cottages and five sawmills will be destroyed. |

# 1879

| | |
|---|---|
| January 22 | The first train runs between Christchurch and Invercargill. It reaches its destination two hours behind schedule after the railway commissioner of the South Island is nearly decapitated when he leans out from the engine. |
| February 21 | A naked flame causes an explosion in the coal mine at Kaitangata. As a result 35 workers die, most of them suffocated by choke damp as they try to escape. The disaster will prompt the introduction of new legislation to improve safety in mines. |
| April 17 | Sir Hercules Robinson assumes office as governor for a brief term. He has previously been governor of Hong Kong, Ceylon and New South Wales. |
| May 26 | Maori plough up the land of European settlers at Oakura under instruction from Parihaka prophet Te Whiti, who is committed to regaining lost Maori land through civil disobedience. |
| June 5 | The first known night game of soccer, at the Basin Reserve in Wellington, is played in front of 8000 curiosity seekers. Two electric lamps provide the floodlighting, but when one lamp fails the other has to be carried up and down the sideline following the action. The game is eventually cut short when the second lamp fails too. |
| July 26 | The Canterbury Rugby Union is formed at a meeting in Timaru following a match between North Canterbury and South Canterbury. The CRU is New Zealand's first rugby union. |
| August 11 | A peaceful community established by prophet and healer Te Maiharoa on reoccupied tribal land at Omarama in South Canterbury is dismantled by police and armed volunteers. Several members of the community will die in winter storms during the heke back down the Waitaki Valley. |
| September 8 | A boarding house in the Octagon, Dunedin, burns to the ground. Twelve die in the inferno, among them Robert Wilson, editor of the *Otago Witness*. |

| October 8 | John Hall, a popular political moderate, assumes office as premier. |
| December 26 | Violence between Protestant Orangemen and Irish Catholics breaks out in Timaru following an Orange parade. |

# 1880

| July 1 | The official opening of the railway between Auckland and Te Awamutu takes place. Here construction of the main trunk line will stall for five years while negotiations with Ngati Maniapoto are undertaken to allow the railway to pass through the King Country, which has been closed to Pakeha since the end of the New Zealand Wars. |
| July 19 | The first 16 students enrol at the new school of agriculture at Lincoln, near Christchurch. The oldest agricultural college in the Southern Hemisphere has W. E. Ivey as its first director. |
| September 7 | The Auckland free public library is officially opened in the old Mechanics' Institute building in High Street. The library will move to purpose-built premises in 1887. |
| September 11 | A train is blown off the rails on the Rimutaka Incline. Three children die and many adults are injured. |

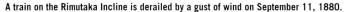

**A train on the Rimutaka Incline is derailed by a gust of wind on September 11, 1880.**

| November 10 | Donald Sutherland and John Mackay find Sutherland Falls, near Milford Sound, Fiordland. They are the first Europeans to see the 585 m falls, which are the highest in New Zealand. |
| November 25 | Ngati Whakaue lease to the crown (represented by Judge F. D. Fenton) the site of the future European settlement of Rotorua. |
| November 29 | Sir Arthur Gordon assumes office as governor. His term will be remembered for his clashes with the government and in particular his disputes with John Bryce, the native minister. |

# 1881

| February 24 | The first cable tram service in the Southern Hemisphere, in Rattray Street, Dunedin, glides effortlessly up the steep hill. |
| April 29 | SS *Tararua* strikes Otara Reef off Waipapa Point at the entrance to Foveaux Strait. Of 151 passengers and crew, only 20 will survive the wreck. |
| July 5 | The Chinese Immigrants Act is passed by the Legislative Council, imposing a poll tax of £10 on Chinese arrivals in New Zealand. The tax will later be raised to £100. |
| July 11 | As a token of peace, King Tawhiao and chief Wahanui lay down their arms before native minister John Bryce at Alexandra (Pirongia). Tawhiao declares, 'This is the end of warfare in this land.' |
| October 1 | A telephone exchange is officially opened in the chief post office at Christchurch. The first manual exchange in the country has 27 private subscribers as well as official subscribers such as the post office, fire service and police station. |
| October 11 | Trials of the new Auckland telephone exchange begin in advance of its official opening on October 24. |
| November 5 | The Maori settlement at Parihaka is broken up in a surprise attack by a force of 1600 armed police and volunteers. |

|  | Pacifist leaders Te Whiti and Kakahi Tohu offer no resistance and are arrested. They will not return from forced exile until March 1883. |
|---|---|
| December 3 | The southernmost horse tram service in the world begins operation in Invercargill. |
| December 9 | For the first time in a general election, voting proceeds on the basis of universal manhood suffrage, the property qualification having been lifted. It is also the first time that voting takes place for a three-year parliamentary term. |

## 1882

| January 18 | A pioneering dairy factory opens at Edendale, Southland, under the supervision of Thomas Brydone. The enterprise will combine production with experimentation and a dairy school. |
|---|---|
| January 23 | A massive fire started deliberately by a grocer destroys property in Queenstown. |
| February 15 | The *Dunedin* sails from Port Chalmers with the first refrigerated cargo. Nearly 5000 frozen sheep carcasses — and a small amount of butter — will arrive in good condition in the United Kingdom on May 24. |
| March 2 | William Spotswood Green, Emil Boss and Ulrich Kaufmann attempt the first ascent of Aoraki/Mt Cook but are forced to retreat minutes from the summit. |
| April 10 | The New Zealand Exhibition is officially opened at Christchurch. The privately funded 14-week show will draw more than 225,000 visitors but still make a heavy loss. |
| April 21 | Frederick Whitaker again assumes office as premier, after a break of more than 17 years. |
| May 14 | The schooners *City of Perth* and *Ben Venue* founder in a storm at Timaru. Nine lives are lost, not in the wrecks themselves but in the attempt to return to the vessels to secure them. |

| August 19 | Sir George Grey presents his library to the city of Auckland. Grey's collection is especially important because it is the largest single repository of Maori-language manuscripts in the world. |

## 1883

| January 20 | Lieutenant-General Sir William Jervois assumes office as governor. The military expert will complete a reorganisation of the defence system before his departure. |
| February 12 | A binding peace between the Ringatu movement and the crown is negotiated by Te Kooti and Native Minister John Bryce. |
| February 13 | Maori political prisoners are released under the Amnesty Act 1882. |
| April 1 | The Salvation Army 'opens fire' in New Zealand with an inaugural meeting at the Cargill fountain, Dunedin. |
| May 16 | Shaw Savill & Albion's *Westmeath* arrives at Auckland with passengers from England. It is the first regular direct steamer link between England and New Zealand. |
| May 21 | Auckland University College is officially opened by the governor. A hundred students will be on the inaugural roll. |
| September 25 | Harry Atkinson assumes office as premier for a second term. |
| October 10 | The first edition of a newspaper, the *New Zealand Herald*, to be printed on a rotary press is published. |

## 1884

| April 1 | King Tawhiao (Potatau II) leaves New Zealand to petition Queen Victoria for a separate Maori parliament and an inquiry into land confiscations. |
| May 28 | The first New Zealand representative rugby team to go |

| | overseas plays its opening game, against Cumberland County at Parramatta. The team will win all eight games during its tour of New South Wales. |
|---|---|
| August 16 | Jurist and humanitarian Robert Stout assumes office as premier, Atkinson's cabinet having resigned nine days after Parliament convened. Stout's first term will last less than two weeks. |
| August 28 | Harry Atkinson assumes office as premier once more, this time for only five days. |
| September 3 | After Atkinson resigns, Robert Stout takes over again as premier with a broader base of support. |
| October 22 | King Tawhiao disembarks from the *Wairarapa* after his visit to England. He has been denied an audience with Queen Victoria, reportedly at the request of the New Zealand government. |
| December 3 | Sale of alcohol in the King Country is forbidden by proclamation of the governor, at the request of Maori in the district. |

# 1885

| January 7 | The first New Zealand Trades and Labour Congress begins in Dunedin. It is the first national expression of organised labour. |
|---|---|
| March 18 | The Mornington–Maryhill cable car extension in Dunedin is launched with bold claims it is the steepest in the world. |
| April 15 | A formal ceremony south of Te Awamutu marks the start of work on the connecting link of the main trunk line. After years of negotiation between Ngati Maniapoto and the government to allow the railway to pass through the King Country, Wahanui Huatare turns the first sod and the prime minister wheels it away. |
| November 8 | The new Jewish synagogue at Princes Street, Auckland, is dedicated. Designed by Edward Bartley, it is described as 'mosque in style, and a little gothic in the details'. |

Wahanui Huatare (tall man with top hat), Rewi Maniapoto (top hat behind barrow) and Robert Stout (between them) officially open work on the railway line through the King Country on April 15, 1885.

| November 9 | Troops stage a mock landing at St Heliers Bay in Auckland to practise for an attack by Russians that will never in fact come. New Zealand is in the middle of the Second Russian Scare. |

## 1886

| March 1 | The Maungatautari Whare Uta opens for business. It is one of several banks set up by Maori to avoid being cheated by Pakeha bankers. |

| May 31 | Probable date tourists see a mysterious canoe on Lake Tarawera. The 'phantom canoe' is later claimed to be an omen of the Tarawera eruption. |

| June 10 | Mt Tarawera, near Rotorua, erupts. During the six-hour event, ash is spread over 4 million acres (16,000 km²), the Pink and White Terraces are destroyed, and three Maori villages — Te Wairoa, Te Ariki and Moura — are buried. It is thought that 153 people died, 15 of them at Te Wairoa. |

| November 3 | The first 100 lb (45 kg) of butter is produced at Henry Reynolds's new factory at Pukekura in the Waikato, and the Anchor brand is born. |

| December 24 | Reefton Electric Light & Power Co., the first public electricity supply authority in the Southern Hemisphere, is registered. |

## 1887

| August 1 | The Kermadec Islands become part of New Zealand. |
| September 23 | Te Heuheu Tukino IV (Horonuku) signs a deed presenting the mountain tops of Tongariro, Ngauruhoe and Ruapehu to the native minister for use as New Zealand's national park. |
| October 1 | The first inland parcel post service begins operation. The service has been made possible by the development of the railways. |
| October 8 | Sir Harry Atkinson begins a fourth and last term as premier. |

## 1888

| February 17 | The Auckland City Art Gallery, the first permanent art gallery in the country, opens in the library building. The core of its collection is 25 paintings donated by Sir George Grey. |
| August 4 | The lights are switched on and Reefton gains a public supply of electricity, the first place in New Zealand to do so. |
| September 1 | The top of the spire of Christchurch Cathedral is destroyed in an earthquake of magnitude greater than 7.0 and centred in North Canterbury. |
| September 27 | Rarotonga and the southern Cook Islands become a British protectorate at the request of chiefs concerned about French empire-building in the Pacific. |
| October 3 | The New Zealand Native team plays its first game in Great Britain, against Surrey at Richmond. The privately organised, mainly Maori rugby team is the first national team to wear the silver fern. During a tour of New Zealand, Australia and the British Isles lasting more than a year, the Natives play 107 games of rugby, eight of Australian rules football and two of soccer. |

**The New Zealand Native rugby team of 1888–89 proudly wears the silver fern emblem.**

## 1889

| | |
|---|---|
| May 2 | The Earl of Onslow assumes office as governor. He will be remembered for his disputes with John Ballance. |
| June 10 | New Zealand's first successful free kindergarten opens at the Walker Street mission hall, in one of the poorest parts of Dunedin. The Froebel kindergarten starts off with 16 children, but enrolments will rise to 60 by the end of the year. |
| July 11 | The Dunedin Tailoresses' Union, the first women's union in New Zealand, is officially formed. Its foundation president is Rutherford Waddell, the clergyman who has drawn national attention to the issue of 'sweating' among women working in the clothing industry. |
| November 26 | The ambitious New Zealand and South Seas Exhibition is officially opened at Dunedin, celebrating the golden jubilee of the proclamation of British sovereignty. |

## 1890

| | |
|---|---|
| January 13 | 'Torpedo' Billy Murphy wins the world featherweight boxing championship in a bout against Ike Weir at San Francisco. The first New Zealander to win a world title in professional boxing will lose the title again within a year. |

| | |
|---|---|
| May 5 | The Royal Commission on Sweating delivers its report. The inquiry into workplace abuses has found many instances of long hours, low pay and the exploitation of women and children, and its findings will support a raft of legislation over the next five years. |
| July 3 | The country's first Arbor Day is observed at Greytown. Introduced to promote the planting of trees, the day will never be taken up as a public holiday. |
| July 9 | A public meeting is held at Auckland to form the Jubilee Institute for the Blind. The organisation is today known as the Royal New Zealand Foundation of the Blind. |
| July 30 | Constable Neil McLeod is shot by gumdigger Henry Funcke on board the steamer *Minnie Casey* off Dargaville. It is the first time a police officer has been killed on duty. |
| August 16 | In the first interprovincial association football match, Canterbury beats Wellington 2–0 at Christchurch. |
| August 29 | New Zealand's first great maritime strike begins in Auckland when watersiders unloading the Union Steam Ship Co.'s *Waihora* are called off in support of striking Australian unionists. Over two months about 10,000 New Zealand unionists will become involved. |
| December 5 | For the first time members of the House of Representatives are elected under the 'one man one vote' principle. |

## 1891

| | |
|---|---|
| January 14 | British-born New Zealand boxer Bob Fitzsimmons knocks out Jack Dempsey in New Orleans to win the world middleweight championship. He will retain the title for seven years and become one of New Zealand's first sporting heroes. |
| January 24 | John Ballance assumes office as premier. His Liberal Party will remain in power for the next 21 years, although progressive, pacifist Ballance's term as premier will be cut short after less than three. |

| | |
|---|---|
| March 11 | A meeting held in Christchurch, at the instigation of Arthur Harper and George Mannering, resolves to form the New Zealand Alpine Club. |
| April 21 | Emily Siedeberg enrols at Otago University as a medical student. Five years later she will become New Zealand's first woman doctor. Other female academic pioneers are Helen Connon, who graduated MA in 1881, and Ethel Benjamin, who will graduate in law in 1897. |
| April 22 | The Cook Islands come under New Zealand control when New Zealand-appointed British resident Fred Moss assumes office. |
| August 14 | A Women's Christian Temperance Union petition (9000 signatures), supporting the proposed introduction of parliamentary votes for women, is presented at Parliament. |
| September 8 | The Land and Income Assessment Act passes into law, giving New Zealand its first taste of income tax. The new legislation also imposes heavy taxes on large landowners, one of a number of measures introduced by minister of lands and of agriculture John McKenzie to spur the break-up of large estates for closer settlement. |
| October 18 | Rudyard Kipling arrives in New Zealand for a visit. The British writer will later describe Auckland as 'Last, loneliest, loveliest, exquisite, apart'. |
| October 29 | General William Booth of the Salvation Army visits Christchurch. His procession around the streets of the inner city is accompanied by the music of three bands. |

# A clearer identity
## 1892-1907

**The 1890s brought something** of a social revolution in New Zealand, with the beginnings of a Maori renaissance, the assertion of some rights for women and the establishment of an old-age pensions scheme. Elsewhere, the changes were more dramatic and more violent. In 1895 China suffered an overwhelming defeat at the hands of Japan. Three years later the Spanish-American War saw Spain lose Cuba, Puerto Rico, Guam and the Philippines to the USA. Just before the turn of the century a renewal of the conflict between Afrikaners and the British gave New Zealand its first chance to fight for Empire overseas, an opportunity eagerly taken up by thousands of volunteers. The relatively low-key South African War would, as it turned out, merely be a dress rehearsal for the epic drama of World War I.

# 1892

| | |
|---|---|
| April 14 | The Paremata Maori (Maori parliament) is established at a hui of 96 chiefs at Te Tiriti o Waitangi marae, Pewhairangi. The most successful manifestation of the kotahitanga movement aims to unify tribes politically and ensure the principles of the Treaty of Waitangi are upheld. |
| April 16 | The New Zealand Rugby Football Union is founded at a meeting in Wellington — although Otago and Canterbury will immediately withdraw their support. |
| June 7 | The Earl of Glasgow assumes office as governor. The navy man will eventually resign office on the grounds the salary is too small. |
| June 14 | The Paremata Maori meets for the first time at Waipatu, Hawke's Bay. |
| July 15 | A second WCTU women's suffrage petition (20,000 women's signatures) is presented at Parliament. |
| October 11 | The Land Act passes into law. Among other things, the legislation enshrines the right of public access to rivers, lakes and coasts, and forests and mountains. |

# 1893

| | |
|---|---|
| April 17 | Te Kooti dies at Te Karaka, on the Ohiwa Harbour. The final 20 years of the great military leader's life have been devoted to peace and faith. |
| April 27 | Premier John Ballance dies from cancer. |
| May 1 | The dynamic Richard Seddon (Liberal) assumes office as premier. During his term the position will be officially retitled 'prime minister'. |
| July 8 | The New Zealand Racing Conference approves the formation of the New Zealand Jockey Club. The new body, which will control horse racing, has taken 20 years to establish. |

| July 28 | A third women's suffrage petition is presented at Parliament. This one contains nearly 32,000 signatures — almost a quarter of the adult European female population in New Zealand. |
| --- | --- |
| September 8 | The Legislative Council votes 20 to 18 to allow all women to vote, despite the opposition of Richard Seddon and several of his ministers. |
| September 19 | The Electoral Act is signed into law by the governor, and New Zealand becomes the first self-governing nation where women have a parliamentary vote. |
| October 2 | The Alcoholic Liquors Sale Control Act passes into law, allowing the public a say in the availability of alcohol. The first poll will be held the following year. |
| November 28 | More than 90,000 women vote for the first time in a general election. In the poll, James Carroll wins Waiapu for the Liberal Party and becomes the first Maori to be elected to a general, rather than a Maori, seat. He will hold the seat for 25 years. |
| December 20 | Elizabeth Yates is installed as mayor of Onehunga, Auckland. She is the first woman in the British Empire to be elected mayor. |

**Women voting in the local body elections of November 29, 1893. In the Onehunga election Elizabeth Yates will be elected the first woman mayor.**

## 1894

| | |
|---|---|
| March 2 | Grace Neill is appointed as the first woman factory inspector. |
| April 12 | The constitution put together by King Tawhiao's kauhanganui (parliament) at Maungakawa in the Waikato is published in the newsletter *Te Paki o Matariki*. |
| June 30 | Urgent legislation is passed to guarantee £2 million to the Bank of New Zealand to enable it to continue banking transactions. |
| August 26 | Tukaroto Matutaera Potatau Te Wherowhero Tawhiao, the second Maori king, dies at Parawera in the Waikato. The tangi will last for nearly two months. |
| August 31 | The Industrial Conciliation and Arbitration Act passes into law. The new legislation makes New Zealand the first country in the world to outlaw strikes in favour of compulsory arbitration. To begin with the system will be a success — there will be no strikes for 11 years and wages and conditions will improve. |
| September 14 | Mahuta Tawhiao becomes the third Maori king. |
| October 29 | SS *Wairarapa* strikes Miners Head, Great Barrier Island, at full speed after a navigation error. At least 121 of the passengers and crew travelling from Sydney to Auckland will die. |
| December 25 | Waimate men Jack Clarke, Thomas Fyfe and George Graham become the first to reach the summit of Aoraki/Mt Cook. The New Zealanders have rushed to complete the ascent before visiting British climbers can beat them to it. |
| December 27 | The New Zealand Cricket Council is formed in Christchurch, and for the first time cricket is organised on a national level. |

## 1895

| | |
|---|---|
| January 24 | Alexander von Tunzelmann becomes the first New Zealander |

|  | — and possibly the first person — to set foot on the Antarctic continent. The crew members of the *Antarctic* making landfall at Cape Adare in what will become the Ross Dependency may have been beaten to it by those of the *Cecilia*, who claim to have landed in 1821. |
|---|---|
| June 18 | Minnie Dean's trial for murder begins at the Invercargill Supreme Court. Accused of murdering babies placed in her care, the 'Winton babyfarmer' is defended by the famous barrister Alfred Hanlon. Three days later she will be found guilty of murder after jury deliberations of half an hour. |
| August 12 | Minnie Dean is executed in the Invercargill jail. She is the first and only woman to be hanged in New Zealand. |
| September 20 | The Family Homes Protection Act passes into law, preventing homes from being mortgaged or sold for debt. |
| November 5 | Samuel Clemens (Mark Twain) lands at Bluff to begin a lecture tour of New Zealand. Locals will later be pleased to discover he is generally enthusiastic about the country. |
| November 29 | Alfred Whitehouse becomes the first person to exhibit motion pictures in New Zealand. The images are displayed through Edison's Kinetoscope, a peep-hole device, at Bartlett's Studio in Auckland. |

## 1896

| March 26 | Sixty-seven men die in the Brunner coal mine on the West Coast. Killed by blast and gas, they make up almost half of the Brunner underground workforce. It is the worst mining disaster in New Zealand history. |
|---|---|
| April 13 | A convention of women's organisations begins in Christchurch. At the conference the National Council of Women will be formed, and resolutions passed for prison reform, against capital punishment and for raising the age of female consent to protect young women from sexually transmitted diseases. |

| | |
|---|---|
| October 13 | A short programme of 'moving figures in life-like action' is shown at the Auckland opera house. The first commercial projected screening of motion pictures in New Zealand takes place 10 months after the world's first public film show in Paris. |
| November 18 | Alfred Hill's cantata *Hinemoa* is premiered at the opening night of the Wellington Industrial Exhibition. It is the first European work to use Maori themes, and it is hailed as a triumph. |

## 1897

| | |
|---|---|
| January 29 | A conference begins at Te Aute College, Hawke's Bay, during which the Te Aute College Students' Association will be formed by Peter Buck, Apirana Ngata and others. The organisation will launch a number of great Maori leaders, and will later become known as the Young Maori Party. |
| March 17 | Bob Fitzsimmons of Timaru becomes the world heavyweight boxing champion by defeating 'Gentleman' Jim Corbett at Carson City, Nevada. It is the first world championship fight to be captured on film. |
| April 16 | In Hawke's Bay the Tutaekuri River breaks its banks. In the flooding 12 men die, including 10 would-be rescuers swept away while trying to help the people of Clive. |
| May 14 | The Pigeongram postal service between Great Barrier Island and Auckland begins. In possibly the world's first airmail service, pigeons carry messages attached to their legs for the 55 miles (90 km) flight. |
| August 10 | The Earl of Ranfurly assumes office as governor. He is perhaps best remembered for his donation of the Ranfurly Shield for rugby. |
| September 26 | The Riot Act is read to a gathering of thousands outside a meeting hall in Lichfield Street, Christchurch. The jeering crowd is preventing the departure of cult leader Arthur Worthington, who has been revealed as a religious imposter. |

| December 8 | A severe earthquake measuring 7.0 on the Richter scale is felt along the Wellington coast as far as Wanganui. |

# 1898

| February 19 | Two Benz motor cars from Paris arrive at Wellington. The first petrol-driven cars in New Zealand, imported by William McLean, MP, pose a problem for the Customs Department, which has no regulations to cover motor vehicles. |
| May 5 | Colonel Stuart Newall and 120 troops march from Rawene to Waima, in the Hokianga, to put down the 'Dog Tax Rebellion'. When they arrive they discover Hone Heke has negotiated a resolution to the conflict between the local council and Nga Puhi people refusing to pay a dog tax. |
| October 12 | William Larnach shoots himself in a committee room at Parliament buildings. The MP's suicide is attributed to worries about money, health — and his wife's rumoured adultery with his own son, her stepson. |
| October 28 | The McLean Motor-car Act passes into law, allowing William McLean to legally drive his new motor cars — although he has already been for a spin around the streets of Wellington with the city council's engineer and inspector of vehicles on board. |
| November 1 | Richard Seddon's Old-age Pensions Act passes into law after two earlier rejections. The new legislation, the first of its kind in the world, allows a small, means-tested pension to be paid to destitute older people — but only if they are deemed to be of good character. Over the next quarter-century the scheme will be extended to cover widows with dependent children, war veterans, miners affected by phthisis and the blind. |
| December 1 | Auckland showman Alfred Whitehouse shoots the first motion-picture footage in New Zealand when he records the opening of the Auckland Mining and Industrial Exhibition. |

# 1899

| | |
|---|---|
| February 23 | Victoria College is formally admitted as an affiliated institution of the University of New Zealand. Lectures at the Wellington College will begin in April. |
| March 11 | In a railway collision at Rakaia four passengers are killed and 40 injured. As a result of the accident all trains will be fitted with the Westinghouse continuous automatic air-braking system. |
| May 29 | Richard Seddon offers the British government 500 troops to respond to an insurgency in Samoa. Militia and volunteers keen to put their training to practical use are enthusiastic about going, but the offer will be declined. |
| September 1 | In Kaitaia, the first farmers' union is set up, with an entrance fee of 6d and an annual subscription of 2 shillings. Concerning itself with land tenure and marketing, it is the forerunner of Federated Farmers. |
| October 11 | War against the South African Republic (Transvaal) is declared. In anticipation of the declaration, New Zealand has already become the first British colony to offer a contingent of troops, and the first volunteers are gathering in Wellington. |
| October 11 | The first Labour Day public holiday is celebrated. It marks the adoption of the concept — if not the practice — of the nationwide eight-hour working day. |
| October 21 | The first contingent leaves Wellington on the troopship *Waiwera* for service in the South African War. An enthusiastic crowd farewells 200 mounted rifles and their horses, the first force raised in New Zealand to represent the country in overseas combat. A total of 10 contingents — nearly 6500 personnel and 8000 horses — will go to South Africa over the next two and a half years. |
| December 9 | In northern Cape Colony, New Zealand troops fire their first shots in anger during the South African War. |

The first contingent of troops for the South African War departs Wellington on board the *Waiwera* on October 21, 1899.

December 28    Private George Bradford, from Paeroa, becomes the first New Zealand soldier to die in the South African War, having been wounded in action and taken prisoner.

# 1900

February 15    New Zealanders participate in the relief of Kimberley after a 124-day siege. They are disappointed with the lack of appreciation shown by the citizens of the town.

March 28    A hui begins at the Basin Reserve, Wellington, to raise money for the Transvaal War Fund. It also protests the exclusion of Maori from service in the South African War on the grounds that 'blacks should not be deployed against whites'. There will be no change in policy, although Maori women will serve with distinction as nurses.

June 22    Aucklander Hugh Kelly dies of bubonic plague. The health scare surrounding his death will spur the passage of the Public Health Act.

| | |
|---|---|
| October 13 | The Public Health Act passes into law, providing for a centralised department of public health that is the first of its kind in the world. |
| October 18 | The Maori Councils Act passes into law. Promoted by native minister James Carroll, the act attempts to reduce support for the kotahitanga movement by setting up regional committees to take over local government and health functions. The scheme will not be a success, partly because of underfunding, and within 10 years most councils will cease to exist. |
| October 18 | The Workers' Compensation for Accidents Act passes into law. The introduction of the 'no fault' scheme makes New Zealand a world leader in providing compensation for work injuries. |
| October 20 | The Maori Lands Administration Act, drafted by James Carroll and Apirana Ngata, passes into law. The legislation provides for the establishment of boards controlled by Maori to administer the sale or lease of their land. |
| October 23 | The first electric tram service in New Zealand begins operation at Maori Hill, Dunedin. |
| November 29 | New Zealand troops of the second and third contingents take part in an attack on Rhenoster Kop, in the last orthodox battle of the South African War. From now on, Boer troops will use guerrilla warfare. |

# 1901

| | |
|---|---|
| January 1 | Penny postage is introduced, making New Zealand the first country in the world to establish universal penny postage. |
| January 22 | Queen Victoria dies and is succeeded by King Edward VII. |
| February 2 | The day of Queen Victoria's funeral is observed with official mourning and private grief. Huge processions are formed, ceremonies are held, and the trains stop for half an hour. |
| February 16 | A thousand troops from Britain's great regiments march |

| | |
|---|---|
| | with Indian Army officers from the wharves to the Auckland Domain. Touring New Zealand after being in Australia for the federation celebrations, after the hot and dusty march the NCOs and men are controversially denied a beer by the prohibitionist-dominated welcoming committee — although the officers are served champagne. |
| May 30 | A royal commission recommends against federation with Australia. The finding is not a surprise, given the prime minister's fierce opposition to the idea. |
| June 10 | The Duke and Duchess of Cornwall and York (later King George V and Queen Mary) arrive at Auckland on the *Ophir*. The royal couple, who are touring Commonwealth countries to thank them for their support in the South African War, have arrived a day early but diplomatically remain aboard the converted liner. |
| June 11 | John Logan Campbell, mayor of Auckland, greets the duke and duchess in a civic ceremony. The 'Father of Auckland' takes the opportunity to formally hand over the deed of gift of land below One Tree Hill to the people of the city. The new park will be named Cornwall Park to commemorate the royal visit. |
| June 11 | The boundaries of the colony of New Zealand are extended by order-in-council to include the Cook Islands, Niue and other small Pacific Islands. |
| June 15 | A great welcome hui for the Duke and Duchess of Cornwall and York reaches its climax at Rotorua. James Carroll, minister of native affairs, has organised the event, which draws more than 3500 Maori from all over the country. The duke's decision to wear a tail feather from the endangered huia in his hat will spark a craze for huia feathers and, it is claimed, precipitate the extinction of the bird. |
| December 21 | Captain Robert Falcon Scott and the *Discovery* depart Lyttelton to explore Antarctica, despite a seaman falling to his death during departure celebrations. The vessel will return in 1904. |

# 1902

| | |
|---|---|
| February 22 | The Kelburn cable tram service commences operations in Wellington, lifting passengers from Lambton Quay to Kelburn at an average grade of 1 in 5.1. |
| February 24 | The battle of Langverwacht Hill in South Africa ends. In the clash, 24 New Zealanders have died when Boer commandos refuse to give up fighting. |
| April 14 | Richard Seddon leaves for London to attend a conference of colonial premiers, and to represent New Zealand at the coronation of King Edward VII. |
| May 31 | The Boers surrender at Potchefstroom and the South African War ends. By the time the New Zealand contingents return home, 71 of their number will have been killed in combat or died of wounds, 133 will have died from illness and a further 30 will have been killed in accidents. |
| June 12 | The New Zealand Ensign Act passes into law, approving the use of the New Zealand ensign with the Southern Cross on the fly as the national flag. |
| June 27 | The description of New Zealand's current national flag is gazetted. |
| October 28 | The *Ventnor* sinks off Omapere, Northland, with the loss of 13 lives. Also lost are 499 coffins containing the remains of Chinese being returned to China for burial. |
| November 9 | The *Elingamite* is wrecked in fog at the wrongly charted Three Kings Islands. Of its nearly 200 passengers and crew, 45 will die, and some of the survivors will not be rescued from their life raft for five days. The steamer has also been carrying more than £17,000 worth of gold and silver coins. |
| November 17 | The first Auckland electric tram rumbles up Queen Street with Sir John Logan Campbell at the controls, although passenger services will not begin for a week. Auckland is the first New Zealand city to get a full electric tram service. Dunedin will |

| | follow in 1903, Wellington in 1904 and Christchurch in 1905. |
|---|---|
| November 25 | Voting takes place in the general election. With the ever-growing population, the number of parliamentary seats has been increased from 74 to 80. |
| December 8 | A cable across the Pacific Ocean from Vancouver Island to Doubtless Bay has its first formal use. The All Red Route allows telegraphic communication with the United Kingdom at the cost of 3 shillings per word. |

## 1903

| | |
|---|---|
| March 31 | Possible date Richard Pearse of Waitohi becomes airborne in a monoplane he designed and built himself — before crashing into the top of a hedge (although it is also possible the flight took place 12 months later). The 1903 date would be more than nine months before the Wright brothers claimed the first controlled powered flight. |
| May 22 | King Mahuta Tawhiao Potatau Te Wherowhero is appointed to the Legislative Council and sworn in as a member of the Executive Council. The appointment has been made in return for his agreement to open up a million acres of land for settlement. |
| May 24 | Empire Day (later Commonwealth Day) is celebrated for the first time. |
| May 26 | The first Automobile Association in New Zealand is formed at Auckland. The touring club hopes to improve public attitudes towards motor cars and will lobby for road building. |
| July 16 | Wanganui fire brigade takes delivery of the first self-propelled fire engine in Australasia. The steam-driven Merryweather appliance will remain in use for 17 years. |
| August 15 | New Zealand plays its first full-scale international rugby match, against Australia at the Sydney Cricket Ground. The New Zealand team, captained by Dave Gallaher, wins 22–3. |

**The first self-propelled fire engine in Australasia, acquired by the Wanganui fire brigade on July 16, 1903.**

| | |
|---|---|
| August 30 | Guide Joseph Warbrick and three tourists are killed instantly when they get too close to the Waimangu geyser at Rotorua and it erupts. |
| September 26 | The Wireless Telegraphy Act passes into law, making New Zealand the first country in the world to have a state monopoly over wireless transmission. The government has been alerted to the potential of radio by the experiments of local youngsters, including schoolboy James Passmore who in 1902 communicated over a distance of 100 yards (90 m). |
| November 25 | Bob Fitzsimmons wins the world light-heavyweight championship in San Francisco by defeating George Gardner. In doing so he becomes boxing's first triple world champion. |
| December 24 | A runaway double-decker tram collides with another tram at Kingsland, Auckland. Three passengers die and many are seriously injured. |

# 1904

| | |
|---|---|
| March 31 | New Zealand's first coin-in-the-slot postage franking machine is given a public trial at Christchurch. The introduction of the machine, designed and built by Christchurch man Ernest Moss, makes it unnecessary to buy stamps for postage. |
| June 3 | The foundation stone of the Dunedin railway station is laid by Joseph Ward. Architect Sir George Troup's Edwardian baroque masterpiece will be officially opened in 1906, although it will not be completed until 1907. |
| June 7 | Otago geology graduate James Thomson is selected as New Zealand's first ever Rhodes scholar at Oxford University. |
| June 20 | Lord Plunket assumes office as governor. The politically conservative Irishman will fulfil his constitutional role and little more. |
| August 6 | Rugby's Ranfurly Shield is contested for the first time. In the match at Alexandra Park, Auckland, the home province, loses to Wellington 3–6. In the early years the Ranfurly Shield will be regarded as a minor event. |
| September 26 | An order-in-council is issued to protect the Risso's dolphin. The move has been made to ensure the safety of the famous Cook Strait dolphin Pelorus Jack, the first marine mammal in the world to be protected by an act of state. |
| November 1 | Christchurch Cathedral is consecrated by Bishop Newall more than 40 years after construction began. The completion has been delayed by a chronic lack of funds. |

# 1905

| | |
|---|---|
| June 9 | Baritone John Prouse cuts 12 songs for the Gramophone & Typewriter Co. while visiting Great Britain. He is the first New Zealander known to have recorded music for commercial release. |
| June 14 | William Pember Reeves is appointed to the newly created |

| | |
|---|---|
| | position of high commissioner for New Zealand in London. The role replaces that of the agent-general. |
| June 15 | The world's first stamp vending machine has a public trial at the chief post office in Wellington. The machine, invented by New Zealander Robert Dickie, is a huge success and will be used all over the globe. |
| September 16 | The New Zealand rugby team plays the first match of its tour of the British Isles, defeating Devon 55–4 at Exeter. The first fully representative New Zealand team to tour in the Northern Hemisphere will become known as the Originals. |
| September 24 | Lionel Terry, the 'Yellow Peril' campaigner, murders Joe Kum Yung in Wellington. The fanatic is trying to draw attention to his crusade to rid New Zealand of Chinese people. |
| October 21 | The New Zealand rugby team is called the All Blacks for the first time. The occasion is the touring team's game against Somerset at Taunton. |
| October 30 | The Workers' Dwellings Act passes into law, heralding New Zealand's first state housing scheme. A competition in 1906 will select 35 designs for houses to be leased to low-income workers. |
| December 16 | Against Wales, the All Blacks have their only loss of the Originals tour. They are controversially beaten 0–3 at Cardiff Arms Park after a last-gasp try is disallowed. On their return to New Zealand (March 7, 1906), the team will be hailed as 'New Zealand's brave sons'. |

# 1906

| | |
|---|---|
| June 10 | Richard Seddon, 'King Dick', dies unexpectedly after a heart attack during a voyage from Sydney to New Zealand. News of the prime minister's death will be greeted with an outpouring of public grief. |
| June 21 | William Hall-Jones (Liberal) assumes office as prime minister, until Sir Joseph Ward's return from overseas. |

| | |
|---|---|
| August 6 | The efficient and articulate Joseph Ward (Liberal), Seddon's protégé, replaces William Hall-Jones as prime minister. |
| September 8 | New Zealand's first motor vehicle fatality due to driver error occurs near Timaru when Janet Meikle crashes her car when she over-corrects after nearly hitting a bank. |
| November 1 | The New Zealand International Exhibition is officially opened in Hagley Park, Christchurch. During the government-funded exhibition, Alfred Hill will conduct the country's first fully professional orchestra in a temporary 1600-seat concert hall, and the Marconi Co. will give a public demonstration of wireless telegraphy. |

## 1907

| | |
|---|---|
| March 7 | The barque *Dundonald* is wrecked at the Auckland Islands. Twelve die, and the remaining 16 are stranded for eight months. |
| April 29 | Ethnologist Elsdon Best completes his mammoth tribal history, *Tuhoe, the children of the mist*, after 12 years. |
| May 23 | Frederic Truby King addresses the inaugural meeting of the Society for the Promotion of the Health of Women and Children, later known as the Plunket Society. The organisation has been established by prominent Dunedin women inspired by Dr King to encourage breast feeding, train nurses and educate parents. |
| July 12 | The House of Representatives resolves to accept New Zealand's transformation from colony to dominion. It is a sign that New Zealand is increasingly thought of as an entity independent of Great Britain — even if New Zealanders themselves are not convinced such a small country can live up to the status of dominion. |
| July 23 | An Australasian team including New Zealander Anthony Wilding defeats the British Isles by 3 rubbers to 2 and wins tennis's Davis Cup. Wilding will also be in the team that successfully defends the trophy in 1908 and 1909, and wins |

| | it again in 1914. New Zealand's greatest ever player will also win the Wimbledon singles title for four years in succession, 1910–13. |
|---|---|
| August 17 | A New Zealand rugby league team plays against a New South Wales team at Sydney, although, lacking a league rule book, the sides play under rugby rules. The New Zealand team, dubbed the All Golds by the New Zealand press in reference to its professional status, is warming up for a tour of Great Britain. |
| September 24 | James Carroll's Tohunga Suppression Act passes into law. It is an attempt to protect Maori from exploitation by people claiming to be healers and prophets — specifically Rua Kenana, who has established a 'new Jerusalem' with his followers at Maungapohatu, north of Lake Waikaremoana. |
| September 26 | On the steps of the general assembly library in Wellington, the governor, Lord Plunket, reads a royal proclamation granting New Zealand dominion status. This first Dominion Day is a full public holiday — and lawyers will continue to take it each year as one of their holidays. |
| September 26 | The first issue of the *Dominion* newspaper is published in Wellington. The new publication has been established to promote conservative interests in the capital. |
| December 11 | Fire destroys all of Parliament buildings except the library — and among the items lost are historical records and the parliamentary mace. For the next 11 years, Parliament will assemble in temporary accommodation in Government House. |
| December 28 | The last confirmed sighting of the endangered huia is made by W. W. Smith. |

# New Zealand and the world
## 1908–1928

**In 1908 New Zealand** was establishing itself on the world stage, producing an Olympic medallist, a world rowing champion and a Nobel prize winner. The recently-established dominion was also developing infrastructure and technology, including public supplies of electricity, rail, road and air transport, wireless and cinema, despite the period also being marked by industrial unrest. Overseas, revolutions in Turkey and Russia, war in the Balkans and a series of crises in Ireland were all overshadowed by the catastrophic 1914–18 war in Europe, Russia, the Middle East, Africa and the Pacific. A subsequent influenza epidemic killed tens of millions of people worldwide. The shakedown after the war saw the inception of the League of Nations, the redrawing of borders and a time of ambition and hope in many places.

# 1908

|  |  |
|---|---|
| January 1 | Explorer Ernest Shackleton and the *Nimrod* are farewelled from Lyttelton by a crowd of as many as 50,000. To save coal the vessel is towed by the Union Steam Ship Co.'s *Koonya*, which will become the first steel-hulled ship to cross the Antarctic Circle. The expedition will be unsuccessful in its attempt to reach the geographic South Pole. |
| January 1 | New Zealand, represented by the All Golds, loses narrowly to Wales at Aberdare in rugby league's first ever international test match. |
| January 20 | The country's first permanent picture show is established at His Majesty's Theatre, Wellington, by the Royal Pictures Syndicate. The venue is packed for the Projectoscope display of a series of short movie subjects that includes the building of a motor car. |
| February 3 | The first wireless telegraphy message from New Zealand to another country is exchanged between Joseph Ward, on HMS *Pioneer* at Wellington, and Alfred Deakin, on HMS *Psyche* at Sydney, via a relay on HMS *Powerful* in the Tasman Sea. |
| February 10 | Auckland at last gets a public supply of electricity, 20 years after Wellington. The steam-powered generator is run in conjunction with the city's destructor at Freemans Bay. |
| February 27 | Seven union members are dismissed from the Blackball mine after instigating a move to extend miners' lunchtime to 30 minutes. The remaining workers embark on an illegal strike that will last for three months before the company relents. The success will inspire confidence in the power of organised labour. |
| March 2 | The Devonport No. 1 troop of boy scouts is formed. It is the first troop in Auckland and probably in New Zealand. |
| May 5 | The first shot is fired in the construction of the Otira railway tunnel. Doing the honours is the prime minister, Joseph Ward. |

| June 13 | The New Zealand All Golds touring rugby league team plays an exhibition match at Wellington. It is the first official league game to be played on New Zealand soil. |
| July 6 | On the *Papanui*, 19-year-old aspiring writer Kathleen Beauchamp leaves New Zealand for the last time — to reinvent herself in London as Katherine Mansfield. |
| July 14 | Representing Australasia, Harry Kerr comes third in the 3500 m walk at the London Olympics, thus winning New Zealand's first ever Olympic medal. |
| August 4 | The Crimes Act passes into law, defining crimes and punishments for New Zealanders. Among many other measures, male homosexual practice is criminalised, with 'buggery' becoming an offence liable to imprisonment with hard labour for life, with the option of flogging. |
| August 4 | The Federation of Miners is formed in Greymouth by delegates representing 2300 miners. The following year the organisation will become the first 'Red' Federation of Labour. |
| August 7 | The 'Parliament Special' leaves Wellington for Auckland, travelling over a makeshift track in some sections of the unfinished main trunk line. The first direct train between the two cities is carrying VIPs to greet the visiting American fleet. |
| August 9 | The 'Great White Fleet', under the command of Admiral C. S. Perry, puts in at Auckland. The arrival of the 16 US navy vessels is greeted with much celebration, and an extensive programme of 'fleet week' entertainment will be put on for the 14,000 sailors. |
| September 10 | Schoolboys Stanton Hicks and Rawson Stark complete a demonstration of wireless telegraphy, with an exchange of greetings between the mayors of Dunedin and West Harbour. The prime minister will offer his congratulations, even though the transmission is illegal. |
| November 6 | Joseph Ward drives the last spike of the North Island main trunk railway line, at Pokaka. Three days later, the first |

| | scheduled passenger trains will set out, with an overnight stay in Ohakune (Wellington–Auckland) and Taumarunui (Auckland–Wellington). |
|---|---|
| December 10 | In Stockholm, Ernest Rutherford is presented with the Nobel Prize in Chemistry. The highly surprising conclusion to his work is that, contrary to all theories at the time, a chemical element is capable of being transformed into other elements. |
| December 11 | New Zealand's last horse tram service, in Invercargill, ceases operation. |
| December 15 | Richard Arnst becomes world rowing champion, defeating fellow New Zealander Billy Webb by a comfortable margin on the Whanganui River. |

## 1909

| February 12 | SS *Penguin* is wrecked in Cook Strait off Cape Terawhiti. The loss of more than 75 lives will be attributed to a strong flood tide and a breach of naval regulations. |
|---|---|
| April 21 | The wedding of Percy Carol Redwood and Agnes Ottaway takes place. Redwood will turn out to be the male impersonator Amy Bock, who days later will be arrested and a month later sentenced to two years' hard labour for her fraud. |
| December 24 | The Defence Act passes into law, providing for, among other things, compulsory military training. |

## 1910

| February 17 | Field Marshal Lord Kitchener arrives at Bluff on HMS *Encounter*. The commander of the British army, invited to New Zealand to advise on defence, will endorse government plans to introduce compulsory military training to feed a territorial force of 20,000 men. |
|---|---|
| March 12 | Alleged thief Joseph Pawelka escapes from custody in Palmerston North on a stolen bicycle. He will be recaptured only to escape again on March 23. |

| | |
|---|---|
| March 13 | J. R. Denniston makes the first recorded ascent of Mitre Peak in Milford Sound. |
| March 16 | New Zealand's first purpose-built picture theatre, the King's Theatre, opens in Wellington with a 'dazzling collection of luminous art gems'. |
| March 20 | A landslide at Waihi village, Lake Taupo, leaves one dead and several injured. The huge slip follows the same track as the one that buried the village of Te Rapa more than 50 years earlier. It hurtles into the lake, sending a 3.2 yard (3 m) high wave to the opposite shore. |
| March 23 | Lord Plunket officially opens the Hocken Library in Dunedin. The library's benefactor, Thomas Hocken, is too ill to attend and will die two months later. |
| April 10 | Joseph Pawelka, on the run for the second time, allegedly shoots and wounds Sergeant McGuire. The officer, who has been among police, soldiers, scouts and volunteers looking for the escaper, will die four days later. |
| April 11 | Pawelka kills a civilian searcher — or so it is claimed at the time. It is more likely that, in the atmosphere of rising hysteria, the dead man has been shot by a fellow searcher. Pawelka himself will be arrested six days later. |
| April 28 | Grafton Bridge, Auckland, is officially opened. Its arch, nearly 98 m wide, makes it the largest single-span concrete bridge in the world at the time. |
| May 6 | King George V succeeds his father, King Edward VII. |
| May 21 | After the end of his term on the Legislative Council, Mahuta Tawhiao Potatau Te Wherowhero resumes his kingship, which has been temporarily entrusted to his younger brother Te Wherowhero Tawhiao. |
| June 8 | Joseph Pawelka is sentenced to 21 years in jail after being convicted of theft, arson and escaping. He has been acquitted on charges of murder and robbery under arms. |

| June 22 | Lord Islington assumes office as governor. |
| November 29 | Captain Robert Falcon Scott sails from Port Chalmers in the *Terra Nova* on his ill-fated Antarctic expedition, with local donations of, among other things, 150 sheep, 500 lb of sheep's tongues and 300 lb of butter. |
| December 3 | Australian climber Freda du Faur, accompanied by guides Peter and Alec Graham, reaches the summit of Aoraki/Mt Cook. She is first woman to make the ascent. |

## 1911

| February 5 | At Papakura, Vivian Walsh makes the first confirmed controlled powered flight in New Zealand. The *Manurewa*, a Howard Wright biplane assembled by Walsh and his brother Leo, reaches an altitude of 60 feet and covers a distance of 400 yards (365 m) before landing safely. |

**The *Manurewa*, the aircraft that made the first controlled powered flight in New Zealand, on February 5, 1911.**

| July 26 | The first government wireless telegraphy station begins broadcasting, from the tower of the Wellington post office to ships at sea — over distances of as much as 600 miles at night. |

| August 26 | The New Zealand armorial bearings are authorised by royal warrant, giving New Zealand its first national coat of arms. |
| --- | --- |
| August 27 | Joseph Pawelka, having made several failed attempts, escapes from custody one last time. He will never be recaptured. |

## 1912

| March 23 | The foundation stone of the new Parliament House in Wellington is laid by the governor, Lord Islington. The building, designed by John Campbell and Claude Paton to be 131 yards (120 m) long, will not be completed according to its original plans. |
| --- | --- |
| March 28 | Thomas MacKenzie (Liberal) assumes office as prime minister of a caretaker administration after the resignation of Sir Joseph Ward. |
| May 13 | The Waihi miners' union calls a strike after 40 engine drivers break away to form a new 'scab' union. The gold miners' action, supported by the militant Federation of Labour, will continue for six months and will be marred by violence. |
| July 10 | William Massey, a shrewd, domineering former farmer, assumes office as the first Reform prime minister. He has masterminded a successful vote of no confidence on July 6, in which several government members crossed the floor to support the opposition. |
| July 15 | Swimmer Malcolm Champion becomes the first New Zealander to win an Olympic gold medal, representing Australasia in the 4 x 200 m relay at the Stockholm games. The winning time is a new world record. |
| August 4 | A conference begins at which the constitution of the New Zealand Political Reform League will be decided. The new political party, which as been operating unofficially for three years as the Reform Party, has the support of right-wing organisations around the country. |
| November 9 | Mahuta Tawhiao Potatau Te Wherowhero, the third Maori king, dies at Waahi. |

| November 12 | On 'Black Tuesday', strike-breakers and police storm the miners' hall at Waihi, and a constable is wounded by gunfire. The officer and several strike-breakers then bludgeon Fred Evans, the miner blamed for firing the shot. When Evans dies the following day he becomes New Zealand's first union martyr. The evening marks the end of the miners' resistance, and most of their leaders will be run out of town. |
| November 24 | Te Rata Mahuta Te Wherowhero is crowned as the fourth Maori king. |
| December 19 | The Earl of Liverpool assumes office as governor. |

## 1913

| March 22 | The world's first electrically operated automatic totalisator operates for the Auckland Racing Club's Easter meeting at Ellerslie. It has been developed by engineer George Julius. |
| April 8 | A Mormon missionary arrives at Auckland on the *Zealandia*, bringing with him the smallpox virus. He will attend a hui in Horahora, Northland, spreading the virus while reassuring his hosts his illness is not infectious. As a result, an epidemic will strike Maori communities in many parts of the North Island, and within a year 55 people will be dead. |
| April 12 | HMS *New Zealand*, the Royal Navy battleship Joseph Ward rashly offered in 1909 to buy for Britain, makes Wellington its first port of call in New Zealand. More than 500,000 people will visit the vessel during its tour of the country. |
| April 13 | The Edison electric-battery tram service begins operation at Gisborne. The new trams, which are quiet, odourless and without unsightly overhead wires, will run until 1929. |
| July 1 | A 'unity conference' of the Federation of Labour and the United Labour Party begins in Wellington. At the conference, the organisations will combine to form the United Federation of Labour and the Social Democratic Party. The new federation is even more militant than the old one, and pledges to overthrow capitalism through strikes. |

| July 31 | A notice is posted in Waihohonu hut that formally announces the existence of Ruapehu Ski Club. The first ski club in New Zealand has been formed just weeks after its founders Bill Mead and Bernard Drake became the first skiers on the mountain. |
| --- | --- |
| October 23 | Waterside workers in Wellington picket the wharves after the Union Steam Ship Co. has locked them out over a pay dispute. The nationwide strike that ensues will threaten the national economy. |
| October 30 | Wellington strikers clash for the first time with mounted special constables. The 'specials', who will soon earn the nickname of 'Massey's cossacks', are young farmers brought in to put down the strike. |

**Four members of Section 1, Troop N, Squadron A of 'Massey's Cossacks' at Customhouse Quay, Wellington, ready for action in the waterfront dispute of 1913.**

| November 5 | In the 'Battle of Featherston Street', 800 mounted special constables charge a crowd trying to prevent racehorses being loaded onto a ship. Twenty people are injured. |
| --- | --- |

| November 10 | A general strike ordered by the United Federation of Labour is observed in Auckland. Christchurch and Dunedin unions do not respond to the call. |
| December 20 | The United Federation of Labour calls off the waterside workers' strike. The humiliating defeat will bring about the demise of the UFL. |

## 1914

| March 6 | Will Scotland flies his Caudron biplane from Timaru to Christchurch, establishing a distance record of 98 miles (158 km). On the way he makes the first unofficial airmail delivery, dropping a small package from the cockpit over Temuka. |
| August 4 | Following the invasion of Belgium, King George V declares that Great Britain and the British Empire are at war with the Central Powers (Germany, Austria-Hungary and Italy). |
| August 5 | The declaration of a state of war is read from the steps of Parliament, and New Zealand offers an expeditionary force to Britain. Crowds cheer at the news, and men rush to enlist. |
| August 15 | An expeditionary force of about 1400 men departs with six nurses for a secret destination. It has been instructed to take the wireless telegraphy station in German Samoa. |
| August 17 | The first New Zealand feature film, *Hinemoa*, premieres at the Lyric and West End Theatres, Auckland. Made by George Tarr, it has an all-Maori cast. |
| August 29 | New Zealand troops land at Apia, Samoa. German forces surrender without a shot being fired, and the New Zealanders claim the first allied occupation of enemy territory during the war. |
| September 10 | Probable date mudslides and volcanic eruptions overwhelm White Island's sulphur works. Its 10 operators are buried by as much as 6.5 yards (6 m) of volcanic debris. |
| September 12 | An explosion at Ralph's coal mine, Huntly, results in the deaths |

| | |
|---|---|
| | of 43 men. The probable cause is a naked flame coming into contact with fire damp. |
| October 16 | The main body of the New Zealand Expeditionary Force leaves Wellington. The 8400 men and 3800 horses are expected to go to the western front in France. |
| November 25 | William Massey officially opens the hydro-electricity works at Lake Coleridge. New Zealand's first major public hydro scheme will start supplying Christchurch the following year. |
| December 3 | New Zealand and Australian troops begin disembarking at Alexandria, Egypt. They have been diverted after the entry into the war of the Ottoman Empire. During their time training at Zeitoun, the two forces will form the New Zealand and Australian Division and later the Australian and New Zealand Army Corps. |

# 1915

| | |
|---|---|
| January 1 | Off Bastion Point, Auckland, a flying boat piloted by Vivian Walsh makes the first seaplane flight in New Zealand. It is the first flying boat to be designed and built in the Southern Hemisphere. |
| February 3 | New Zealand troops join an Indian brigade to defend the Suez Canal from a Turkish attack south of Ismailia. Private William Ham, age 22, will die of wounds two days later, becoming New Zealand's first casualty of the war. |
| February 14 | A Maori contingent of 500 volunteers, among them Peter Buck, departs Wellington for Egypt. The men will form the core of Te Hokowhitu a Tu, the Pioneer Battalion. More than 2000 men will serve in the battalion, among them 410 Cook Islanders and 148 Niueans. |
| April 25 | The Australian and New Zealand Army Corps, including 3100 New Zealanders, is landed at Anzac Cove, Gallipoli, only to find the Royal Navy has put them ashore in the wrong place. They are on a narrow beach surrounded by steep hills that will prove to be impossible territory for infantry. |

**The landing at Anzac Bay, Gallipoli on April 25, 1915.**

| | |
|---|---|
| May 8 | The New Zealand Brigade makes two desperate charges across the 'Daisy Patch' at Gallipoli. In one day there are 835 casualties. |
| May 15 | In Wanganui, a 3000-strong mob attacks shops with German names. The mayor and several police officers are injured when they try to quell the worst anti-German violence of the war. |
| August 8 | In a heroic effort, the Wellington Battalion secures Chunuk Bair. Two days later it will be recaptured in a Turkish counter-attack. |
| August 12 | A coalition national war cabinet is formed, with William Massey as prime minister. Despite the vigorous animosity between them, party leaders Massey (Reform) and Ward (Liberal) will work together for the duration of the war. |
| October 2 | The Walsh brothers' New Zealand Flying School begins training pupils at Orakei in Auckland (the following month it will move to Kohimarama). By January 1918, 50 pilots will have gained their pilot's licence and joined the Royal Flying Corps in Great Britain. |

| | |
|---|---|
| October 11 | The Discharged Soldiers Settlement Act passes into law. The government will buy up land to resell to returned servicemen with state loans, causing a real-estate boom. The poor quality of much of the land will cause resentment, and one-third of the soldier-farmers will give up their land within 20 years. |
| October 23 | The troopship *Marquette* is torpedoed in the Gulf of Salonika, and 10 New Zealand nurses are drowned. |
| December 19 | Troops are evacuated from Anzac Bay and Suvla in what proves to be the only successful action of the Gallipoli campaign. Of the 8556 New Zealand troops that have served in Gallipoli, 2721 have died. Those that remain will be taken back to Egypt to be reinforced and reorganised. |

## 1916

| | |
|---|---|
| January 23 | The New Zealand Mounted Rifle Brigade leaves Cairo for deployment at the Suez Canal. The Sinai and Palestine campaign will continue until 1918. |
| April 2 | More than 60 armed police come onto the marae at Maunga-pohatu to arrest prophet Rua Kenana for sedition. Shots are fired by both sides and Rua's uncle and son are killed. |
| May 13 | The New Zealand Division moves into the trenches on the western front near Armentières in northern France. It is during their time in Europe that the New Zealand troops will gain a reputation as 'diggers'. |
| June 9 | Rua Kenana and his followers go on trial at Auckland for sedition and, among other things, resisting arrest at Maungapohatu. The trial will run for 47 days — at the time it is one of the longest in British history — before Rua is found guilty of 'moral' resistance to the police. |
| July 1 | The first Somme offensive begins. |
| July 8 | The New Zealand Labour Party is formed at a joint conference of the United Federation of Labour and the Social Democratic Party at Wellington. |

| July 13 | Vivian Walsh becomes the first New Zealander to obtain an aviator's certificate. |
| --- | --- |
| August 1 | The Military Service Act passes into law. The new legislation means compulsory enrolment of Pakeha men between the ages of 20 and 46 for war service. Hundreds will refuse to serve, and conscientious objectors will be interned and punished, with a few forced to go to the front. |
| September 20 | The Canterbury (New Zealand) Aviation Co. is registered by Sir Henry Wigram. The flying school will train military pilots. |
| October 4 | The New Zealand Division is relieved from the frontline at Somme, having sustained more than 7000 casulties. |
| December 22 | Peter Fraser appears in a Wellington Magistrates' Court charged with sedition after making an anti-conscription speech. The future prime minister, who is among a number of Labour leaders charged with the same crime, will serve 12 months in jail. |

# 1917

| January 16 | A procession of 33 cars with more than 100 passengers, including parliamentary representatives and businessmen, sets out from Devonport in Auckland on a two-week tour of Northland to draw attention to transport problems in the 'roadless north'. |
| --- | --- |
| February 27 | The National Efficiency Board is established to advise on economic and industrial issues during the war. |
| June 2 | The *Wairuna* is sunk off the Kermadec Islands by the German raider *Wolf*, and the crew is captured. |
| June 7 | The New Zealand Division attacks at Messines. In two days the division will succeed in all its initial objectives, but nearly 3700 men will be casualties. |
| June 26 | Conscription is extended to include Maori, with the first ballot to be held in February 1918. Maori conscription will be |

selectively imposed, with only Waikato Maori forced to enlist as punishment for the separatism of the region's Kingitanga movement. Te Puea Herangi will organise a vigorous campaign of passive resistance.

| | |
|---|---|
| June 28 | Lord Liverpool assumes office as New Zealand's first governor-general. He has previously been the governor. |
| July 13 | Colonel H. R. Potter elects to force 14 conscientious objectors held at Trentham military camp to go to the front line. Among them is Archibald Baxter, who when he refuses to fight will for 28 days in a row be subjected to No. 1 Field Punishment, in which he is tied to a pole with his hands held behind his back. |
| September 18 | The steamer *Port Kembla* is sunk by a mine laid by the German raider *Wolf* off Farewell Spit, but the entire crew of 60 is able to escape in lifeboats. |
| October 7 | The debonair German naval captain Count Felix von Luckner arrives at Auckland for internment on Motuihe Island. Von Luckner has been captured in Fiji after sweeping through the Pacific with the raider *Seeadler*, sinking a number of ships and taking more than 200 prisoners without the loss of a single life. |
| October 12 | In one day at Passchendaele in Belgium, the New Zealand Division sustains 3296 casualties, including 1190 dead. With casualty rates of 85 per cent in some units, it is New Zealand's worst ever military disaster. |
| October 31 | The New Zealand Mounted Rifle Brigade seizes the redoubt at Tel el Saba and Beersheba is captured from the Turkish. |
| December 1 | Hotels are forced to close at six o'clock for the first time. The 'temporary' war measure will last for 50 years. |
| December 13 | Count Felix von Luckner and other German prisoners make a daring escape from Motuihe Island on the commandant's launch. |

| | |
|---|---|
| December 16 | Von Luckner and his men board the sailing scow *Moa* off the Coromandel. They set sail in the captured vessel to the Kermadec Islands, where they will surrender to the captain of the *Iris* after a shell is fired in their direction. Von Luckner will attempt two more escapes before being repatriated in May 1919. |

# 1918

| | |
|---|---|
| March 17 | Tahupotiki Wiremu Ratana receives the first intimation of his calling as a prophet when two whales are washed up on the beach at Whangaehu, near Wanganui, where the Ngati Apa ploughman is camping with his family. |
| March 19 | A huge bush fire starts at Raetihi. The fire will destroy buildings at Raetihi, Ohakune, Horopito and Rangataua, and kill one family. |
| June 26 | The *Wimmera* sinks north of Cape Maria van Diemen. Twenty-six of the 151 passengers and crew die after the steamer strikes a mine laid the year before by the German raider *Wolf*. |
| August 21 | The ceremony of the breaking down of the headings of the Otira tunnel is performed. The eastern and western ends of the tunnel, which is more than 5 miles long, have missed being perfectly in line by only 1¼ inches (3.2 cm) in level and ¾ inch (1.9 cm) in line. |
| October 3 | The *New Zealand Herald* reports that influenza of 'a rather virulent character' has been in Auckland for three or four weeks. |
| October 12 | The passenger liner *Niagara* arrives at Auckland with 26 serious cases of 'Spanish influenza' but the ship, with the prime minister on board, is not quarantined. As many as 8500 people — including a disproportionate number of Maori — will be killed by the virus in New Zealand. |
| October 30 | A massive petition is presented at Parliament seeking prohibition of the sale of alcohol. |

| November 4 | In New Zealand's last action of World War I, the Rifle Brigade captures Le Quesnoy using ladders to climb the 22 yards (20 m) high ramparts. |
| November 8 | Ratana has his most significant revelation, in which he is charged with uniting Maori and turning them towards God. Maori, resentful of being treated as a lesser race and reeling from the influenza epidemic, will be drawn to the faith healer's religious movement in great numbers. |
| November 8 | Unofficial — and inaccurate — reports are received that the armistice has been signed. Word spreads and joyful pandemonium takes over the streets, giving perfect conditions for the transmission of the influenza virus. |
| November 11 | The armistice is signed and the war ends. |
| November 12 | On the steps of the parliamentary library, the governor-general announces the signing of the armistice. The second time around, celebrations are muted. |
| December 10 | The Electric-power Boards Act passes into law, providing for the creation of power boards to control electricity distribution. |
| December 10 | The Repatriation Act passes into law. Under it a repatriation board will help returned soldiers go back to civilian life, encouraging training and further education. |

## 1919

| March 25 | The New Zealand Division is disbanded in Europe. |
| April 10 | A national referendum on prohibition is held. A majority of voters in New Zealand favour prohibition, and it is only when the votes of overseas servicemen are counted that a total ban on alcohol is avoided. |
| June 28 | At the Paris peace conference, William Massey signs the Treaty of Versailles as a representative of a separate and independent country. The treaty brings World War I to a formal end. |

| July 2 | New Zealand gets a joint mandate (with Great Britain and Australia) for the administration of phosphate-rich Nauru. The mandate, which will later be confirmed by the League of Nations, gives the country access to cheap phosphate for fertilisers. |
| --- | --- |
| August 20 | HMS *New Zealand* arrives at Wellington on its second visit to New Zealand. It is commanded by admiral of the fleet Lord Jellicoe, whose report on the country's naval defences will prompt the formation of the New Zealand Division of the Royal Navy. |
| August 24 | William Massey assumes office as prime minister after the dissolution of the national war cabinet. He heads a Reform government. |
| October 29 | The Women's Parliamentary Rights Act passes into law, allowing women to stand for Parliament. |
| November 1 | The New Zealand Expeditionary Force ceases to exist. Of the more than 100,000 New Zealanders who have served in the war, in excess of 18,000 have died — more than 7 per cent of all New Zealand men aged between 18 and 45. Four men have also been shot for refusing to fight. |
| November 25 | The first children's health camp begins at Turakina with 55 undernourished youngsters. School medical officer Dr Elizabeth Gunn has instigated the camp to improve health through sunshine, fresh air, activity and regular healthy meals, and the concept will take off throughout the country in following years. |
| December 16 | The first official airmail flight is made, from Auckland to Dargaville. The pilot for the experimental service is George Bolt, chief pilot of the Walsh brothers' flying school. |

# 1920

| January 16 | The League of Nations, of which New Zealand is a founding member, is officially inaugurated. After a year, the Paris peace conference has finally come to an end. |
| --- | --- |

| April 24 | The Prince of Wales (later King Edward VIII) arrives at Auckland to thank New Zealand for its support during the war. Over the course of a four-week visit the dashing prince will win the hearts of women all over the country. |

**Wellington crowds await the Prince of Wales during his 1920 tour of New Zealand.**

| May 15 | Charles Mackay, mayor of Wanganui, shoots poet D'Arcy Cresswell and seriously injures him. Cresswell, possibly acting on behalf of the mayor's political enemies, has invited Mackay to make a homosexual overture then tried to force him to resign over it. The mayor will be found guilty of attempted murder and sentenced to 15 years in jail with hard labour. |

| May 28 | In the Supreme Court, Auckland, Dennis Gunn is convicted of the murder of the Ponsonby postmaster and is sentenced to death. He is the first person to be convicted on fingerprint evidence. |

| June 28 | The Alexander Turnbull Library in Wellington, bequeathed to the crown by the book collector, first opens to the public. The collection will form the core of the national library. |

| August 25 | Captain Euan Dickson flies from Christchurch to Trentham, Wellington, with some stops for refuelling. The flight, in an Avro 504K, includes the first airplane crossing of Cook Strait. |
| September 27 | Viscount Jellicoe assumes office as governor-general. |
| December 17 | New Zealand's mandate to administer Western Samoa is confirmed by the League of Nations, although the islands are not part of New Zealand territory. |

## 1921

| April 2 | The buildings of the Cawthron Institute in Nelson are officially opened. The country's first privately endowed scientific research institution has been established with a bequest from Thomas Cawthron. |
| April 25 | The first Anzac Day is marked. The full public holiday has been introduced after lobbying by the Returned Soldiers' Association. |
| May 9 | A six-days-a-week airmail service begins operating between Auckland and Whangarei. George Bolt makes the first flight in an Avro floatplane, but the uneconomic service will soon be discontinued. |
| June 7 | Rotary Club begins in New Zealand with the formation of a Wellington branch. An Auckland arm of the service club will open within a week. |
| June 20 | The New Zealand Division of the Royal Navy is established, with HMS *Chatham* as its first vessel. |
| August 20 | On the *Eastern Planet*, Ralph Lawrence uses a radio telephone set to play records for the benefit of the radio operator on the *Wairuna*. One of the very first radio broadcasts in New Zealand, it is also heard on land in Christchurch. |
| October 4 | George Bolt, in a Supermarine flying boat, completes the first one-day flight from Auckland to Wellington. |

| November 17 | Professor Robert Jack of Otago University uses a small transmitter he has assembled to broadcast New Zealand's first radio programme, including the popular song 'Hello My Dearie'. Within a year there will be radio stations operating in Wellington, Dunedin, Auckland and Christchurch. |
| --- | --- |
| December 25 | The new pa Turangawaewae, established by Te Puea Herangi at Ngaruawahia, hosts its first hui. |

## 1922

| February 11 | The Forests Act passes into law, providing for the establishment of the New Zealand Forest Service. The new body will engage in large-scale plantings of radiata pine trees. |
| --- | --- |
| June 28 | The new Parliament buildings in Wellington are officially handed over, although the building has been in use since 1919 while work was under way. |
| September 16 | The cabinet offers to send New Zealand military support to Britain in a confrontation with Kemal Ataturk in Turkey. |
| October 6 | Enlisting of volunteers for the British–Turkish crisis closes with 13,481 men having stepped forward to return to Gallipoli. They will not be needed as the conflict will be resolved through negotiation. |

## 1923

| June 21 | The Canterbury Aviation Co. is taken over by the government with the gift of £10,000 from Sir Henry Wigram. It will become the New Zealand Permanent Air Force. |
| --- | --- |
| July 6 | The Auckland–Wellington express train is derailed at Ongarue in the early hours of the morning when it hits a landslip. In the accident, the first major loss of life on New Zealand railways, 17 people die and many more are seriously injured. |
| July 30 | The Ross area of Antarctica is declared a British settlement administered by New Zealand and named the Ross Dependency. |

| August 4 | The Otira tunnel is officially opened by William Massey, connecting Greymouth with Christchurch by rail. It takes 15 minutes to pass through the tunnel. |

## 1924

| March 18 | On a visit to Mt Taranaki and Parihaka, Tahupotiki Wiremu Ratana finds omens that lead him to take his religious message to the wider world. The faith healer and Maori spiritual leader is by now known as the Mangai ('mouthpiece of God'). |
| May 21 | The New Zealand Association of Basketball is formed at a meeting in Wellington. The organisation is a forerunner of the national netball association. |
| September 13 | The All Blacks play the first game of their rugby tour of the British Isles, France and British Columbia. Against Devon at Devonport they emerge the winners, as they will in every match over the next five months of the tour. The team will become known as the Invincibles. |
| October 18 | Otago farmer and amateur radio pioneer Frank Bell calls a student in London from his shed, making headlines around the world. It is the first ever trans-global radio transmission. |
| December 13 | General Sir Charles Fergusson assumes office as governor-general. He is the son of the eighth governor, Sir James Fergusson. |

## 1925

| March 17 | The touring All Blacks are fêted on their return to Wellington. The band plays 'See, the Conquering Hero Comes' as they disembark before a motorcade carries them along Lambton Quay. |
| April 1 | It becomes illegal under the Motor-vehicles Act 1924 to pilot a motor vehicle without a driver's licence. |

| | |
|---|---|
| May 10 | Prime minister William Massey succumbs to cancer while still in office. |
| May 14 | Sir Francis Dillon Bell (Reform) assumes office as prime minister in a caretaker administration. Having effectively been the country's leader since Massey became ill in 1924, the successful lawyer is the first New Zealand-born prime minister. |
| May 30 | Gordon Coates (Reform) assumes office as prime minister. |
| May 31 | Ratana announces the existence of his own church, Te Hahi Ratana, separate from the conventional church. As a result, the Anglican church will declare the movement schismatic, and excommunicate any Anglicans who join the new church. |
| October 1 | New Zealand formally takes over the administration of the Tokelau Islands from Great Britain, through the League of Nations mandate for Western Samoa. |
| November 17 | A second New Zealand and South Seas Exhibition opens on reclaimed land at Logan Park, Dunedin. In 24 weeks it will draw over 3.2 million visitors — and nearly 84,000 people (more than the city's whole population) will attend the closing festivities and fireworks. |

# 1926

| | |
|---|---|
| February 11 | Tokelau is disannexed from the Gilbert (Kiribati) and Ellice Islands (Tuvalu). |
| August 7 | The radio station 1YA is officially opened in Auckland. It is the first of four government-controlled local stations. |
| September 9 | Gordon Coates's Family Allowances Act passes into law, providing an allowance for the third and subsequent children in a family. Over the past 30 years New Zealand's developing welfare system has gained it a reputation as the world's social laboratory. |

| December 3 | Nine workers die in a coal mine explosion at Dobson on the West Coast. It is the worst mining disaster since the Brunner mine tragedy in 1896. |

## 1927

| January 21 | The first of the national yearling sales takes place at Trentham during the Wellington Racing Club's summer meeting. |
| February 22 | The Duke and Duchess of York (later King George VI and Queen Elizabeth) arrive at Auckland on HMS *Renown*. The duchess will win over New Zealanders with her warmth and charm. |
| February 26 | In Rotorua, the royal couple attend a concert of Maori entertainments. The recording of a duet by Ana Hato and Deane Waretini will launch the international career of the cousins. |
| April 27 | New Zealand's last steam tram service, between Bayswater and Milford on Auckland's north shore, ceases operation to be replaced by motor buses. |
| June 29 | A royal commission reports on the confiscation of Maori lands following the New Zealand Wars. It finds fault with government behaviour on many occasions. |
| October 14 | Dale Austen wins the Miss New Zealand contest by popular vote. Part of the prize is a three-month contract with MGM in Hollywood. |
| November 6 | New Zealand summer time starts, with the clocks advanced by an hour to GMT plus 12 hours. The following year daylight saving will be reduced to half an hour. |

## 1928

| January 10 | New Zealand flyers George Hood and John Moncrieff disappear without trace while attempting the first trans-Tasman flight. |
| January 25 | The new temple at Ratana pa is officially opened on Ratana's |

birthday. The occasion marks the official end of the prophet's spiritual mission and the beginning of his secular one.

March 20    Massey Agricultural College, Palmerston North, is officially opened with 85 students on its inaugural roll. It will become an autonomous university in 1964.

July 26     New Zealander Tom Heeney fights Gene Tunney for the heavyweight championship of the world. Heeney loses the contest at Yankee Stadium, New York, by technical knock-out in the 11th round, in what is described as a 'mauling'.

August 11   Despite an injured hand, boxer Ted Morgan wins the gold medal in the welterweight class at the Amsterdam Olympic Games. It is the first time New Zealand has won Olympic gold in its own name.

September 11 Australian Charles Kingsford Smith and his crew land at Wigram in the *Southern Cross* after the first successful trans-Tasman flight. Kingsford Smith will become an instant celebrity, and his achievement will revive interest in the potential of commercial aviation in New Zealand.

**Charles Kingsford Smith and the *Southern Cross* are mobbed at Wigram after the first trans-Tasman air crossing on September 11, 1928.**

| December 2 | Commander Richard Byrd leaves Dunedin to map the South Pole. The US aviator's expedition includes the ships *City of New York* and *Eleanor Bolling*. New Zealand has become the usual base for expeditions to the Antarctic. |
| December 2 | At Napier, Frederick Bennett is consecrated as the first Bishop of Aotearoa. Maori now have their own bishop within the Anglican church. |
| December 10 | Sir Joseph Ward again assumes office as prime minister 22 years after his first term began. This time at the head of a United government, his election success is put down to a rash promise to borrow £70 million to boost the economy. |

# A test of national character
## 1929–1945

**The collapse of the US stock market** in 1929 sent shockwaves around the world. The Great Depression spread as far as New Zealand, where unemployment brought poverty and social unrest. In 1935 election of the first Labour government saw the introduction of an extensive social security system. In the 1930s there was suffering on a breathtaking scale in China, where Mao Zedong's communists were forced on their Long March, and in the Soviet Union, where millions died in a famine before Stalin conducted a 'purge' of his opponents. In Spain, civil war raged from 1936 to 1939, serving as a prelude to Hitler's 1939 invasion of Poland. World War Two once more saw New Zealanders lining up at recruitment offices to defend the interests of Empire, even as the dominion celebrated the 100th anniversary of the signing of the Treaty of Waitangi.

# 1929

| | |
|---|---|
| March 8 | At the Paramount Theatre, Wellingtonians enjoy the opening night of the first successful season of talking pictures. An interview with George Bernard Shaw and other talking short films are shown before the feature presentation of the silent *Street Angel*. |
| March 11 | An 11-day hui begins at Turangawaewae that will be described as 'the most historic assembly of tribes since the Maori wars'. During the hui there will be three separate opening ceremonies for Mahinarangi, the newly completed whare whakairo (carved meeting house). |
| June 17 | An earthquake shakes the country from Auckland to Dunedin. The quake, which measures 7.8 on the Richter scale, is centred in the Lyell Range just west of Murchison. Seventeen people die, many in landslips and floods, and Karamea will be cut off for two weeks. |
| November 28 | The Auckland War Memorial Museum and cenotaph are consecrated. The Greek revival building is opened in an impressive ceremony during which the governor-general knocks on the door with a mere before leading in 10,000 people. The following day he will join with Tutanekai Taua to reopen Hotunui, a whare runanga relocated from near Thames to the Maori section of the museum. |
| December 1 | Len Lye's ground-breaking *Tusalava* animation premieres at the London Film Society. It will nearly be banned from general release by censors who don't understand what it is about and think it therefore may well be objectionable. |
| December 11 | The first issue of health postage stamps is made, with half of the value of the two-penny stamps going into a fund for the prevention of tuberculosis. From 1931 they will be used to raise money for children's health camps. |
| December 20 | The Civic Theatre in Auckland, a grand new 'atmospheric' picture palace with Moorish, Persian and Indian decoration, opens its doors to its first audience. |

| December 28 | Eight Samoans and one police officer are killed or mortally wounded during a Mau demonstration at Apia. Among those shot by police is leading chief Tamasese Lealofi III. |

# 1930

| January 3 | *Coubray-tone News* is screened at the Plaza, Auckland. It is the first time New Zealand-made talking pictures have been publicly exhibited. |
| January 19 | Four women trampers and their guide die in a blizzard on the Tasman Glacier. Having found the bodies, guide C. Hilgendorf crawls 8 km over ice to get help and is hailed as a hero. |
| March 19 | Viscount Bledisloe, a former lawyer and agriculturalist, assumes office as governor-general. |
| May 28 | George Forbes (United) assumes office as prime minister after Sir Joseph Ward has been persuaded to retire because of poor health. The country's new leader is a former farmer and captain of the Canterbury rugby team. |
| October 11 | The Unemployment Act passes into law. It provides for relief payments for registered unemployed, but does not cover women or Maori who do not live 'in the same manner as Europeans'. |
| October 29 | The Thermette is patented by John Hart. Later known to soldiers as the 'Benghazi Boiler', it can boil 12 cups of water in five minutes, using any fuel that comes to hand. |
| November 4 | Phar Lap wins the Melbourne Cup by two lengths from Second Wind. It is one of the New Zealand-bred galloper's greatest victories. |
| November 25 | The first official international telephone call is made. Minister of native affairs Sir Apirana Ngata, in Kirkcaldie & Stains in Wellington, speaks to the acting prime minister of Australia, J. E. Fenton. |

# 1931

**January 7**   Australian Guy Menzies completes the first trans-Tasman solo flight. The trip from Sydney ends in an undignified fashion at Harihari on the West Coast, where the plane lands in a swamp and flips over.

**January 31**   The chair of the Unemployment Board announces new make-work schemes for the unemployed involving local authorities and private businesses. Within two weeks an extra 11,000 men will put their names down on the register.

**February 3**   A massive earthquake of magnitude 7.8 on the Richter scale devastates Napier, Hastings and rural Hawke's Bay. Rivers are dammed, the Ahuriri Lagoon is drained and huge chasms are formed — and 256 people are killed, most by falling buildings. Tens of thousands of residents will be without running water, electricity and communications for weeks.

**Twelve women died when the nurses' home in Napier collapsed during the earthquake of February 3, 1931.**

**February 13**   A major aftershock of the Hawke's Bay earthquake shakes the region. Just one of many continuing tremors, this one measures 7.3.

| April 1 | Public service wages and salaries are reduced by 10 per cent in a desperate attempt to cut government spending. |
| June 1 | Under a general order issued by the president of the Arbitration Court, wages are reduced by 10 per cent to reduce costs of production and combat the economic depression. |
| July 23 | The New Zealand–United Kingdom telephone link is officially inaugurated, at the daunting cost of £6 15s for a three-minute call. |
| September 12 | The Bledisloe Cup is contested for the first time at a New Zealand–Australia rugby match at Wellington — even though the trophy has not yet been designed and made. |
| September 22 | George Forbes begins his second term as prime minister, leading a United–Reform government. The coalition has been formed to better combat the problems of the depression. |
| December 11 | The royal assent is given to the Statute of Westminster, which establishes New Zealand as an autonomous community within the Commonwealth. New Zealand, anxious about cutting ties with Great Britain, has tried to obstruct the legislation, and will not ratify it until 1947. |

# 1932

| January 9 | Unemployed workers riot in Dunedin, trying to storm a grocery store after the hospital board refuses relief for starving families. Eventually it is announced that private individuals have subscribed to supply 800 food parcels, which are duly distributed. |
| March 20 | New Zealand-bred Phar Lap wins the Agua Caliente Handicap, North America's richest horse race, by two lengths and in record time. |
| April 1 | Public servants suffer a second round of salary cuts, and pensions and benefits are reduced. To compensate, rents, interest rates and other fixed charges are reduced as well. |

| April 5 | Phar Lap dies of a mystery illness in California. It is suspected that the racehorse, at the time the greatest stake winner in Australasian racing history, has been poisoned. |
| April 8 | Unemployed Dunedin workers stone the relief depot and attack the mayoress's car. The disorder will continue for several days. |
| April 14 | Unemployed workers and men from relief camps riot in central Auckland after Jim Edwards, a leader of the Unemployed Workers' Movement, is batoned by police at a demonstration. About 200 people are injured in conflicts with police and navy personnel, and Queen Street shops are looted. The following night in Karangahape Road there will be further conflict between demonstrators and newly recruited special constables. |
| May 10 | Three thousand Wellington relief workers vote to go on strike rather than be moved to country camps. Later that day, a crowd of 5000 relief workers gathers at Parliament but Gordon Coates, the minister of public works, refuses to address them. A small breakaway group lets loose on Lambton Quay, Willis Street and Cuba Street, breaking 160 windows as they go. The following day, a meeting of 2000 relief workers will be broken up by police wielding batons. |
| September 16 | An earthquake of magnitude 7.25 on the Richter scale rocks the East Coast. Despite its being among the most powerful quakes recorded in New Zealand, few people are injured because it occurs in a sparsely populated area. |
| December 28 | The lighter *Tu Atu* and the launch *Doris* collide at Napier. Ten watersiders are drowned, but there are 21 survivors. |

## 1933

| January 20 | The sterling bank rate is raised from parity to £NZ125 for £100. Going against the advice of trading banks, the government is trying to protect primary producers from a disastrous fall in export prices. |

| | |
|---|---|
| July 15 | At Princeton University, Jack Lovelock breaks the world record for the mile by almost two seconds. The run is dubbed the 'greatest mile of all time'. |
| July 22 | The number of registered unemployed reaches its depression peak of 57,352. When male minors, Maori and women are added, the figure for those seeking work is more like 85,000. |
| September 21 | Elizabeth McCombs is sworn in as New Zealand's first woman MP after winning a by-election at Lyttelton. |
| October 1 | Te Rata Mahuta Potatau Te Wherowhero, the fourth Maori king, dies at Waahi. |
| October 8 | Koroki Mahuta Te Wherowhero is crowned fifth Maori king on the same day as his father's burial. His coronation comes in spite of a campaign to appoint Te Puea Herangi as leader of the Kingitanga, and the new king's doubts about his ability to live up to the position. |

## 1934

| | |
|---|---|
| February 5 | Ceremonies of dedication begin at Waitangi National Reserve, on land donated to the nation by Lord and Lady Bledisloe. The celebrations will continue into the following day. Te Ti marae has become a temporary township of 6000, with representatives of all tribes attending a hui. |
| February 17 | Charles Ulm completes the first official trans-Tasman airmail flight. The *Faith in Australia* makes the trip from Auckland to Sydney in a little over 14 hours. |
| February 27 | The New Zealand Permanent Air Force is redesignated as Royal New Zealand Air Force with the permission of the king. It is still, however, under the control of the army. |
| March 15 | George Bernard Shaw arrives in Auckland. The highlight of his visit will be a radio broadcast on April 12 to New Zealand and Australia in which he gives his frank opinion on New Zealand. On his departure, nonetheless, he will describe it as 'the best country I've been in'. |

| August 1 | The newly established Reserve Bank of New Zealand makes its first issue of New Zealand bank notes, replacing trading bank notes. The Reserve Bank now has the sole right to produce bank notes in New Zealand. |
| --- | --- |
| December 18 | Air Travel becomes the first licensed airline in New Zealand to begin scheduled services, south from Hokitika. |

# 1935

| February 1 | British silver coins cease to be legal tender in New Zealand. They have been gradually replaced by local coinage since 1933. |
| --- | --- |
| April 12 | Viscount Galway assumes office as governor-general. |
| May 2 | *Down on the Farm*, New Zealand's first successful talkie feature film, premieres at the Empire De Luxe Theatre in Dunedin. It is not a critical success. |
| June 29 | The Christchurch *Sun* and the *Times* both stop publication after a price-cutting newspaper war with the *Star* and the *Press*. |
| November 24 | The popular radio programme of Uncle Scrim (Colin Scrimgeour) is mysteriously beset by a technical problem. The government may have jammed the signal of the Friendly Road station, fearing the outspoken broadcaster would advise listeners to vote Labour in the upcoming election. |
| November 27 | Labour has a decisive victory in the general election, allowing the formation of the first Labour government. |
| December 6 | Michael Joseph Savage (Labour) assumes office as prime minister. His wide appeal as a warm, benign, sincere, seemingly saintly man will become a force for national unity. Meanwhile, the first act of the incoming cabinet is to authorise a 'Christmas box' of money for the unemployed. |

# 1936

| | |
|---|---|
| January 16 | Union Airways begins operating New Zealand's first trunk air service, with daily flights between Palmerston North, Blenheim, Christchurch and Dunedin. |
| January 20 | King Edward VIII succeeds his father. |
| February 1 | A violent storm begins that will, over the course of two days, see at least six people killed in the North Island and Marlborough, and the interisland steamer *Rangatira* holed off Wellington Head. |
| February 8 | The announcement is made that Sir Peter Buck (Te Rangi Hiroa) has been appointed chair of anthropology at Yale University. |
| March 16 | The first regular official airmail trunk service begins. The inaugural flight from Palmerston North to Dunedin carrying 10 bags of mail battles headwinds but arrives in time for the afternoon delivery of letters posted in Auckland two days earlier. |
| March 26 | Parliamentary debate is broadcast on radio for the first time, making New Zealand the first place in the world to begin regular parliamentary broadcasts. The tone of discussion will quickly change as MPs learn to play to the radio audience. |
| April 22 | T. W. Ratana meets with the prime minister, Michael Joseph Savage, to formalise an alliance between the Ratana movement and the Labour Party. By 1943, the Mangai's prediction that his representatives would hold all four Maori seats will be fulfilled. |
| May 13 | A conference begins during which the New Zealand National Party will be formed out of the coalition of the United and Reform parties. The aim of the new party is to promote 'good citizenship and self-reliance', stamp out socialism and encourage private enterprise. |
| August 1 | Guaranteed basic prices for butter and cheese are introduced, |

and all dairy products for export become the property of the crown.

August 1    The Dominion Museum and National Gallery (incorporating the New Zealand Academy of Fine Arts) open to the public in Wellington.

August 6    At Berlin, Jack Lovelock streaks away from the pack in the 1500 m to win Olympic gold. His time is also a world record.

**Jack Lovelock runs easily during the early stages of the 1500 m final at the Berlin Olympics, August 6, 1936.**

September 1    The 40-hour week becomes compulsory 'where practicable'. The same law change makes union membership compulsory in most industries.

| | |
|---|---|
| October 16 | New Zealand aviatrix Jean Batten lands at Mangere, Auckland, to be greeted by an emotional crowd of 6000. She has completed the first ever solo direct flight from England to New Zealand. Along the way she has broken the England–Australia solo record, become the first woman to fly the Tasman, and broken the record for any flight between Australia and New Zealand. |
| October 29 | The first government-owned commercial radio station, 1ZB, is officially opened in Auckland. Regular broadcasts, under the direction of Colin Scrimgeour, will begin the following day. |
| December 11 | King Edward VIII is succeeded by King George VI after Edward's abdication. |

## 1937

| | |
|---|---|
| March 1 | The free milk in schools scheme, the first such scheme in the world, begins in Auckland. It will supply daily half-pint bottles of milk to the country's schoolchildren for 30 years. |
| March 30 | Captain Edwin Musick brings the Pan-American flying boat *Samoan Clipper* in Auckland after the first survey flight from San Francisco. His arrival begins the bridging of the travel gap between New Zealand and the rest of the world. |
| April 1 | The Royal New Zealand Air Force becomes an autonomous branch of the defence forces. |
| April 14 | The National Industrial Conference begins. During the meeting, a new Federation of Labour will be formed, with Angus McLagan as the inaugural president, healing a long-standing rift in the labour movement. |
| September 18 | The first state house, in Miramar, Wellington, is officially opened by Michael Joseph Savage. The prime minister and most of the Labour cabinet then help the McGregor family carry in the furniture. The Department of Housing Construction, under the leadership of John A. Lee, has embarked on a great campaign to rid New Zealand of sub-standard housing by building 5000 new dwellings each year. |

| December 27 | *Centaurus*, an Imperial Airways flying boat commanded by Captain J. W. Burgess, arrives at Mechanics Bay, Auckland, after a survey flight from Sydney. The success of this flight clears the way for the first scheduled trans-Tasman air services. |

## 1938

| January 2 | Pan-American takes off for the first official Auckland–San Francisco airmail flight. The flying boat piloted by Captain Musick is carrying 25,000 items posted by eager New Zealanders. Musick and the crew of the *Samoan Clipper* will be lost later in the year when the aircraft crashes into the Pacific. |
| February 19 | In the early hours of the morning, a railway construction camp at Kopuawhara, north of Wairoa, is hit by a flash flood. In the disaster 21 people drown, some of them losing their lives while trying to save others. |
| February 26 | The Summit Road, in the Port Hills near Christchurch, is officially opened. It has been under construction for nearly 30 years. |
| March 18 | Five thousand people attend a hui at Turangawaewae. During the gathering, Te Puea Herangi is invested as a CBE, Turongo — the Maori monarch's new residence — is opened, and the canoe *Te Winika* is relaunched after damage inflicted in the New Zealand Wars has been repaired. |
| March 26 | A weekend excursion train is derailed at Ratana. Six lives are lost immediately, and the train's fireman will die later. |
| April 2 | Michael Joseph Savage issues a statement outlining the planned establishment of a free and universal health service, national superannuation and increased pensions. It is seen as the beginning of the welfare state. |
| April 25 | Floods sweep through Hawke's Bay. No human lives are lost, but there is extensive damage to property and the silt-covered Esk Valley will be a dustbowl for a year. |

| September 14 | The Social Security Act passes into law, providing a welfare programme for New Zealanders 'from the cradle to the grave'. It introduces a revised pensions structure and extended benefits for families, invalids and the unemployed. Over following years further benefits will be introduced, along with free medical care for all and free dental care for children. |
| December 5 | The export and import of goods are forbidden except under government licence. |

## 1939

| March 25 | A new 1900 yard (1743 m) road bridge over the Rakaia River is opened. |
| April 19 | Heavy rain begins to fall after months of severe drought all over the country, offering relief to desperate farmers. |
| June 30 | The first edition of the *New Zealand Listener* is published, free to holders of a radio licence. Oliver Duff is the foundation editor. |
| July 27 | Snow falls in Auckland for the first time since meteorological records began. It is as much as 2 inches (5 cm) deep on the heights, with just a sprinkling at lower levels. Days later, snow will fall as far north as Cape Maria van Diemen in Northland. |
| September 1 | Germany invades Poland, precipitating World War II. |
| September 3 | The 'first shots' of World War II are fired from Fort Dorset, Wellington, before war has even been declared. The shells are launched into the path of the *City of Delhi*, a British freighter that has ignored signals. |
| September 3 | Just before midnight the New Zealand cabinet agrees to declare war on Germany. |
| September 4 | Christian pacifist Ormond Burton is arrested after denouncing the war to a crowd of 200 outside Parliament. Burton and other pacifists will be charged repeatedly for anti-war protests, and |

| | |
|---|---|
| | will be sentenced to jail terms of up to two and a half years. |
| September 5 | Michael Joseph Savage addresses the nation in a radio broadcast. The ailing prime minister, speaking from his bed, famously says of Britain, 'Where she goes, we go; where she stands, we stand.' |
| September 12 | Voluntary enlistment begins for what will become known as the 2nd New Zealand Expeditionary Force (2NZEF). |
| September 24 | Eleven men die of asphyxiation while investigating an underground gas leak in the Glen Afton mine, Huntly. |
| November 8 | The New Zealand Centennial Exhibition is opened at Rongotai, Wellington. The centrepiece of New Zealand's centennial commemorations, with its sleek art deco temporary pavilions, shows off New Zealand's cultural, industrial and agricultural achievements — while a 10 acre (4 ha) amusement park provides light relief. |
| November 22 | Bernard Freyberg assumes command of the expeditionary force. The World War I hero is British born but New Zealand raised. |
| December 13 | The Royal Navy cruiser *Achilles*, manned mainly by New Zealanders, takes part in an attack on the *Admiral Graf Spee* in the battle of the River Plate off Uruguay. Four ratings are killed on the *Achilles*, and four days later the *Admiral Graf Spee* will be scuttled by its commanding officer. |

# 1940

| | |
|---|---|
| January 2 | The memorial to the Arawa canoe, commemorating the arrival of the Maori in New Zealand, is unveiled at Maketu. It is the first of seven national events organised by the national centennial committee. The anniversary of the signing of the Treaty of Waitangi will also be marked with books, exhibitions, art, music, theatre and film. |
| January 5 | The first echelon of the 2NZEF (6529 men) departs. A convoy of six ships leaves Wellington Harbour for training in Egypt. |

| | |
|---|---|
| February 6 | Ten thousand people gather at Waitangi for centennial celebrations, although the event is boycotted by Waikato Maori. The signing of the Treaty of Waitangi is re-enacted, speeches are made and memorials to Hobson, Busby and the Maori signatories are unveiled. The new whare runanga is dedicated and the waka taua *Ngatokimatawhaorua* is launched with 100 paddlers. |
| February 23 | A civic reception is held at Auckland for Captain W. E. Perry and the men of HMS *Achilles*. Fresh from their success in the Battle of the River Plate, they are welcomed by a crowd of about 100,000. |
| March 27 | Michael Joseph Savage dies at Wellington after a long illness. News of the death of a beloved prime minister prompts widespread mourning. |
| March 31 | Savage is buried at Bastion Point, Auckland. The special train carrying his body has stopped at 20 train stations on the way to allow North Islanders to pay their respects, and massive crowds line the route of the funeral cortège in Auckland. |
| April 1 | Peter Fraser (Labour), a former watersider and union official, assumes office as prime minister. He will put firm controls on the economy so that the country's wealth is available for the war effort. |
| April 26 | Tasman Empire Airways Limited (TEAL) is formed as a limited liability company. The airline, the forerunner to Air New Zealand, is owned jointly by the New Zealand government, Union Airways, BOAC and Qantas. |
| April 30 | TEAL begins the first regular Auckland–Sydney flying boat service (passengers and mail) with a flight commanded by Captain J. W. Burgess. TEAL's inaugural commercial service makes New Zealand–UK airmail delivery possible. |
| May 1 | The government buys the copyright of 'God Defend New Zealand' at the recommendation of the national centennial council. It becomes the national hymn, while 'God Save the King' remains the anthem. |

| May 2 | The second echelon of 2NZEF, including 28 (Maori) Battalion, leaves Wellington. |
| June 13 | The German raider *Orion* arrives in New Zealand waters and lays mines in Mercury Bay, off the Coromandel. In two days it will lay 228 mines, including barrages in the Hauraki Gulf. |
| June 19 | The Canadian–Australian mail steamer *Niagara*, also carrying passengers and £2.5 million in gold, is sunk by a German mine off Northland. There is no loss of life but the gold sinks to the seabed with the ship. |
| July 16 | Prime minister Peter Fraser announces the formation of a war cabinet that includes Gordon Coates and Adam Hamilton representing the opposition. |
| July 18 | Pan-American's first regular trans-Pacific flight, a Boeing 314 flying boat that left San Francisco on 12 July, arrives at Auckland. |
| July 22 | Enlistment ceases to be voluntary, replaced by ballots for call up for military service. The first conscription will occur in October. |
| August 2 | The war cabinet approves the establishment of the Home Guard as an integral part of the military forces. By the end of the war more than 100,000 men will volunteer to serve to protect New Zealand from invasion. |
| November 23 | The National Broadcasting Service transmits a concert entirely of New Zealand music, including the works by Douglas Lilburn that have won three of the four composition prizes in the centennial music competition. |
| November 25 | The passenger ship *Holmwood* is captured and scuttled off the Chatham Islands by the German raider *Komet*. The passengers and crew will eventually be landed in the Bismarck Archipelago, New Guinea. |

# 1941

| | |
|---|---|
| January 16 | The air force opens its doors to women with the foundation of the Women's Auxiliary Air Force. The WAAFs are New Zealand's first female military personnel but will within 18 months be joined by the Women's Army Auxiliary Corps and the Women's Royal Naval Service. More than 1000 women in these three services will serve overseas. |

**The Women's Auxiliary Air Force, formed on January 16, 1941, trained wireless operators for the war effort.**

| | |
|---|---|
| February 2 | The *Niagara* is found at a depth of 439 feet (134 m). Salvage operations will recover almost all the gold bars lost when the vessel sank. |
| February 22 | Marshal of the RAF Sir Cyril Newall assumes office as governor-general. His term will be best remembered for his controversial reference in a speech to the 'men of the navy, men of the army and gentlemen of the air force'. |
| March 6 | The first New Zealand units leave Alexandria for the invasion of Greece. By the end of the month the entire division will be there. |

| | |
|---|---|
| April 29 | The last of the New Zealand forces leave Greece in a hasty evacuation to Crete that leaves thousands behind. The campaign has seen 261 New Zealanders killed, 387 wounded and 1856 taken prisoner. At least 400 will find their own way out of Greece. |
| May 20 | The German airborne invasion of Crete begins. Within a week the battle will be lost and New Zealand troops will be withdrawn to North Africa. |
| June 3 | The first intake of women police recruits enters the training depot. Although they will have the same legal powers as male officers, at first they will be used as typists and clerks. Uniforms will not be issued to women officers until 1952. |
| July 3 | The National Film Unit's first production, *Country Lads*, is released as the first in a weekly series of newsreels. The unit will produce films for government departments, specialising in high-quality tourism films. |
| July 29 | The Finnish barque *Pamir* arrives at Wellington from the Seychelles Islands. It will be seized as a prize of war because Finland is deemed to be an enemy power, and will sail under the New Zealand ensign until 1949. |
| September 17 | The death penalty for murder is abolished and replaced with life imprisonment with hard labour, although the Labour government began commuting death penalties in 1935. The law change also brings an end to flogging and whipping as punishments. |
| October 1 | The Royal New Zealand Navy is formed and the dominion's naval forces cease to be a division of the Royal Navy. |
| October 8 | West Coast farmer Stan Graham, paranoid and delusional, kills three police officers at Kowhitirangi. A fourth officer is mortally wounded. An agricultural instructor is also shot and will die from his wounds 17 months later. Graham escapes into the bush. |
| October 9 | Stan Graham returns to his house. During an exchange of |

| | shots, two home guardsmen are fatally injured before Graham flees into the hill country. The manhunt that follows involves hundreds of police, military and volunteers. |
|---|---|
| October 20 | Stan Graham is at last found and is shot by a police officer. He will die in hospital the following day. |
| November 1 | The general medical services benefit is introduced, providing free GP visits for beneficiaries. |
| November 18 | New Zealand troops enter Libya as part of the Eighth Army. Over the next 18 months they will be involved in a series of actions, including Sidi Rezegh, Belhamed, Tobruk, Minqar Qaim, Ruweisat Ridge and Takrouna. |
| December 8 | New Zealand declares war on Japan following the surprise attack on the US Navy at Pearl Harbor, Hawaii. Japan also invades the Philippines, Malaya and Thailand, and within eight weeks Singapore will have fallen. |
| December 19 | HMS *Neptune* sinks off Tripoli after striking mines. Of the more than 750 who perish, 150 are New Zealanders. Only one man, an English rating, survives. |

## 1942

| | |
|---|---|
| January 10 | Amendments to the national service regulations provide for the complete mobilisation of manpower. Civilians can now be required to register for work and workers can be directed into industries of national importance. |
| February 23 | 2 New Zealand Division is deployed to Syria. |
| March 29 | Confidence trickster Sydney Ross has a meeting with Peter Fraser and Bob Semple, and he convinces them there is a fifth column operating in New Zealand. Ross will dupe the Security Intelligence Bureau for several months, living the high life at government expense as he pretends to work as a counter espionage agent. When the hoax is revealed, the head of the SIB, Major Kenneth Folkes, will be dismissed and responsibility for security intelligence handed over to the police. |

| April 27 | Sugar rationing of 12 oz (1½ cups) weekly begins. |
| --- | --- |
| May 7 | A Wellington–Nelson flight crashes on Mt Richmond. The five dead are the first civilian casualties on a regular passenger flight in New Zealand. |
| May 13 | Lieutenant-Colonel Edward Love is appointed commander of the Maori Battalion. He is the first Maori to hold this position. |
| June 3 | At the instigation of MPs Paraire Paikea, Eruera Tirikatene and H. T. Ratana, the government approves the establishment of the Maori War Effort Organisation. It will oversee Maori recruitment for war service and later use its effective national structure of tribal committees to advise on education, training and land use. |
| June 14 | Without public notice, thousands of US marines, the advance echelon of the 1st Division, put in at Wellington. Between 1942 and 1944, more than 100,000 US servicemen will be based in New Zealand, allowing 2 New Zealand Division to remain in the Middle East and North Africa rather than return to defend their country from Japanese invasion. |
| June 16 | 2 New Zealand Division begins the move from Syria to Egypt to rejoin the North African campaign. |
| June 24 | An earthquake strikes Wellington and the Wairarapa. Masterton is especially badly damaged. |
| July 22 | A US amphibious force of 12 transports escorted by five cruisers sails from Wellington for an assault on the Japanese-held Solomon Islands. New Zealand forces will also be involved in the campaign. |
| August 2 | A second major earthquake in six weeks hits the Wellington, Wairarapa and Manawatu districts. |
| October 26 | The Women Jurors Act passes into law, allowing women to sit on judicial juries. The first female juror will not be selected until the following year. |

| November 2 | 2 New Zealand Division, with three British brigades, makes a decisive breakthrough at El Alamein. The success will push the Axis forces into retreat. |
| December 8 | Fire sweeps through Ward 5 of Seacliff Mental Hospital, Otago. Thirty-seven of the 39 female patients in the locked ward die in the fire. |
| December 15 | The director and committee of the Economic Stabilisation Commission are appointed. They are charged with controlling the nation's economy by fixing prices and wages through subsidisation, regulation and rationing. |

## 1943

| February 25 | Japanese prisoners revolt at Featherston prisoner-of-war camp. Guards shoot dead 48 prisoners and one New Zealand guard is killed by a ricochet. |
| April 3 | Hundreds of US and New Zealand servicemen clash in the 'Battle of Manners Street' in Wellington. It is claimed the brawl began when US men tried to stop Maori entering a club. Rumours will circulate that two men have been killed but this will never be proved. |
| May 13 | The campaign in North Africa ends when General Freyberg accepts the surrender of the Italian and German forces. |
| June 4 | The Cromwell–Dunedin express train, travelling at speed, is derailed at Hyde. In the crash 21 people are killed and 47 injured. The driver will later be found guilty of manslaughter. |
| July 12 | The first draft of volunteers returns from overseas on furlough. After January 1944 more than 800 of them will be convicted of desertion when they refuse to go back to the war until all single men have been conscripted. |
| July 13 | HMNZS *Leander* is torpedoed during the invasion of the Solomon Islands. |

**Soldiers of 2NZEF return to New Zealand on furlough on July 12, 1943. Many will be reluctant to return to the front line.**

| | |
|---|---|
| August 2 | A cargo plane carrying Japanese internee families crashes on take-off from Whenuapai, Auckland, and 15 crew and passengers die. As with several military plane accidents in New Zealand, there is no media coverage because of wartime secrecy. |
| August 11 | Flying Officer L. A. Trigg, a New Zealander serving in the RAF, earns the Victoria Cross for his actions over the Atlantic Ocean. Uniquely, he will be put forward for the medal by the captain of the U-Boat he was targeting when his aircraft was hit and crashed. |
| September 18 | A New Zealand force lands at Vella Lavella (Solomon Islands) to clear Japanese forces from the island. Over the next few months, 3 New Zealand Division will take part in assaults on Mono, Stirling and Nissan Islands. |
| October 9 | The first main convoy of New Zealand troops lands at Taranto, Italy. 2 New Zealand Division will finish the war clearing German troops out of Italy. |

| October 28 | The introduction of butter rationing is announced. Butter will continue to be rationed until 1950 so that more can be sent to the United Kingdom. |

# 1944

| January 21 | Australia and New Zealand sign the Canberra Pact, undertaking to co-operate on international matters, especially in the Pacific. It is an assertion of growing independence from British and US influences. |
| February 5 | US forces at Cassino, Italy, are relieved by units of 2 New Zealand Division. |
| March 15 | Castle Hill is captured on the first day of the newly-formed New Zealand Corps's assault on Cassino. |
| March 26 | The New Zealand Corps is disbanded, having lost more than 200 dead and 100 missing in its seven-week life. |
| August 16 | The New Zealand Council of Organisations for Relief Overseas is formed. The first project for CORSO is to gather and dispatch clothes for refugees in Europe. The charity will become controversial as it becomes increasingly politicised. |
| August 21 | Two RNZAF Lockheed Hudson bombers disappear on a Fiji–Auckland flight. Fourteen lives are lost. |
| October 20 | 3 New Zealand Division ceases to exist at the conclusion of its role in the Pacific. |
| November 1 | The first wartime refugees arrive at Wellington in the form of 732 Polish children who will stay in a refugee camp in Pahiatua for up to five years. By the end of the 1940s, New Zealand will have accepted more than 5000 child and adult refugees. |
| December 15 | The poll tax is abolished when the Finance Act (No. 3) passes into law. The tax on Chinese immigrants, although it has been waived for the past 10 years, is described by Walter Nash as a 'blot on our legislation'. |

# 1945

| | |
|---|---|
| April 25 | 2 New Zealand Division makes an Anzac Day crossing of the River Po in Italy. |
| April 25 | The United Nations Conference on International Organisation begins at San Francisco. New Zealand is fully represented, and Peter Fraser particularly will impress the other delegates. |
| May 2 | New Zealand forces enter Trieste, and the German army in Italy surrenders. |
| May 8 | VE Day is celebrated in Europe. |
| May 9 | Morning papers announce the end of the war in Europe. Throughout the country there is dancing and singing in the streets, and the celebrations continue into the night in bars. |
| June 26 | New Zealand is one of 50 nations to sign the United Nations Charter at San Francisco. They pledge to 'save succeeding generations from the scourge of war' and 'reaffirm faith in fundamental human rights'. |
| July 14 | Snow settles to a depth of a foot over much of Christchurch. The city is paralysed by power and telephone failures. |
| August 15 | Peter Fraser announces VJ Day. Japan has surrendered following the atomic explosions at Hiroshima and Nagasaki, and World War II is over. More than 200,000 men and women have served in the country's armed forces, nearly three-quarters of them overseas, and more than 11,500 have died. |
| August 21 | The war cabinet is dissolved, putting Peter Fraser's Labour Party back in full control. |
| September 2 | On behalf of New Zealand, Air Vice-Marshal Leonard Isitt signs the instrument of Japanese surrender aboard USS *Missouri* in Tokyo Bay. |

| | |
|---|---|
| November 1 | The Bank of New Zealand is nationalised, with all shares being vested in the crown. |
| December 7 | The government appoints the Dominion Population Committee to suggest the best ways to increase New Zealand's population. Its 1946 report will favour growth by natural means — but states that if immigrants are to come, priority should be given to the British. |
| December 15 | The last section of the South Island main trunk line, north of Kaikoura, is officially opened. Picton and Bluff are now linked by rail. |

# Good times – for some
# 1946–1957

**The international jubilation** accompanying the end of World War Two was short-lived as a colonial war broke out in Vietnam and the Cold War stand-off between the USA and the Soviet Union began. In New Zealand spirits were high as the newly-independent country looked forward to better times. Prosperity did come aided by a wool boom and extensive industrialisation, but not without a shift to the political right and a bout of union-wrecking in 1951. Around the world a number of colonies and territories, among them India in 1945, became independent nations. The state of Israel was founded as a homeland for Jews in 1948. Mao Zedong came to power in China in 1949 and Soviet troops invaded Hungary in 1956. But in 1957 all eyes turned to space as the Sputnik satellite orbited Earth and the space race began.

# 1946

| January 1 | New Zealand Standard Time is set at GMT plus 12 hours, making permanent the emergency regulations introduced in 1941. |
|---|---|
| January 23 | 28 (Maori) Battalion returns as a unit to Wellington. Described by its commander, Lieutenant-Colonel James Henare, as 'the remnants of a proud force', the battalion has lost more than 600 dead and about 2000 wounded. |
| January 31 | Mary Dreaver and Mary Anderson are appointed to the Legislative Council. They are the first women to serve. |
| February 7 | A fire begins near Taupo that will sweep over 247,000 acres (100,000 ha), destroying pine plantations and threatening the township. Although it is regarded at the time as a national calamity, in the months that follow regeneration will occur at a rate of as many as 500,000 seedlings per acre. |
| March 29 | The main body of J-Force reaches Kure in Japan to join the British Commonwealth Occupation Force. |
| June 17 | Lieutenant-General Sir Bernard Freyberg assumes office as governor-general. During his term he will be raised to the peerage. |
| December 13 | The United Nations approves New Zealand's trusteeship agreement for Western Samoa. The new arrangement provides for internal self-government. |

# 1947

| January 19 | The passenger ship *Wanganella* runs aground on Barrett Reef, Wellington. It will remain there for more than two weeks before floating clear on a heavy southerly swell. |
|---|---|
| March 6 | The New Zealand National Orchestra gives its first public performance, at Wellington town hall. The orchestra, under the baton of Anderson Tyrer, is the predecessor of the New Zealand Symphony Orchestra. |

| | |
|---|---|
| March 24 | On behalf of New Zealand, the high commissioner in London signs a cheque for a £10 million gift to Great Britain in recognition of the burden carried by the country during World War II. |
| March 26 | A tsunami hits the East Coast, with two waves as high as 10 m. No one is hurt because the main forces strike in a thinly populated area. |
| April 1 | The government-owned National Airways Corporation (NAC) begins operating under licence, having purchased Union Airways, Cook Strait Airways and Air Travel (New Zealand). |
| May 13 | Mabel Howard is selected by the Labour caucus to become the first woman in cabinet. A tireless advocate for women and children and a supporter of trade unions, she will be given the health portfolio. During her time in Parliament she has constantly challenged the male domination of facilities in Parliament buildings. |
| June 5 | New traffic lights on the corner of Customs Street and Albert Street, Auckland, are officially switched on after several days of trials. Drivers quickly become accustomed to the first automatic traffic lights in the country, and before long will learn to start accelerating on an amber light. |
| July 10 | The advisory committee of the State Literary Fund meets for the first time. The fund has been established to assist serious writers and publishers, and one of the earliest beneficiaries will be *Landfall*, the literary journal established by Charles Brasch. |
| July 31 | The Dairy Products Marketing Commission Act passes into law, giving the dairy industry and government shared responsibility for export marketing. |
| August 23 | The *Rangitata* arrives at Auckland with the first 118 assisted immigrants from Great Britain, all of them single people aged between 20 and 35. Large numbers of British immigrants are also arriving independently, although 'non-European' people (including Greeks and Italians) are not encouraged. |

| October 10 | The last major outbreak of typhoid begins at Kaikoura, and three people will die. The outbreak is traced back to unpasteurised milk. |
| November 18 | A fire destroys Ballantyne's department store in Christchurch. In the blaze 41 staff members, most of them women, die. A commission of inquiry will later find that fire crew training and leadership were sub-standard, the building was unsafe, and store management did not take the fire risk seriously. |
| November 23 | A civic funeral is held for the victims of the Ballantyne's fire and the service broadcast nationwide. The dead are buried in a mass grave at Ruru lawn cemetery. |
| November 25 | The Statute of Westminster Adoption Act passes into law, ratifying the Statute of Westminster 16 years after it was passed. New Zealand is now a sovereign nation independent of Great Britain but still part of the Commonwealth. |
| November 25 | The Rabbit Nuisance Amendment Act passes into law, setting up the Rabbit Destruction Council to supervise attempts to control a nationwide plague of rabbits. |
| November 27 | The Maori Purposes Act passes into law, replacing the term 'native' with 'Maori' for official use. |
| November 28 | North Island schools close early for the summer to slow the progress of a poliomyelitis epidemic. The schools will not reopen for nearly five months, and children will also be banned from cinemas and other public places. |

## 1948

| February 25 | The Picton–Christchurch express train is derailed at Seddon. Six people will die in a crash caused by excessive speed. |
| May 1 | For the first time in recorded history Ruapehu and Ngauruhoe are in simultaneous eruption — although Ruapehu's eruption is brief and unspectacular. |
| May 7 | Sir Apirana Ngata, who was in 1894 the first Maori to be |

awarded a bachelor's degree, receives an honorary DLitt degree at Victoria University College. His son Henare also receives his BA, making this the first time in New Zealand a father and son have been capped together.

| | |
|---|---|
| August 25 | A tornado at Frankton Junction, Hamilton, kills three people and wrecks nearly 150 houses. |
| September 21 | The RNZAF conducts aerial topdressing trials using an adapted Avenger aircraft. The encouraging results are well publicised, and the first commercial drop will take place less than a year later. The idea of aerial sowing and topdressing was first raised in the 1920s by John Lambert, and the public works department also did some experiments in the 1930s. The practice will revitalise pastureland all over the country. |
| September 27 | Meat rationing is abolished. |
| October 3 | Recording of the first locally recorded and manufactured disc is completed. The Ruru Karaitiana Quintette's performance of 'Blue Smoke', with vocals by Pixie Williams, will be released on the TANZA label in 1949. |
| October 11 | The last big draft of J-Force returns from Japan, leaving behind only a small rear party. |
| October 23 | An NAC Lockheed Electra airliner crashes on Mt Ruapehu. All 13 occupants are killed in this, New Zealand's first major passenger plane accident. A recovery party will not reach the wreckage until a week after the plane goes missing. |
| November 20 | A party led by Dr Geoffrey Orbell photographs and catches a takahe in a valley above Te Anau. It is the first time the flightless species of bird has been seen for 50 years, and it has long been thought to be extinct. |

# 1949

| | |
|---|---|
| January 1 | Under the Tokelau Islands Act 1948, Tokelau becomes part of the territory of New Zealand. |

| | |
|---|---|
| January 1 | New Zealanders become New Zealand citizens, and the words 'New Zealand' are added to the front of their British passports. Citizenship can be acquired by birth, descent, naturalisation or registration. |
| January 5 | The first four of the navy's six newly acquired frigates arrive at Auckland. They have been bought second-hand from the British government. |
| February 9 | Mt Ngauruhoe erupts violently, throwing glowing rocks 330 feet (100 m) into the air. The display will continue for more than a week. |
| March 9 | A two-issue referendum supports the introduction of off-course betting through the totalisator and the retention of six o'clock closing. |
| March 18 | An NAC Lodestar aircraft crashes into the Tararua foothills on approach to Paraparaumu. Thirteen passengers and two crew members die in the accident. |
| August 3 | A referendum on peace-time conscription is resoundingly successful, with 568,000 voting for it and 161,000 against. The first intake will begin compulsory military training in May the following year. |
| September 20 | The New Zealand pound is devalued against the US dollar by about 30 per cent in concert with Commonwealth countries. |
| September 24 | A trolley bus service to Herne Bay begins in Auckland. The introduction of the more manoeuvrable vehicles in Auckland and Wellington marks the beginning of the end for tram services. |
| November 29 | In the poll for the Western Maori seat, Iriaka Ratana is elected to Parliament. She is the first Maori woman MP. |
| November 30 | The 14-year-old Labour government is defeated in a general election. Voters have tired of wartime shortages and regulations, and have found the National Party promise of |

|  | free enterprise in place of state control attractive. National will be in power for 29 of the next 35 years. |
| --- | --- |
| December 13 | Businessman Sidney Holland (National) assumes office as prime minister. His term will be remembered as New Zealand's worst time for industrial relations. |
| December 28 | Jack Lovelock is killed when he falls under a subway train in New York. The reason for the death of the 'Golden Miler', who has been working as a surgeon in Manhattan, is unexplained. |

## 1950

| February 4 | The British Empire Games, the first to be held in New Zealand, begin at Auckland. Forty thousand people attend the opening ceremony, and about a quarter of a million spectators will be drawn to the sporting events. |
| --- | --- |
| June 1 | Petrol rationing ends nearly 11 years after it was introduced at the beginning of World War II. |
| June 4 | Butter rationing ends, and New Zealand is completely free of rationing. |
| July 1 | The Colombo Plan, first mooted by Commonwealth foreign ministers in January 1950, comes into force. The plan is designed to address the development needs of Asian countries, and through it many Asian students will take up scholarships in New Zealand. |
| July 3 | The navy frigates *Tutira* and *Pukaki* depart Auckland for Korea to join the United Nations intervention in the civil war. |
| November 13 | Wool prices at Auckland reach nearly three times the previous year's rate. The boom, which has been brought on by the US policy of buying all available wool for military uniforms, will end within a year. |
| December 1 | The Legislative Council adjourns for the last time. Just before 6 pm, the government-appointed 'suicide squad' of members |

| | |
|---|---|
| | links arms and sings 'Auld Lang Syne' and 'God Save the King' before leaving. |
| December 1 | The death penalty for murder is reinstated, although expectant mothers are now exempt. Eight men will be hanged before the Labour government begins commuting the death sentences in 1958. |
| December 10 | A New Zealand artillery regiment, nicknamed K-Force, departs for Korea on the liner *Ormonde*. It is the first of many embarkations of military personnel, most of whom have enlisted specially for this conflict. |
| December 23 | The Johnsonville section of the Wellington–Foxton motorway is opened to traffic. It is the first limited-access road in New Zealand. |
| December 28 | The passenger launch *Ranui*, carrying holidaymakers on a day trip, is overturned by a rogue wave off Mt Maunganui. One man struggles to shore but the remaining 22 on board will die. |

# 1951

| | |
|---|---|
| January 1 | The Legislative Council officially ceases to exist. The New Zealand Parliament now has just a single house. |
| January 23 | The Wellington–Lyttelton centennial yacht race begins. Only one yacht out of 20 starters will complete the event — in a violent storm 17 will turn back or limp into harbour along the way, and the remaining two will sink with the loss of 10 lives. |
| January 24 | K-Force fires its first shots in anger, when 163 Battery unleashes artillery rounds at an enemy party south-east of Seoul. |
| February 15 | The Port Employers' Association begins a partial lockout of waterside workers who have refused overtime as part of industrial action over a wage increase. The waterfront dispute will last four months and divide the nation. |

**1951**

| | |
|---|---|
| February 19 | The wharves are closed after the employers, in contravention of a Waterfront Industry Commission order, sack all workers who refuse overtime. The employers and the government see it as an illegal strike; the unions as a lockout. At its height, more than 20,000 unionists will be involved. |
| February 21 | A state of emergency is declared over the waterfront dispute. The government will introduce draconian regulations imposing censorship, increasing police powers and making it an offence to help the strikers in any way — even feeding their children will be illegal. |
| February 27 | The government orders the armed forces to unload cargo at the ports of Auckland and Wellington. |
| March 7 | In the first official public demonstration of television, closed-circuit transmissions are made from broadcasting service studios in Wellington. Viewers are treated to a programme with, among other things, a violin recital, a tennis lesson and an appearance by Aunt Daisy. |
| March 16 | The last Maori land at Orakei in Auckland is compulsorily taken by the crown for a recreation ground. The residents will be evicted, installed in overcrowded state houses and the marae burnt. Ngati Whatua of Tamaki are now landless, save for the ¼ acre (1000m$^2$) urupa (burial ground) at Okahu Bay. |
| March 28 | Trial branches of the government's Totalisator Agency Board are set up to offer off-course betting at Dannevirke and Feilding, in opposition to illegal bookmakers. |
| May 3 | Strike-breaking workers represented by a new union begin work in the port at Auckland. They have the support of the Federation of Labour and the protection of the military and police. |
| May 8 | The first New Zealand Writers' Conference begins at Christchurch. Among those attending are James K. Baxter, who presents an acclaimed paper on trends in poetry, and Denis Glover, who announces there is no such thing as a New Zealand school of writers. |

| June 1 | On 'Bloody Friday', police break up a peaceful union demonstration in Auckland using batons. On a number of occasions during the waterfront dispute, unionists will report police violence and harassment. |
|---|---|
| July 15 | The Waterside Workers' Union concedes defeat after a 151-day strike/lockout. It advises its members to reapply for any jobs that are still open, but many unionists will never find work on the wharves again. |

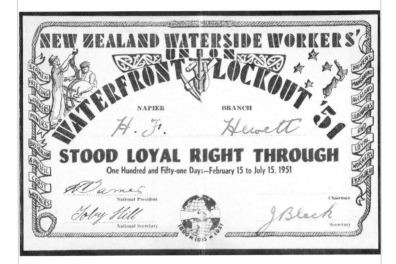

**Certificate issued to a staunch unionist involved in the waterfront dispute of February 15 to July 15, 1951.**

| August 13 | The Meals on Wheels service begins at Wellington. Voluntary workers deliver hot meals prepared in hospital kitchens to elderly people at home. |
|---|---|
| August 15 | The troopship *Wahine* is wrecked on a reef at Masella Island in the Arafura Sea while taking 570 servicemen to Japan. No lives are lost. |
| September 1 | In a snap election, the National government is re-elected with a massive majority, confirming popular support for its rigid stance in the waterfront dispute. |

| September 1 | The draft ANZUS Agreement, between Australia, New Zealand and the USA, is signed at San Francisco. It is the first time New Zealand has signed a treaty with a foreign power without British involvement. The defence treaty will come into force in the following year. |
| September 8 | At Leicester Square Hall, London, Timaru man Clark McConachy wins the world professional billiards championship for the first time at the age of 56. He will retain the title until 1968. |
| September 24 | The Maori Women's Welfare League is set up at a national conference in Wellington. The league, led initially by Whina Cooper, will tackle health issues and social problems caused by discrimination and urbanisation. |
| December 11 | An RNZAF Airspeed Consul crashes on Mt Ruapehu, sparking a huge search involving more than 20 aircraft as well as mountain guides, police and volunteer searchers on foot. The wreckage will not be found for five days. |
| December 27 | TEAL begins operating the Coral Route flying boat service, from Auckland to Papeete via Suva and Aitutaki. |

# 1952

| February 6 | Queen Elizabeth II succeeds King George VI following his death from cancer. |
| July 23 | Yvette Williams wins the long jump at the Helsinki Olympic Games with an Olympic record leap. She is New Zealand's first female gold medallist — and her win comes in spite of an injured knee. At the medal ceremony, 'God Defend New Zealand' is played after 'God Save the Queen'. It is the first time the national hymn has been heard at the Olympics — and the last for 20 years. |
| September 1 | A Lancashire schoolboy disembarks from the immigrant ship *Captain Hobson* to become the official two-millionth New Zealander. |
| September 9 | A rock fall in the partly constructed Rimutaka rail tunnel traps |

| | |
|---|---|
| | 27 men. All but one are rescued within 10 hours. The last man is released 30 hours later but will die in hospital. |
| October 12 | Princess Te Puea Herangi dies at Ngaruawahia. The much-admired leader has for over 40 years helped the fragmented and dispirited Waikato tribe regain its focus and embrace its cultural traditions. Her tangi at Turangawaewae marae will last seven days and draw 10,000 mourners. |
| December 2 | Sir Willoughby Norrie assumes office as governor-general. |

## 1953

| | |
|---|---|
| January 6 | Godfrey Bowen establishes a world record by shearing 456 full-wool sheep at Opiki, Palmerston North, in a nine-hour working day. |
| January 10 | The Social Credit Political League is formed. The new political party advocates the monetary doctrine of the Douglas Credit Movement and will offer the first serious threat to the two-party system. It will have a good showing in the 1954 election, but will not win a seat until 1966. |
| May 8 | Richard and Edith Campion's New Zealand Players begins a first national tour with a production of *The Young Elizabeth* at the Grand Opera House in Wellington. The pioneering theatre company will entertain more than a million people, making New Zealand voices on stage familiar, before its financial collapse in 1960. |
| May 29 | New Zealander Edmund Hillary and Nepalese Sherpa Tenzing Norgay reach the summit of Everest. Another New Zealander, George Lowe, is also part of the British team that is the first to climb the world's highest mountain. |
| June 8 | Auckland becomes the first place in New Zealand — and possibly the first place outside North America — to have parking meters. More than 420 meters begin operation in the city, at a cost of 3d for half an hour. |
| June 30 | The New Zealand Ballet gives its first public performance, at |

the Playhouse Theatre, Auckland. Founded by Danish dancer Poul Gnatt, the company will not add the 'Royal' to its name until 1984.

| | |
|---|---|
| July 26 | Four women and two men lose their lives climbing on Mt Taranaki. Roped together, they fall off a bluff and slide down a rock-strewn snow slope. Within a week two more climbers will die on a mountain that will gain a reputation as New Zealand's most dangerous peak. |
| July 27 | Fighting in Korea ends with the signing of the armistice between the United Nations and the communists at Panmunjon. New Zealand troops will stay on until 1957, by which time 21 men will have been killed in action and 22 will have died of illness or in accidents. |
| August 15 | An imposing red-granite memorial to Sir Peter Buck (Te Rangi Hiroa) is unveiled at Urenui, Taranaki. The renowned Maori anthropologist, who died in Hawaii in 1951, is described at the time as 'the greatest New Zealander to emerge since Rutherford'. |
| October 12 | US vice-president Richard Nixon arrives in New Zealand for a short goodwill tour. He is the most senior US official to have visited while still in office, and his presence cements the defence alliance between the two countries. |
| November 28 | The Family Planning Association opens New Zealand's first birth-control clinic, in Remuera Road, Auckland. |
| December 23 | The newly crowned Queen Elizabeth II, accompanied by Philip, Duke of Edinburgh, arrives at Auckland on the *Gothic*. The first reigning British monarch to set foot on New Zealand soil will be greeted everywhere by cheering crowds. |
| December 24 | The Wellington–Auckland express plunges into the Whangaehu River after a lahar on Mt Ruapehu has swept away the rail bridge at Tangiwai. In the country's worst railway disaster, 151 of the 285 believed to be on board the train lose their lives. |
| December 25 | Queen Elizabeth II gives her Christmas radio message from |

Auckland. It is the first time the monarch's holiday message has been broadcast away from Great Britain.

# 1954

| | |
|---|---|
| January 1 | New Zealand takes its seat for a two-year term on the United Nations Security Council. |
| January 2 | Selwyn Toogood hosts the first *It's in the Bag* show. The touring quiz show quickly becomes the most popular radio programme in the country, and will continue to run for 11 years. It will later transfer to television. |
| January 12 | Queen Elizabeth II opens a special session of the New Zealand Parliament in the centennial year of parliamentary government. Her arrival in the government precinct in her coronation gown elicits gasps of delight from a crowd of 50,000. |
| January 16 | The Kiwi Concert Party performs for the last time. Formed in March 1941 as a military concert party, it has continued after war's end as a professional revue troupe. |
| January 30 | Queen Elizabeth II and the Duke of Edinburgh leave from Bluff at the end of a royal visit that has left New Zealanders breathless with praise. |
| February 20 | Yvette Williams breaks the world long jump record at Gisborne, surpassing Fanny Blankers-Koen's record of more than 10-years' standing. |
| May 22 | A DC-3 crashes at Raumati Beach after the engines stop on the approach to the airport at Paraparaumu. Three children are killed in NAC's third serious crash in 10 years. |
| June 22 | Teenagers Pauline Parker and Juliet Hulme, caught up in a *folie à deux*, kill Pauline's mother, Honora, at Cashmere Hills, Christchurch. The story of their relationship and the murder will shock and enthral New Zealanders. |

| June 27 | The last TEAL flying boat flight travels between Sydney and Mechanics Bay, Auckland. The Solents have been replaced on the trans-Tasman route by DC-6 land planes. Since the service began in 1940, they have completed more than 11 million accident-free miles. |
| --- | --- |
| August 15 | The government-owned Franz Josef Glacier Hotel in South Westland is destroyed by fire. |
| August 28 | Pauline Parker and Juliet Hulme are found guilty of murder are and sentenced to be detained 'at Her Majesty's pleasure'. |
| September 8 | The South-East Asia Collective Defence Treaty, also known as the Manila Pact, is signed. Out of it will grow the South-East Asian Treaty Organisation (SEATO) to foster stability in the region. |
| September 20 | Oswald Mazengarb delivers his special committee report on juvenile 'moral delinquency'. The report blames the perceived promiscuity of the nation's youth on the absence from the home of working mothers, on the availability of contraceptives and on young women who entice men into having sex. A copy of it will be delivered to every family home. |
| October 18 | The New Zealand Opera Group, soon to be renamed the New Zealand Opera Company, has its first opening night. The performance of *The Telephone* in Wellington is also broadcast live on radio. |

## 1955

| March 28 | New Zealand scores 26 runs against England in the second innings of the second cricket test at Eden Park. It is the lowest ever score by any team in a test innings. |
| --- | --- |
| May 1 | The New Zealand Special Air Service is formed as part of New Zealand's contribution to the British Commonwealth Far East Reserve. In November, the SAS will depart for active service in Malaya, where it will specialise in jungle warfare against communist insurgents. |

**Recruits for the Special Air Service, formed on May 1, 1955, stand to attention on their first day of training for the conflict in Malaya.**

| | |
|---|---|
| May 1 | The RNZAF has its first operational strike mission since World War II, with 14 Squadron pilots flying Vampires in Malaya. The RNZAF will mount 115 missions in three years. |
| May 10 | A helicopter is used for the first time to transfer a patient to hospital — from Waiheke Island to Auckland Hospital. The demonstration flight prompts calls for a helicopter to be bought for the ambulance service. |
| July 24 | New Zealand's first electrified passenger rail service, from Wellington to Upper Hutt, is completed. |
| September 23 | Ruth Page leads a sit-in on the railway line at Kiwi, Nelson, to prevent it from being demolished. The protest, which gains international attention, will continue until the women are arrested a week later. |
| October 29 | The first commercial newsprint is manufactured at the Tasman Pulp & Paper mill at Kawerau, using wood from planted Kaingaroa pines. |

| November 3 | The Rimutaka rail tunnel, between the Wairarapa and the Hutt Valley, is opened. The tunnel bypasses the famously steep Rimutaka incline. |
|---|---|

## 1956

| March 8 | A special fisheries regulation is enacted making it an offence to 'take or molest any dolphin in Hokianga Harbour'. The regulation is designed to protect Opo, the 'gay dolphin' that has spent the summer frolicking with children and adults in shallow water at Opononi. |
|---|---|
| March 9 | Opo is found dead at Opononi. It is thought the dolphin may have fallen victim to illegal fishing explosives. |
| March 13 | New Zealand has its first ever cricket test victory, over the West Indies at Eden Park. The win, which comes in New Zealand's 45th test match, puts a halt to talk that New Zealand should not be allowed to take part in international competition. |
| March 29 | The last electric tram in the South Island makes its final trip in Dunedin. |
| June 5 | The Springboks arrive at Whenuapai, Auckland. The epic battles of their tour of New Zealand will captivate the nation. The South Africans will play 23 matches, winning 16, losing 6 and drawing 1. The All Blacks will win the test series 3–1. |
| July 22 | The gates of the dam on the Clutha River are closed to fill Lake Roxburgh. Thousands of prospectors gather to search for gold in the dry river bed but will have little success. |
| September 17 | An exhibition of Henry Moore drawings and sculptures opens in Auckland to a flood of publicity when the mayor describes the work as 'a nauseating sight'. His revulsion will inspire record attendance for an art exhibit, with 36,000 people curious enough to view it in Auckland, and nearly 20,000 in Christchurch. |
| September 24 | Immunisation begins using the newly developed Salk anti-polio vaccine. Forty-four thousand schoolchildren will be |

| | |
|---|---|
| | injected, bringing to an end a series of six major outbreaks of the disease, in 1916, 1925 (in which 173 people died), 1937, 1947–49, 1952–53 and 1955–56. The vaccine will be phased out from 1961, when it is replaced by the safer and more effective Sabin vaccine. |
| November 24 | British-born New Zealander Norm Read wins a gold medal in the 50 km road walk at the Melbourne Olympic Games. His success excites interest in road walking as a sport — for a while. |
| November 28 | The New Zealand Security Service (later the Security Intelligence Service) is established by order in council. Modelled on Britain's MI5, its task is to defend New Zealand from internal and external danger from sabotage, espionage and subversion — and its immediate focus will be the Cold War. |
| December 13 | The first 66 Hungarian refugees land at Whenuapai, Auckland. They are fleeing Russian oppression in their homeland. |
| December 17 | The New Zealand Antarctic Expedition sails from Lyttelton to establish Scott Base in McMurdo Sound as part of New Zealand's commitment to International Geophysical Year. |

## 1957

| | |
|---|---|
| January 16 | Swimmer Philippa Gould sets New Zealand records in the 200 m and 220 yards backstroke at the 50 m Olympic Pool, Newmarket in Auckland. The times will in 1960 be recognised as world records when times swum in shorter pools are removed from the record books. |
| January 20 | Scott Base at Pram Point, Ross Island, is officially opened as a New Zealand base in Antarctica. Sir Edmund Hillary is the first base commander. |
| February 18 | Walter Bolton is hanged at Mt Eden jail for murdering his wife by poisoning her with arsenic. It is the last time capital punishment will be used in New Zealand before the death penalty is abolished. |

| | |
|---|---|
| July 10 | A royal commission reports favourably on the addition of fluoride to the water supply. A trial in Hastings has shown a significant reduction in childhood tooth decay, and fluoridation will soon spread to other parts of the country. |
| September 5 | Viscount Cobham assumes office as governor-general. He will quickly become a popular figure. |
| September 16 | The Hermitage Hotel at Mt Cook is destroyed by fire. Coming so soon after the loss of the Franz Josef Glacier Hotel, the destruction of the biggest tourist hotel in the South Island is a serious blow to the tourism industry. |
| September 18 | Sir Leslie Munro is elected to the presidency of the United Nations General Assembly. He will preside over Cold War stand-offs between the Soviet Union and the USA over the Middle East, disarmament and Cyprus. |
| September 20 | Keith Holyoake (National) takes over as prime minister from Sidney Holland, who has retired because of ill health. |
| December 12 | Walter Nash assumes office as prime minister after a Labour victory in the November general election. The 75-year-old stalwart of the labour movement is the country's oldest ever leader. |

# Broadening perspectives
## 1958–1969

**A brief return to Labour** government in the late 1950s, while proving generally unpopular, did signal a shift to a more international outlook in New Zealand as Walter Nash travelled the world meeting major leaders. In the 1960s the rest of the world seemed to be in permanent tumult: the Berlin wall went up, the Bay of Pigs fiasco and the Cuban missile crisis played out, Nelson Mandela was jailed, John F. Kennedy, Martin Luther King and Robert Kennedy were assassinated, the Vietnam War began, the cultural revolution took place in China, and the Soviet invasion of Czechoslovakia ended the Prague Spring. Back in New Zealand the boom times continued and horizons were expanded with the introduction of television and long-haul jet travel.

# 1958

| | |
|---|---|
| January 3 | A Commonwealth team led by Sir Edmund Hillary reaches the South Pole using modified tractors. It is the first land team to reach the pole since Scott's ill-fated expedition in 1912. |
| February 3 | An NAC Vickers Viscount turboprop airliner has its inaugural flight. It is the first jet-assisted aircraft to run a service in New Zealand. |
| February 17 | The newly constituted separate, permanent Court of Appeal sits for the first time, at Wellington. |
| February 20 | Opotiki in the Bay of Plenty is overwhelmed by floods. Several days of torrential rain will see the North Island inundated from Kaitaia to the Central Plateau. |
| March 15 | Seventeen-year-old Philippa Gould breaks two world backstroke records — in the 100 m and 110 yards — in the Olympic Pool at Auckland, despite blustery conditions disturbing the water in the outdoor pool. |
| April 1 | The PAYE (Pay As You Earn) income tax system is introduced. |
| April 20 | Dedication services begin for the first Mormon temple in the Southern Hemisphere, at Tuhikaramea near Hamilton. The service is conducted by the world president of the church, David McKay. |
| June 18 | The new 'all-convenience' Foodtown opens at Otahuhu, Auckland. The store, owned by Tom Ah Chee and Norm Kent, is the country's first full-size supermarket. Shoppers trample food underfoot and break fittings in their rush to make the most of opening day bargains. |
| June 26 | Labour minister of finance Arnold Nordmeyer delivers a budget quickly named the 'Black Budget' by the opposition. It cuts back imports, and increases sales tax on beer, tobacco and petrol — and is widely seen as an over-reaction to a balance of payments crisis. |

| June 28 | The first live beef export leaves Tauranga for the USA. The shipment is a forerunner in the developing trade relationship with the USA. |
| August 21 | The 'Barnes dance' — diagonal crossing by pedestrians at an intersection — becomes legal. |
| September 3 | At Green Lane Hospital in Auckland, Brian Barratt-Boyes performs the first open heart surgery in New Zealand using a heart-lung bypass machine. The patient is a 10-year-old girl with a hole in her heart. |
| November 15 | The first commercial thermal power production begins at Wairakei at an output of 1.7 megawatts. Wairakei, which has been running trials for three years, is the second geothermal power station in the world. |
| December 17 | Power restrictions in the North Island are lifted after 17 years of shortages and cuts. |
| December 31 | The first night trotting meeting in New Zealand draws 30,000 spectators to Alexandra Park, Auckland. |

## 1959

| January 27 | The first Kapuni oil well, near Hawera in Taranaki, is 'spudded in' and drilling begins. Gas under pressure will be found five months later. |
| February 23 | The first NZBS experimental television signal is broadcast by 1YA in Shortland Street, Auckland. Since 1957, however, the privately owned Bell Radio & Television has been transmitting variety and educational shows to entice people to buy its television sets. |
| April 2 | US Christian evangelist Billy Graham arrives in Auckland for a tour of the North Island. He will attract large crowds to stadium events, and thousands will pledge their lives to Christ. |
| May 24 | The Auckland Harbour Bridge between Northcote Point |

and Herne Bay is opened to pedestrians only, and more than 100,000 take the opportunity to walk over the new landmark.

| | |
|---|---|
| May 30 | The harbour bridge is officially opened by the governor-general, Lord Cobham. The opening of the bridge brings about the end of all cross-harbour ferry services except Devonport's. Two days later, a 20-mile (32 km) celebratory parade through central Auckland and over the bridge will attract the biggest crowds ever seen in New Zealand — and create the biggest traffic jam. |
| June 15 | Grahame Turner of Turners & Growers writes to a US agent with the news that, after a brief spell as the melonette, the Chinese gooseberry has been renamed the kiwifruit. The fruit has been grown in New Zealand since 1904. |
| July 20 | The first commercial aircraft fly into the new Wellington Airport at Rongotai. More than 3 million cubic metres of earth and rock have been moved to create an airport for the modern age. |
| October 25 | The official opening of Wellington Airport at Rongotai is celebrated with an air pageant after a postponement for bad weather. The event is marred by two mishaps with aircraft involved in the display. |
| November 8 | In Wellington, Methodist Phyllis Guthardt becomes the first woman to be ordained a minister in any mainstream church. |
| November 24 | MV *Holmglen* sinks without apparent cause near Timaru. The entire crew of 15 is lost. |
| December 1 | The Antarctic Treaty is signed by 12 nations, including New Zealand. The treaty sets aside territorial claims, bans military activity and preserves Antarctica for scientific research. |
| December 1 | TEAL's inaugural turboprop Lockheed Electra flight travels between Auckland and Sydney, taking about one and a half hours off the crossing time. |

| December 7 | Rowena Jackson hangs up her ballet shoes in Auckland after her last performance. She has had an outstanding international career, including being prima ballerina of the Royal Ballet Company. |
| December 12 | Racing driver Bruce McLaren of Auckland becomes the first New Zealander to win a grand prix. His victory in the US event at Sebring comes as a surprise to almost everyone. |

## 1960

| February 8 | At Christchurch, Mrs H. L. Garrett becomes the first woman to serve on a jury in a criminal case, and the first jury forewoman. |
| March 7 | Bruce Mason begins a lengthy nationwide tour of *The End of the Golden Weather* at Wyndham, Southland. He will perform his one-man play nearly 1000 times. |
| April 11 | Two hundred prisoners begin a riot at Mt Eden Prison that will last for 17 hours. It is the first of a series of disruptions in the prison that will go on for two decades. |
| May 10 | The All Blacks depart Auckland for a tour of Australia and South Africa with all white players, despite protests demanding 'No Maoris, no tour', a petition to Parliament, demonstrators invading the pitch at the trial matches and a last ditch attempt to block the take-off of the plane. |
| May 23 | The first of a series of tsunami waves caused by a massive earthquake in Chile hits the East Coast of the North Island. Three days later Whakatane, Whitianga and Whangamata are evacuated for fear of further waves. |
| June 1 | The first regular two-hour programme is transmitted by Channel 2 from Shortland Street, Auckland. The country's first official television broadcast begins with an episode of *The Adventures of Robin Hood*. By August 1962, there will also be local stations in Christchurch, Wellington and Dunedin. |
| July 31 | The Malayan emergency officially comes to an end. Fifteen |

|  | New Zealand servicemen have lost their lives in Malaya, including three killed in action. |
|---|---|
| August 1 | The first television licences are issued. They cost £4. |
| August 31 | The telex service is officially opened, using high frequency radio links to connect New Zealand with 23 other countries. |
| September 2 | In the space of one 'golden hour' at the Rome Olympic Games, athletes Murray Halberg and Peter Snell win gold medals, in the 5000 m and 800 m respectively. |
| September 10 | Young people riot at the Hastings Blossom Festival. There are dire warnings of degeneracy and licentiousness among the nation's youth and the imminent collapse of law and order. The disturbance will be an issue at the general election later in the year. |
| September 14 | TEAL's only remaining Solent flying boat, the *Aranui*, lands for the final time at Mechanics Bay, Auckland. The Coral Route service has been the last scheduled international flying boat service in the world. |
| October 31 | Canterbury University becomes the first tertiary institution to order a high-speed electronic computer. The IBM machine will be used for research. |
| December 12 | Keith Holyoake (National) assumes office as prime minister after the November general election. This time his term will last more than 12 years. |

## 1961

| January 1 | Telecasting is extended to seven nights a week in Auckland. |
|---|---|
| February 6 | The first national Waitangi Day celebration takes place. It is, however, a 'day of thanksgiving' and not a public holiday. |
| April 1 | The New Zealand government assumes full ownership of TEAL, taking over the 50 per cent share the Australian |

| | |
|---|---|
| April 12 | Writer and publisher A. H. Reed completes a walk from North Cape to Bluff. The 85-year-old is the first person known to have walked the length of the country. |

**In Wellington, A. H. Reed displays the sole of one of the shoes carrying him on his 1960–61 walk from North Cape to Bluff.**

| | |
|---|---|
| April 17 | New Zealand makes preliminary moves to join the International Monetary Fund, the World Bank and the International Finance Corporation. |
| May 9 | A plebiscite is held in Western Samoa to determine its political future. An overwhelming majority vote in favour of independence. |
| October 12 | In a conscience vote, 10 National MPs cross the floor to support the abolition of capital punishment in cases of murder. The vote is won. |
| November 1 | Capital punishment for murder is abolished. |
| November 21 | An Aero-Commander passenger plane crashes on Mt Ruapehu. The pilot and five passengers are killed. |
| December 13 | Gourmet in Auckland becomes the first restaurant to legally serve wine, breaking the stranglehold of the hotels. With the granting of alcohol licences to 10 restaurants around the country, a trend to eating out more often will begin. |
| December 14 | A colourful closing ceremony for the University of New |

Zealand takes place at Wellington town hall. On January 1 it will be replaced by four self-governing universities in the main centres.

| December 18 | The first Golden Kiwi lottery is drawn, and £12,000 is won by an Auckland customs inspector. The last draw will be made in 1989, after the introduction of Lotto. |

# 1962

| January 1 | Western Samoa becomes a fully independent Polynesian state, New Zealand's mandate having lapsed the day before. It is the first Pacific nation to regain independence. |
| January 14 | An ambitious plan to build a £5 million cotton mill in Nelson is officially abandoned. |
| January 27 | Runner Peter Snell breaks the world mile record at Wanganui. His time of 3 minutes 54.4 seconds is greeted with 'endless din and confusion' until it is officially confirmed as a new world mark. He has disproved experts who thought that world records could not be set on grass tracks. |
| February 3 | Peter Snell shatters the world records for both 880 yards and 800 m in the same race at Christchurch. |
| February 22 | Gas is burnt off at Kapuni and golden fluid pours out on the ground. |
| March 2 | The first stage in making union membership non-compulsory is implemented, with new accords and agreements not allowed to have provisions for compulsory unionism. Compulsory union membership will not end completely until June 2, 1963. |
| May 17 | George Wilder escapes from New Plymouth jail. The convicted burglar will evade capture for more than two months and become a renegade folk hero in the process. He will escape twice more, including one stint of nearly six months on the run in 1963 during which he will allegedly commit 40 crimes. |
| July 12 | Two Soviet diplomats leave New Zealand after being expelled |

| | for spying. They have tried to obtain secrets by bribery. |
|---|---|
| August 11 | The *Aramoana*, the first roll-on, roll-off vehicle and rail ferry, makes a demonstration run from Wellington to Picton with 300 VIP passengers. It is damaged when it collides with the wharf in Picton while trying to avoid crushing a small craft. |
| August 23 | In Green Lane Hospital in Auckland, Brian Barratt-Boyes performs the first aortic homograft replacement operation using a technique he has developed himself. He will later discover the surgery is not the world first it was thought to be — a British team has beaten him to it by 30 days. |
| September 1 | The Outward Bound School at Anakiwa in the Marlborough Sounds is officially opened by its patron, Lord Cobham. The school has been established to train young people in self-discipline and self-confidence through outdoor experiences. |
| October 1 | The first ombudsman, Sir Guy Powles, takes office. His role is to investigate complaints about government administrative acts and decisions. |
| November 9 | Brigadier Sir Bernard Fergusson assumes office as governor-general. The monocled English military man, the third generation of his family to be viceroy, is the first governor-general to be fluent in Maori. |
| November 20 | Worser Bay lifesaver Barrie Devenport completes a swim across Cook Strait, becoming the first to do so since Whakarua-tapu achieved the feat while fleeing Te Rauparaha in about 1831. Devenport has made the crossing from Ohau Point to the rocks of Wellington Head in a little over 11 hours. |
| December 10 | New Zealand-born Maurice Wilkins, alongside Englishman Francis Crick and American James Watson, is presented with the Nobel Prize in Physiology or Medicine. The award is for their discovery of the three-dimensional molecular structure of DNA, findings first published in 1953. Wilkins's contribution was to use x-rays to show the shape of the double helix. |

# 1963

| January 1 | The branch of Victoria University of Wellington at Palmerston North combines with Massey Agricultural College to form Massey University of Manawatu. |
| --- | --- |
| February 7 | A chartered bus plunges off the road in the Brynderwyn Hills near Maungaturoto in Northland after its brakes fail, and 15 of the 35 passengers are killed. The bus is returning from Waitangi celebrations attended by Queen Elizabeth II. |
| February 8 | The first computer for use in industry arrives at Auckland. Tasman Pulp & Paper's acquisition for its Kawerau mill weighs almost 4 tons. |
| April 1 | The Queen Elizabeth II Arts Council is founded to promote and develop the arts. |
| April 4 | BOAC's regular international pure jet service between Auckland and the United Kingdom begins. With the flying time reduced to 37 hours, New Zealand has entered the jet age. |
| July 3 | An NAC DC-3 Skyliner crashes in the Kaimai Range near Tauranga, killing all 25 aboard. In the search for the missing plane, helicopters are used for the first time in a search and rescue operation in New Zealand. |
| July 14 | Maud Basham (Aunt Daisy) dies at Wellington. The 83-year-old 'first lady of radio' has greeted listeners with 'Good morning, everyone!' for the last time just a few days earlier. |
| July 14 | Golfer Bob Charles wins a play-off to secure the British Open championship at Royal Lytham St Anne's. |
| September 8 | Sylvia Ashton-Warner's book *Teacher* is featured in the *New York Times Book Review*, sparking worldwide interest in her 'organic' teaching methods. |
| September 20 | Grant Liley McLeod is born in Auckland. He is the first baby in the world to be born after receiving pre-natal blood transfusions, a procedure developed by William Liley. |

| | |
|---|---|
| October 16 | The Indecent Publications Act passes into law. The legislation establishes the Indecent Publications Tribunal, which will make available previously banned material such as D. H. Lawrence's and Henry Miller's work. |
| October 30 | Lynnmall, the country's first American-style shopping centre, opens in west Auckland. |
| December 3 | The COMPAC cable linking New Zealand with the United Kingdom, Australia, Fiji and Canada is officially opened when a recorded message from Queen Elizabeth II is sent the length of the 16,000-mile (25,000 km) circuit. The cable has capacity for telephone, telegraph, telex and facsimile communication. |
| December 7 | The bodies of two men believed to be sly-groggers are found in a house in Remuera, Auckland. Ron Jorgensen and John Gillies will later be convicted of the 'Bassett Road machine-gun murders', New Zealand's first gang-style killings. |

## 1964

| | |
|---|---|
| February 27 | The Lyttelton–Christchurch road tunnel is opened. Vehicles no longer have to make the long slog over the Port Hills. |
| May 2 | The last scheduled tram service in New Zealand ends at Wellington with a ceremonial run from Thorndon to the Newtown car sheds. |
| May 21 | A volunteer force of 20 New Zealand police officers arrives at Cyprus for peacekeeping duties with the United Nations. |
| May 30 | Marsden Point oil refinery is officially opened and declared onstream. The construction and operation of the refinery has brought a wave of prosperity to the Whangarei area. |
| June 21 | The Beatles arrive at Wellington to tour New Zealand. Police dogs have to be used to control thousands of screaming fans. |
| August 3 | The first police officers begin training for the armed offenders' |

| | |
|---|---|
| | squad. The new unit has been set up in response to the deaths of four police officers within a month in early 1963. |
| September 4 | 1 Royal New Zealand Infantry Regiment is deployed in Malaysia when Indonesian infiltrators enter the Malay Peninsula. |
| October 16 | Athlete Peter Snell wins gold in the 800 m at the Tokyo Olympic Games. |
| October 21 | Peter Snell becomes New Zealand's most successful Olympian, and one of the greatest middle distance runners ever, by winning gold in the 1500 m at Tokyo. It is his third gold medal in two Olympic games. Within a month he will have broken the world mile record again. |
| December 21 | The last whale to be killed in New Zealand waters by New Zealand whalers is harpooned, and the Perano whaling station in Tory Channel, the last whaling station in the country, ceases to operate. |

## 1965

| | |
|---|---|
| February 5 | The last steam express train on the North Island main trunk line leaves Auckland for Wellington. |
| February 26 | Waikato University at Hamilton is officially opened by Sir Bernard Fergusson. The new institution will become New Zealand's leading centre for Maori studies. |
| March 12 | A xenon light presented by Sir Ernest Davis is switched on at the Tiritiri Matangi lighthouse in the Hauraki Gulf. The 11-million candlepower light, 50 times brighter than the old one, is now one of the most powerful in the world. |
| April 1 | TEAL changes its name to Air New Zealand. |
| May 15 | With a flick of a switch, the Benmore hydro scheme is switched on and electricity sent to the North Island via the newly inaugurated inter-island cable. |
| May 27 | Prime Minister Keith Holyoake announces that New |

| | |
|---|---|
| | Zealand will send an artillery unit to Vietnam. The commitment will eventually extend to include infantry brigades, SAS and medical teams. It is opposed by Labour, which sees the conflict in Vietnam as a civil war, and will be the subject of vigorous public protest. |
| July 20 | Air New Zealand's jet base at Mangere is officially opened and the first direct jet flight from Long Beach, California, lands. The acquisition of jet aircraft allows the airline to expand its services to North America and Asia, enabling it to become a truly international airline. It also means cheaper travel overseas. |
| July 20 | Prisoners riot at Mt Eden jail, Auckland. The disturbance will last into the next day, during which time warders will be taken hostage and part of the jail burnt. |
| July 24 | Prisoners make a failed attempt to set fire to Mt Crawford jail, Wellington. |
| July 25 | At Paparua jail, Christchurch, prisoners riot and set fire to the eastern wing. |
| July 27 | The Lawson quintuplets are born at Auckland. They are the first set of quintuplets to survive in New Zealand. |
| August 4 | The Cook Islands achieve self-government in free association with New Zealand. The islanders remain New Zealand citizens. |
| August 31 | A limited free trade agreement between New Zealand and Australia is signed. NAFTA will become effective on January 1, 1966. |
| November 6 | The final link in the Haast Pass road is opened. The road between the east and west coasts of the South Island has been under spasmodic construction since 1929 and has cost £4.5 million. |
| November 24 | The first commercial services fly in and out of the new Auckland International Airport at Mangere. Passengers |

are full of praise — even though a cargo shed is used as a terminal.

# 1966

| | |
|---|---|
| January 29 | Auckland International Airport is officially opened. The occasion is celebrated with a three-day air pageant. |
| March 6 | *Country Calendar* begins its long run on television as a programme of news and information for farmers. |
| April 1 | The Alexander Turnbull Library, National Library Service and General Assembly Library are combined to become the National Library of New Zealand. |
| May 18 | Koroki Te Rata Mahuta Tawhiao Potatau Te Wherowhero, the fifth Maori king, dies at Ngaruawahia. |
| May 23 | Princess Piki is crowned as Te Arikinui Te Atairangikaahu, the first Maori queen, a few hours before Koroki's burial. |
| May 23 | The collier *Kaitawa* is swamped off Cape Reinga in a storm. None of the crew of 29 will survive the sinking. |
| July 4 | An Air New Zealand DC-8 jet on a training flight crashes at the newly opened Auckland airport and two crew members are killed. It is Air New Zealand's second major training accident in 16 months. |
| October 19 | US president Lyndon B. Johnson arrives at Ohakea for an overnight visit to New Zealand. Anti-Vietnam War protesters are drowned out by the cheering of otherwise enthusiastic crowds. |
| December 2 | The first Trekka rolls off the assembly line. The jeep-style farm vehicle, which uses Czech mechanicals, is the only vehicle ever to have been designed and mass produced in New Zealand. |
| December 4 | Radio Hauraki makes it to the airwaves. The pirate radio station, broadcasting from the ship *Tiri* in international |

waters between the Hauraki Gulf and the Coromandel, is unwelcome competition in an industry monopolised by the government.

# 1967

| | |
|---|---|
| January 19 | An explosion at the Strongman coal mine, near Greymouth, kills 19 men. The blast will be found to have occurred when safety regulations were not followed and shot was incorrectly fired. |
| February 10 | The government announces the removal of subsidies on flour and butter. On the same day, the last delivery of free milk in schools takes place. |
| July 10 | On DC Day the change is made to decimal currency. Pounds, shillings and pence are replaced with 27 million new notes and 165 million new coins — and confusion will reign for some time. |
| September 23 | A referendum is held that comes out in favour of the end of six o'clock closing in pubs. Another referendum held on the same day will lead to the parliamentary term being reduced again to three years. |
| October 8 | The last six o'clock swill takes place. |
| October 22 | Denny Hulme of Te Puke wins the formula one world drivers' championship by taking third place in the Mexican grand prix event. |
| November 6 | Professor Lloyd Geering is tried and acquitted on charges of heresy and doctrinal error by the Presbyterian General Assembly. The principal of Knox Theological Hall has challenged traditional beliefs about the resurrection of Christ and the immortality of the human soul. |
| November 15 | The Natural Gas Corporation Act passes into law, providing for the establishment of a corporation to purchase, distribute and market Kapuni gas. |

| | |
|---|---|
| November 21 | The New Zealand dollar is devalued by 19.45 per cent, bringing it to parity with the Australian dollar and making exports cheaper. |
| December 1 | Former Olympian Sir Arthur Porritt assumes office as the country's first New Zealand-born governor-general. |

## 1968

| | |
|---|---|
| January 31 | Nauru becomes independent of New Zealand, Australia and Great Britain — but not before two-thirds of the island has been dug up for phosphate. |
| April 9 | Cyclone Giselle hits the northern part of New Zealand. As the cyclone travels south through the country it will join with a storm coming up the West Coast to become one of the most disastrous storms in New Zealand's recorded history. |
| April 10 | Winds in Wellington reach a maximum speed of about 270 km/h and there is extensive damage and loss of life. The inter-island steamer express *Wahine* founders after striking Barrett Reef in Wellington Harbour and, of the 610 passengers and 123 crew, 51 die as they struggle to make it to shore. |

The ferry *Wahine* stranded on Barrett Reef, Wellington Harbour, on April 10, 1968.

| May 24 | An earthquake measuring 7.1 on the Richter scale hits Inangahua Junction, on the West Coast. Three people are killed in a landslip, and three more die when a rescue helicopter crashes. The aftershocks will continue for four weeks. |
| --- | --- |
| June 13 | MV *Maranui* sinks in a hurricane about 25 miles (40 km) from Great Mercury Island. Nine lives will be lost out of the 15 who escape in an inflatable raft. |
| September 14 | Cardigan Bay wins $US7500 at New Jersey, becoming the first horse in the history of trotting to win $US1 million. The Mayor of Yonkers will declare a Cardigan Bay Day, while the racehorse will retire shortly after and return to New Zealand. |

## 1969

| March 12 | An announcement is made that oil condensate, natural gas and traces of heavy oil have been discovered at the Maui I well, 27 miles (38 km) off the Taranaki coast. It is New Zealand's first major oil strike. |
| --- | --- |
| April 28 | Peter McKeefry, Catholic archbishop of Wellington, is proclaimed as New Zealand's first cardinal. |
| May 1 | Blood and breath alcohol limits are introduced for drivers and the Breathalyser begins to be used. |
| August 1 | Hamilton pilot Cliff Tait completes a round-the-world trip in his tiny locally built Airtourer aircraft. The solo journey has taken 81 days. |
| September 14 | The Manapouri hydro scheme makes its first contribution of electricity to the national grid. The scheme will supply electricity to Comalco's aluminium smelter at Tiwai Point, Bluff. |
| September 15 | New Zealand Steel announces that the first steel has been produced at Glenbrook, Waiuku. The new mill at first smelts scrap iron in electric arc furnaces, although iron sand will be used later in the year. |

| September 23 | An extension to the Auckland Harbour Bridge is opened by Sir Arthur Porritt. The 'Nippon clip-on' converts the bridge from four lanes to eight, but there is already talk of the need for a second harbour crossing. |
| October 5 | Drilling for oil at Maui II begins off the Taranaki coast. The well is being sunk to investigate the commercial value of the field. |
| October 20 | The Save Manapouri campaign kicks off at an Invercargill meeting, with Ron McLean as leader, after it has been revealed that a planned change to the lake level will drown 800 hectares of forest and 26 islands, and destroy the lake's ecology. Save Manapouri is New Zealand's first nationwide conservation campaign. |
| November 29 | Twenty-year-olds vote in a general election for the first time. The number of MPs has also been increased to 84 (there will continue to be frequent upwards adjustment because of population growth in the North Island). |
| December 10 | The first pellets of iron sand are fed into the kiln at Glenbrook to make the first New Zealand steel smelted from local raw materials. |

# Unsettled times
## 1970–1979

**In the 1970s** life in New Zealand did not seem so rosy as it once had, as the economy faltered with the United Kingdom's entry into the European Economic Community and the country's defence allies withdrew into the background. A series of oil crises shook the world, Richard Nixon was disgraced in the Watergate scandal, and Arab-Israeli hostilities dominated the news. Demonstrations were staged on New Zealand's streets on a number of issues, including the war in Vietnam, conservation, South African rugby tours, nuclear warships, Maori grievances and the rights of women. Many of these protests were successful in their aims, and it was in this decade that New Zealanders discovered people power.

## 1970

| | |
|---|---|
| January 15 | US vice-president Spiro Agnew arrives in New Zealand for talks with government leaders. His two-day stay is accompanied by disruptive anti-war protests. |
| February 19 | Shell, BP and Todd Services announce that the Maui field has substantial reserves of gas and condensate (light oil suitable for petrol). |
| February 24 | Four men are killed when the Kaimai rail tunnel collapses during construction. It will take three days to rescue seven survivors. |
| March 24 | Privately-owned commercial radio is reinstated with the issue of warrants to Radio Hauraki and Radio i in Auckland. |
| April 8 | The Post Office begins its Datel service, transmitting computer data along telephone lines at 2400 bits per second. |
| April 14 | The government announces that the replacement of imperial measures with metric will be completed by the end of 1976 — as indeed it will. |
| May 17 | The RNZAF's 14 new Skyhawk jet fighter-bombers arrive. |
| May 26 | A Save Manapouri campaign petition with more than 250,000 signatures is wheeled into Parliament. |
| June 2 | Racing driver Bruce McLaren is killed while testing his Can Am car at Goodwood, in the United Kingdom. The death of the 32-year-old New Zealander shocks the racing world. |
| June 13 | After a cancelled tour in 1967, the All Blacks depart for South Africa with Maori and Pacific Islands players in the team for the first time. There are protests nonetheless, by those who believe South Africa should be isolated until it gives up its policy of apartheid. |
| June 22 | An infant girl is found alone in a blood-spattered house at Pukekawa, south of Auckland. The bodies of her missing |

parents, Harvey and Jeanette Crewe, will be found in the Waikato River seven weeks later. The mystery surrounding their deaths will never be satisfactorily explained.

| June 30 | A ban on the use of DDT on farmland comes into force, after concerns have been raised about the effects of the pesticide's residues on the environment. |
| --- | --- |
| October 2 | A commission submits a report about the Manapouri hydro scheme that states that the government is contractually bound to raise the lake level in terms of its agreement with Comalco. |
| October 7 | At Government House, Wellington, Keith Holyoake is dubbed as a knight grand cross of the Order of St Michael and St George. He is the first prime minister to be knighted while still in office. |
| November 7 | John Glasgow and Peter Gough become the first to climb Mt Cook by the treacherous Caroline Face. It has until now been the last great unclimbed route in New Zealand's mountains, and the young Christchurch climbers declare their achievement to be 'a triumph for the hippies'. |

## 1971

| February 6 | Waitangi Day celebrations at Waitangi are disrupted by Nga Tamatoa protesters. The young Maori activists will be prominent in a movement to challenge the Pakeha establishment during the 1970s. Later the same year, the Polynesian Panthers, based on the US Black Panthers, will advocate the overthrow of the capitalist system. |
| --- | --- |
| March 2 | After a two-week trial, Arthur Allan Thomas is convicted of the murder of his neighbours, Jeanette and Harvey Crewe, at Pukekawa in 1970. |
| May 12 | A civic reception is staged at Auckland for 161 Battery and the SAS on their return from Vietnam. Their parade up Queen Street is watched by a crowd of supporters mixed with protesters chanting and throwing red paint. |

An anti-war demonstrator is apprehended during the procession for soldiers returning from Vietnam, in Auckland on May 12, 1971.

| | |
|---|---|
| June 19 | The *Columbus New Zealand* calls at Wellington. It is the first container ship to be loaded at a New Zealand port. |
| July 17 | The Post Office opens the first satellite earth station at Warkworth. It is used for phone, data transfer and television. |
| August 18 | The prime minister announces that New Zealand troops will be withdrawn from Vietnam. The last combat troops will leave in December 1971. |
| August 23 | The last issue of the photographic magazine *Auckland Weekly News* is published. After more than a century it has succumbed to competition from television. |
| October 26 | The last steam locomotive on a regular main line service, a Ja class operating as the South Island Limited express, has to be towed into Christchurch after it breaks down at Rolleston on its last run. |
| November 30 | Comalco's Tiwai Point aluminium smelter is officially opened, although the first aluminium was produced in April 1971. |

| | |
|---|---|
| December 1 | Kiri Te Kanawa's debut as the countess in *The Marriage of Figaro* at Covent Garden, London, makes her an instant international star. |
| December 17 | The Race Relations Act passes into law, legislating against discrimination on the basis of race and allowing the government to ratify the International Convention for the Elimination of All Forms of Racial Discrimination. The office of the race relations conciliator will be set up in 1972. |

# 1972

| | |
|---|---|
| February 7 | Jack Marshall (National) assumes office as prime minister after Sir Keith Holyoake steps down. |
| March 10 | Visiting feminist writer Germaine Greer appears in the Auckland Magistrates' Court charged with using obscene language during a public meeting. She is fined $40. |
| March 23 | Having viewed the musical *Hair*, an Auckland jury throws out an indecency case against the show, which includes scenes with nudity and simulated sex. The publicity the case has attracted has ensured a sell-out season for the show. |
| April 27 | The ketch *Vega*, later renamed *Greenpeace III*, leaves New Zealand for the French nuclear testing area around Moruroa atoll. More private protest yachts will leave in July. |
| September 2 | The New Zealand rowing eight wins the gold medal at the Munich Olympic Games. At the medal ceremony 'God Defend New Zealand' is played in place of 'God Save the Queen' — in contravention of Olympic rules because it is not the official anthem. |
| September 27 | Sir Denis Blundell assumes office as governor-general. |
| October 22 | James K. Baxter dies unexpectedly in Auckland at the age of 46. Acknowledged as New Zealand's most accomplished poet, Baxter has devoted the last years of his life to social work among alcoholics and drug addicts. |

**1972**

| December 8 | Norman Kirk assumes office as prime minister after Labour's heavy defeat of National in the November general election. During his term he will show a particular flair for foreign affairs. On this day the government also announces that Lake Te Anau and Lake Manapouri will be held at their natural levels, a decision that will be confirmed in 1973. |
| December 11 | The newly elected government declares an end to compulsory military training. It also resolves to bring home the last of the training troops from Vietnam by Christmas. Thirty-seven New Zealanders have died in the Vietnam conflict. |
| December 22 | New Zealand establishes diplomatic relations with the People's Republic of China, enabling trade negotiations to begin. |

**1973**

| January 1 | The United Kingdom joins the European Economic Community. New Zealand, which has always relied on preferential trade treatment from 'Home', will be forced to find new markets in Australia, the USA, Asia and the Middle East. |
| February 6 | At the Waitangi Day celebrations, Norman Kirk announces that from the following year the day will be a public holiday called New Zealand Day. |
| February 27 | A chemical spill causes a civil emergency in Parnell, Auckland. Over four days 643 people will receive hospital treatment and 6000 will be evacuated from their homes. There will later be speculation that the incident may have had an element of mass hysteria. |
| March 1 | Passports are not needed for travel between Australia and New Zealand. The 'open door' policy will be revoked from July 1, 1981. |
| March 17 | More than a thousand runners take part in the first Round the Bays fun run in Auckland. The event is inspired by the work of athletics coach Arthur Lydiard, who invented the concept of jogging in Auckland in the early 1960s. |

| April 1 | The first stage of the Equal Pay Act 1972 comes into effect, ensuring men and women doing the same work receive equal remuneration. |
| --- | --- |
| April 3 | The crown agrees in principle to a joint venture with Shell, BP and Todd Services to develop the Maui gas field. The agreement will be executed in October 1973. |
| April 10 | Norman Kirk writes to the New Zealand Rugby Football Union requiring it to defer Springbok rugby tours until teams are selected purely on merit. |
| April 16 | Arthur Thomas is convicted for a second time of the murders of Harvey and Jeanette Crewe, and again sentenced to life imprisonment. |
| May 27 | New Zealand joins the Organisation for Economic Cooperation and Development (OECD). |
| June 23 | In a case brought by New Zealand, the World Court issues an interim injunction against French nuclear testing in the Pacific. The decision is ignored by the French. |
| June 28 | HMNZS *Otago* departs Auckland for the French nuclear-testing zone. Its presence in international waters around Moruroa atoll is an official protest against testing. |
| September 15 | The first United Women's Convention begins at the YMCA stadium in Auckland, bringing a feminist perspective to such issues as education, abortion and legal rights for women. Feminism is increasingly gaining traction in New Zealand society. |
| October 31 | The first colour television broadcasts are made from Auckland, Wellington and Christchurch. Within days a more expensive colour-television licence will be introduced. |
| November 14 | A Social Security Amendment Act passes into law, providing for a domestic purposes benefit for adults caring alone for dependants. Particularly aimed at solo parents, the benefit will be paid from May 1, 1974. |

| December 3 | The government introduces measures to reduce petrol and oil consumption in what will later be identified as the 'first oil shock'. The speed limit is reduced to 50 mph (80 kph), and car pooling is encouraged. |

# 1974

| January 25 | On the first day of competition in the Commonwealth Games in Christchurch, Canterbury man Dick Tayler unexpectedly wins the 10,000 m. The success of the 'Friendly Games' is seen as a sign of New Zealand's growing confidence on a world stage. |
| January 30 | Queen Elizabeth II officially closes the Commonwealth Games. Also present are the Duke of Edinburgh, Princess Anne and Captain Mark Phillips. |
| April 1 | The Accident Compensation Commission begins operation, promoting safety from accidents, providing rehabilitation for the injured and providing compensation to accident victims. The scheme, the first of its kind in the world, supersedes the legal right of the injured to sue for damages in cases of negligence. |
| May 17 | The Auckland Medical Aid Centre, New Zealand's first abortion clinic, opens its doors in Remuera, Auckland. Patients will be harassed by pro-life protesters and the clinic damaged by arson. |
| July 1 | The Auckland Hospital Board dismisses Milan Brych after the 'Town Hall Inquiry' report is highly critical of the cancer therapist and finds he has never used any 'real' immunotherapy in his treatments. Brych, who has gained a cult following among patients, will continue to treat privately. |
| August 31 | Charismatic prime minister Norman Kirk dies at the age of 51 in his second year in office. He has suffered complications following varicose vein surgery. |
| September 3 | A referendum in Niue chooses self-government for the island. |

| September 6 | Bill Rowling (Labour) assumes office as prime minister. |
|---|---|
| September 8 | Pizza Hut is officially opened at Lynnmall, west Auckland. It is the first convenience-food franchise to be launched in New Zealand. |
| September 16 | Police raid the Auckland Medical Aid Centre and take all patient files, causing the clinic to close temporarily. The availability of abortion will remain a hot topic while the Contraception, Sterilisation and Abortion Bill is debated and eventually passed in 1977. |
| September 26 | Witi Ihimaera wins the Sir James Wattie book award for *Tangi*, the first published novel in English by a Maori author. |
| September 27 | Dr W. B. Sutch, a former secretary of industries and commerce, is charged with spying under the Official Secrets Act. It is claimed he has met with a staff member of the Soviet embassy. |
| October 19 | Niue achieves self-government in free association with New Zealand when its new constitution comes into force. |
| November 3 | Summer time is reintroduced on a trial basis. The experiment will prove a success, and daylight saving of one hour will be made permanent in 1975. |

## 1975

| February 17 | Bill Sutch goes on trial under the Official Secrets Act. He will be acquitted when it cannot be shown that any privileged information was exchanged in his meetings with a Soviet diplomat. |
|---|---|
| April 1 | Television One begins regular programming — in colour — on its national network with an opening special that is something of a flop. The functions of the New Zealand Broadcasting Corporation have been split to create two channels instead of one. |
| May 31 | Eighteen-year-old Mona Blades vanishes while hitchhiking |

between Hamilton and Hastings. Her body is never found and her disappearance never explained.

| | |
|---|---|
| June 30 | Television 2 is launched. In its first week it will hold the first telethon, in which more than $500,000 is pledged for St John Ambulance. |
| August 12 | In Gothenburg, Sweden, John Walker becomes the first man to run a mile in less than 3 minutes 50 seconds. |
| September 14 | Te Ropu o te Matakite, the Maori land march led by Whina Cooper, sets out from Te Hapua in Northland. It is part of a larger Maori land rights movement. |
| September 16 | Augusta Wallace becomes New Zealand's first woman stipendiary magistrate. |
| October 10 | The Treaty of Waitangi Act passes into law, setting up the Waitangi Tribunal to hear Maori grievances over the treaty and make recommendations for government action. |
| October 13 | Te Ropu o te Matakite, the land march, arrives at Parliament to deliver a memorial of rights requesting the government prevent the further sale or taking of Maori land. Whina Cooper will become known as 'Te Whaea o te Motu', or 'The Mother of the Nation'. |
| November 7 | The country's first marine reserve, Cape Rodney–Okakari Point, is established off Northland. |
| November 29 | For the first time permanent residents are permitted to vote in the general election, whether or not they have New Zealand citizenship. More than 120 years after the first parliamentary election, almost everyone over the age of 18 has the chance to vote. |
| December 12 | Robert Muldoon (National) assumes office as prime minister. During his nine-year term, he will become known as a proponent of market intervention — and as a fierce political adversary. |

# 1976

| | |
|---|---|
| April 9 | Subscriber toll dialling (STD) is introduced, with Upper Hutt the first locality to bypass the operator when making telephone toll calls. |
| June 7 | The first McDonald's restaurant in New Zealand opens at Cobham Court, Porirua. Within 20 years there will be 100 of the American fast-food outlets around the country. |
| June 22 | The New Zealand rugby team leaves for a tour of apartheid South Africa in spite of international disapproval. African nations will boycott the following month's Montreal Olympics in protest. |
| July 30 | The New Zealand men's hockey team upsets the favoured Australian team to win the gold medal at the Montreal Olympic Games. The following day John Walker will win gold in the 1500 m. |
| August 27 | The nuclear warship USS *Truxtun* enters Wellington Harbour and is greeted by an anti-nuclear protest fleet of small vessels. The port unions withdraw labour until the *Truxtun* departs. |

**Members of the Campaign Against Nuclear Warships prepare to sail in opposition to the planned visit of USS *Truxtun* to Wellington on August 27, 1976.**

| September 1 | The first stage of the Wanganui computer centre is implemented. Civil libertarians will watch warily as information from the departments of justice, police and transport is stored together to help police combat crime. |
| September 14 | The Lyttelton–Wellington ferry *Rangatira* begins its final run. On the steamer express 267 passengers and an unknown number of non-paying extras party the night away. |
| September 23 | New Zealand agrees to extend NAFTA, the limited free trade agreement with Australia, to the end of 1985 — even though Australia sells two to three times as much to New Zealand as it buys. |
| October 21 | Police start a campaign of dawn raids to find Pacific Islanders who have overstayed their visas. They storm homes late at night or early in the morning, and stop Pacific Islanders and Maori in the street and demand to see proof of legal residence. The campaign will be called off four days later after an outcry at the violation of human rights. Similar, less publicised raids have been taking place since 1973. |
| December 20 | Floods and landslides hit the Wellington area after heavy rain. One man loses his life. |

## 1977

| January 5 | In Auckland, Maori and Pakeha led by Joe Hawke pitch tents and occupy Takaparawhau (Bastion Point reserve). The crown wants to sell the land for housing construction, but the Orakei Marae Committee insists this is Ngati Whatua land that has been unlawfully taken. |
| February 6 | The first Waitangi Day national public holiday is celebrated, replacing New Zealand Day. Urban Maori have been particularly active in the campaign to change the name. |
| February 15 | The first commercial flight from New Zealand to Antarctica, Auckland to Christchurch via McMurdo Sound, is operated as a day trip by Air New Zealand. |

| February 22 | Queen Elizabeth II and the Duke of Edinburgh arrive in New Zealand. They are on a silver jubilee tour of the Commonwealth. |
| --- | --- |
| April 10 | Colin Quincey of Hokianga reaches Queensland in the *Tasman Trespasser* to become the first person to row across the Tasman Sea. He has been blown 400 km off course and has almost run out of food. |
| May 11 | The New Zealand Medical Council publishes its evidence against cancer therapist Milan Brych, whom it has been trying to have struck off since 1974. It is revealed that Brych is an ex-convict with fraudulent qualifications. Brych, meanwhile, has already set up a new clinic in Rarotonga. |
| May 30 | The first Waitangi Tribunal case, WAI 1, is heard. Joe Hawke's claim of a right to gather shellfish irrespective of the method will not be supported by the tribunal. |
| June 12 | In Scotland, Robert Muldoon is one of the Commonwealth heads of government to agree on the text for the Gleneagles agreement. The document, which discourages sporting contacts with South Africa, will be signed in London several days later. |
| July 11 | Eight men involved in the failure of the JBL investment company five years earlier are convicted on fraud charges. Thousands of small investors lost their money in the collapse. |
| September 22 | Two hundred Vietnamese refugees arrive in New Zealand for settlement. The first 'boat people' arrived in 1976, and by 1990 New Zealand will have accepted more than 9000 south-east Asian refugees. Many, however, will move on to other countries. |
| September 26 | The Territorial Sea and Exclusive Economic Zone Act passes into law, establishing a 200-mile zone around the coast of New Zealand where foreign vessels must be licensed to fish. |
| October 26 | Former prime minister Sir Keith Holyoake assumes office as governor-general. |

| November 21 | It is announced in the *New Zealand Gazette* that 'God Defend New Zealand' will become a national anthem of equal status to 'God Save the Queen'. |

## 1978

| January 1 | Under the Citizenship Act 1977, the words 'British subject' disappear from passports, and Commonwealth citizens start to be treated no differently from other foreigners. |
| February 3 | Meda McKenzie, a 15-year-old schoolgirl, becomes the first New Zealand woman to swim Cook Strait. She will make the return crossing two weeks later. |
| February 12 | Eva Rickard leads 150 land rights activists in an attempted occupation of the Raglan golf course, which is on land taken from Tainui Awhiro in World War II and never returned. Seventeen protesters are arrested, but in 1979 the land will be returned to the tribe. |
| February 15 | The New Zealand cricket team become national heroes when they achieve their first ever test win over England, at the Basin Reserve, Wellington. |
| February 18 | Bruce Beetham of the Social Credit Party wins a by-election in Rangitikei. The newly revived party will win a second seat in a 1980 by-election and will at times ride high in the polls. |
| April 1 | Air New Zealand and NAC merge to become the first New Zealand carrier to offer both international and domestic services. |
| May 25 | The 'squatters' are cleared from Bastion Point, Auckland, after 506 days of occupation. During the operation involving 600 police officers, more than 200 protesters are charged with wilful trespass. There will be two more occupations in 1982 before in 1987 the Waitangi Tribunal recommends that Bastion Point be returned to Ngati Whatua. |
| June 8 | Rotorua's Naomi James arrives at Dartmouth, England, at the conclusion of her 272-day sea voyage around the world. She |

| | has broken the record for a solo sailor by two days. |
|---|---|
| August 16 | A series of articles begins in the *Auckland Star* that will reveal the workings of the 'Mr Asia' drug ring. New Zealanders will be enthralled by the inside story of murder, smuggling, high living and the relationship between one of the syndicate members and an Auckland barrister. |
| August 31 | National superannuation jumps to 80 per cent of the average weekly wage, amid widespread doubts the very generous scheme can be sustained. |
| September 1 | The Human Rights Commission is set up under the 1977 act that legislates against discrimination on grounds of gender, marital status or religious beliefs. |
| November 13 | The New Zealand Film Commission is established to fund and promote the movie industry. |
| December 31 | A television crew records pictures of 'UFOs' from a plane over Kaikoura. The aircraft is retracing the course of a cargo plane flight 10 days earlier after which the crew reported seeing unexplained lights that also showed up on radar. The footage will be broadcast internationally. |

## 1979

| April 6 | Price control is replaced by price surveillance on many products and services, reducing the level of government intervention. |
|---|---|
| April 23 | New Zealand-born teacher Blair Peach is beaten to death by members of the police special patrol group at an anti-fascism rally in Southall, London. No public inquiry will be held and no officer brought to account, and Blair Peach will become a symbol of unjustified police violence in Britain and around the world. |
| May 1 | Auckland University engineering students rehearsing a racist and obscene parody of a haka are assaulted by a Maori and Polynesian protest group who will later call themselves He |

Taua. The incident and the controversy that follows will lead to a report by the race relations conciliator, *Race Against Time*.

| | |
|---|---|
| July 30 | Carless days for motor vehicles are introduced to combat the second oil shock. They will do little to reduce petrol consumption and will be scrapped in December. |
| August 8 | A massive landslide sweeps through the Dunedin suburb of Abbotsford. The hillside, which has been gradually slipping for months, becomes a 75 m wide chasm that swallows houses. No one is killed because residents have been evacuated in time, but dozens of homes have to be demolished or relocated. |
| September 10 | Cabinet ministers and their staff move into the executive wing of the not-quite-completed Beehive in Wellington. The building has already been labelled a white elephant and Robert Muldoon has expressed his distaste for the structure. |
| September 20 | The first nationwide general strike called by the Federation of Labour is marked by a procession of workers in Queen Street, Auckland. The unionists are angry at government intervention in drivers' pay talks. |
| October 14 | The handless body of New Zealander Martin Johnstone, one-time leader of the Mr Asia drug ring, is found in a quarry in Lancashire, England. His associate Alexander Sinclair (aka Terry Clark) will be convicted, with others, of the crime. |
| November 28 | An Air New Zealand DC-10 on a sightseeing flight from Auckland crashes into Mt Erebus, Antarctica. In New Zealand's worst ever disaster, all 237 passengers plus 20 crew are killed. |
| December 17 | Arthur Thomas is granted a free pardon for his conviction in the Crewe murders nine years earlier and released. Robert Adams-Smith, QC, has released a report that identifies serious flaws in the prosecution's case against him. A later commission of inquiry will find that police planted evidence and award him nearly $1 million in personal compensation. |

# Re-engineering a nation
## 1980–1990

**In the 1980s** New Zealand finally drew the attention of a world otherwise occupied with the Falklands War, IRA violence, and the disasters at Bhopal and Chernobyl. In 1981, the South African rugby team's tour of New Zealand divided this country. Street battles involving protesters, police and rugby fans made international headlines. Also in the international news were the government's unifying anti-nuclear stance and the sinking of the *Rainbow Warrior*. Perestroika in the Soviet Union at the end of the decade saw the beginning of the fall of communism. New Zealand underwent its own radical economic restructuring at the hands of Roger Douglas and the fourth Labour government. Outrage at the garage sale of government assets, and Maori protest over treaty issues, failed to dampen celebrations of the 150th anniversary of New Zealand's founding document, the Treaty of Waitangi, in 1990.

# 1980

| | |
|---|---|
| January 9 | The ANZ bank installs the country's first ATMs in its Lambton Quay branch. |
| January 16 | Otago and Southland are hit by heavy flooding for the second time in less than two years. These are the region's worst floods in more than 100 years. |
| January 27 | Vsevolod Sofinski, the Soviet ambassador to New Zealand, departs the country. He has been given 72 hours to leave after being expelled for interfering with domestic politics by giving money to the Socialist Unity Party. Full diplomatic relations will not be re-established until 1984. |
| February 16 | TVNZ begins operation. It has been formed out of Television One and South Pacific Television. |
| March 31 | An 80-day strike at the Kinleith pulp and paper mill ends when the government backs down and allows a negotiated pay rise to stand. |
| April 1 | The Supreme Court becomes the High Court, shedding much of its civil jurisdiction, and magistrates' courts become district courts. |
| July 19 | An unofficial team of four New Zealanders marches under the games association flag at the opening ceremony of the Moscow Olympic Games. They are the only New Zealand athletes not to join a US-led boycott, which protests the Soviet invasion of Afghanistan. |
| November 6 | Sir David Beattie assumes office as governor-general. |
| November 15 | Saturday morning shopping becomes legal again 45 years after the advent of the 40-hour week ruled it out. |
| December 23 | The 'Independent State of Aramoana' secedes from New Zealand over plans to wipe out the Otago Harbour villages of Aramoana and Te Ngaru to build an aluminium smelter. Protests and declining prices for aluminium will lead to the |

# 1981

| | |
|---|---|
| January 5 | Challenge Corporation, Fletcher Holdings and Tasman Pulp & Paper are legally constituted together as Fletcher Challenge, New Zealand's largest industrial company. |
| February 1 | At Melbourne, Australia wins a one-day cricket match with an underarm ball bowled by Trevor Chappell to Brian McKechnie. There is national uproar at the unsporting behaviour. |
| February 6 | The Waitangi Day investitures of Sir Graham Latimer and Dame Whina Cooper are disrupted by members of the Waitangi Day Committee who see the acceptance of Pakeha honours by Maori leaders as a sell-out. |
| March 3 | Young Auckland sales rep Tania Harris leads the 50,000-strong 'Kiwis Care' march down Queen Street, Auckland. The demonstration calling for national unity is a response to a period of industrial unrest and a recent march by unionists. |
| April 27 | The full report of a royal commission of inquiry into the Erebus air crash is released to the public. In it Justice Peter Mahon clears the crew of blame and controversially accuses Air New Zealand of a cover-up — the 'orchestrated litany of lies'. |
| May 1 | Protest groups in 27 towns and cities stage an evening of demonstrations against the upcoming tour of New Zealand by the Springboks rugby team. The issue of sport, politics and South Africa will divide New Zealand. |
| June 27 | A telethon begins that will see nearly $6 million distributed to charities for the disabled. The total is hailed as a world record per head of population. |
| July 1 | Passports are again required for travel between Australia and New Zealand. |
| July 25 | Anti-tour demonstrators invade the rugby pitch at Hamilton and the Springboks–Waikato match is abandoned. There |

are many injuries in violence involving rugby supporters, protesters and police.

July 29        Protesters against the Springbok tour march on the South African consulate in Wellington. They are halted by police wielding batons.

**One of many anti-Springbok tour demonstrations, in Willis St, Wellington, in July 1981.**

July 29        Kiri Te Kanawa sings at the wedding of the Prince of Wales and Lady Diana Spencer in St Paul's Cathedral, London.

September 12   The South Africa–New Zealand test match at Eden Park, Auckland, is interrupted when flour bombs are dropped onto the pitch from a light plane. Outside the park, 10,000 protesters are caught up in violence between citizens and police on a scale never before seen in New Zealand.

October 25     Aucklander Allison Roe wins the women's section of the New York marathon in a world-record time of 2 hours 25 minutes 28 seconds. Earlier in the year she has won the Boston marathon.

| | |
|---|---|
| December 22 | A Court of Appeal decision on the inquiry into the Erebus disaster determines that some of Justice Mahon's findings violate natural justice. It is declared that there has been no 'pre-determined plan of deception' by Air New Zealand and the order of costs against the airline is quashed. The decision will be upheld by the Privy Council in 1983. |

## 1982

| | |
|---|---|
| January 10 | In Singapore, the All Whites soccer team qualifies for the World Cup finals by beating China 2–1 at the end of a 15-month campaign. |
| March 27 | The Round the Bays fun run in Auckland attracts 80,000 participants, making it the largest jogging event in the world. |
| April 2 | Kokiri Pukeatua, the first kohanga reo, opens in Wainuiomata. |
| May 20 | In London, Robert Muldoon offers HMNZS *Canterbury* in non-combative support of the United Kingdom's effort in the Falklands War. The offer will be accepted, and the frigate will patrol the Indian Ocean, freeing up a Royal Navy ship for the conflict. |
| June 15 | The All Whites play their first game at the soccer World Cup in Spain, losing 2–5 to Scotland. They will not win a game in the tournament. |
| June 23 | An across-the-board wage, rent and price freeze comes into force. The measure, intended to stop high inflation, will continue until 1984. |
| July 19 | The Privy Council rules that all Samoans born between 1924 and 1948 are entitled to New Zealand citizenship. The government will act with unseemly haste to over-ride the decision. |
| September 15 | Western Samoans lose the automatic right to New Zealand citizenship as the Citizenship (Western Samoa) Act comes into force. However, all Western Samoans in New Zealand |

on this day are granted the right to citizenship, and in the future Western Samoans with permanent residence will be permitted to apply.

September 30    The Clyde dam legislation is pushed through the House of Representatives with the help of Social Credit, despite the earlier quashing of the government's water right. There have been years of controversy over the hydro scheme, which involves raising the Clutha River level by 69 m and drowning the business centre of Cromwell.

November 29    Mountaineers Phil Doole and Mark Inglis are rescued after spending nearly two weeks trapped in a snow cave on Aoraki/Mt Cook. Both men will have their feet amputated because of frostbite.

December 14    The heads of agreement for Closer Economic Relations (CER) with Australia are signed. The free trade package removes duty on many goods and will come into effect on January 1, 1983.

## 1983

April 13    Zhao Ziyang becomes the first Chinese premier to visit New Zealand. He will be sent home with a canister of bull semen, a gift described by a Chinese official as the 'seeds of friendship'.

April 17    The Prince and Princess of Wales arrive in New Zealand with their infant son Prince William. During their visit they will be mobbed by enthusiastic crowds.

April 23    Prince William has a photo-opportunity with a Buzzy Bee toy on the lawn at Government House, Auckland. A picture of the prince crawling across a rug will become the first colour image to be transmitted digitally from New Zealand to the rest of the world.

May 21    In the middle of a three-day Wellington storm, winds start to rage at 74 km/h and will continue at that level or above for 32 consecutive hours. It is the longest gale recorded in New Zealand.

| July 3 | Unseeded New Zealand tennis player Chris Lewis loses the Wimbledon men's singles final in straight sets to US player John McEnroe. |
| July 11 | In St Louis, Missouri, 19-year-old Aucklander Lorraine Downes becomes the first New Zealander to win the Miss Universe contest. |
| August 2 | A visit to Auckland by the nuclear-powered USS *Texas* prompts anti-nuclear rallies on land and an armada of protest vessels in the harbour. |
| August 22 | The New Zealand Party is launched by a group including Bob Jones. Described by David Lange as 'a club for rich playboys', the libertarian party will gain more than 12 per cent of the vote at the 1984 general election without winning a seat. |
| September 1 | Schoolgirl Kirsa Jensen disappears while horseriding near Napier. Her body has not been found, and no one has been convicted of her murder. |
| October 23 | Rod Dixon wins the prestigious New York marathon, the first non-American to do so. His victory comes in spite of cramp and a hamstring injury. |

# 1984

| January 26 | A storm hits Fiordland and Southland, causing devastating flooding. Over the next 36 hours, thousands will be evacuated, more than 1000 houses will be made unliveable and more than 12,000 livestock will be lost. |
| February 6 | Eva Rickard leads a hikoi to Waitangi to demonstrate about Maori land grievances, but the marchers are prevented from entering the marae by police. |
| March 27 | A bomb explodes at the Wellington trades hall, killing the caretaker. There is no clear motive for the attack on the trade union headquarters and no one will be charged with the crime. |

| | |
|---|---|
| March 31 | Tolls are charged on the Auckland Harbour Bridge for the last time. |
| April 1 | The first known New Zealand victim of AIDS, a 30-year-old man who contracted HIV overseas, dies at Taranaki Base Hospital. |
| April 10 | Rotorua 20-year-old Susan Devoy wins the British Open for the first time. She will go on to win the world's premier squash event a further seven times. |
| June 14 | Prime minister Robert Muldoon calls a snap election after National MP Marilyn Waring announces she will not promise to vote with her own caucus on the issues of rape legislation and nuclear disarmament. |
| July 4 | Professor Denis Bonham announces the birth several days earlier at National Women's Hospital, Auckland, of New Zealand's first test-tube baby. The child's identity is kept a secret. |
| July 14 | Labour wins the general election by a landslide. The Muldoon era is over, although the outgoing prime minister will do his best to sabotage the transfer of power. |

David Lange and his wife Naomi enjoy election night on July 14, 1984.

| | |
|---|---|
| July 18 | The incoming government announces a package of urgent economic measures to combat a currency crisis, including the devaluation of the dollar, the removal of interest rate controls and a three-month price freeze. |
| July 26 | David Lange (Labour) assumes office as prime minister. The former lawyer's term will be remembered partly for the development of anti-nuclear legislation, but mostly for finance minister Roger Douglas's radical restructuring of the economy to fit a free market model. |
| August 12 | The New Zealand team marches at the closing ceremony of the Los Angeles Olympic Games. New Zealand has had its best ever Olympics, coming eighth on the medal table with 11 medals, including eight golds. The competitions have, however, been affected by a boycott by communist bloc countries. |
| September 10 | *Te Maori*, a high-profile exhibition of traditional Maori art, opens with a dawn ceremony at the Metropolitan Museum of Art in New York. |
| December 7 | A riot in Queen Street, Auckland, starts after the power goes off during a free rock concert in Aotea Square. Cars are burnt and shops looted as young people battle with police, injuring 23 officers. |

## 1985

| | |
|---|---|
| February 1 | New Zealand's anti-nuclear policy leads to the refusal of a visit by a nuclear-capable ship, USS *Buchanan*. The decision will gall the Americans and lead to the breakdown of the ANZUS pact. |
| February 10 | The major trading banks operate a pilot scheme for eftpos through 19 Auckland petrol stations. Eftpos will have its ups and downs, with banks pulling out and re-entering the cashless transaction scheme at various times, before becoming a permanent feature of New Zealand life. |
| March 1 | David Lange participates in a debate at the Oxford Union |

that is broadcast live in New Zealand. He leads a team that successfully argues that 'Nuclear weapons are morally indefensible', and famously remarks that he can smell the uranium on the breath of one of his opponents.

| March 4 | The New Zealand dollar is floated for the first time, with the exchange rate determined by supply and demand in the foreign exchange markets. It immediately — but temporarily — floats down. |

July 10 — Two bomb explosions rip through the Greenpeace vessel *Rainbow Warrior* in the Waitemata Harbour, Auckland, and one crew member is killed. The culprits will turn out to be French secret agents sabotaging Greenpeace's efforts to prevent nuclear testing in the Pacific.

July 14 — An All Blacks tour of South Africa is cancelled after a High Court injunction is granted against the New Zealand Rugby Football Union. The grounds are that the tour would not be good for the sport in New Zealand, and thus would be in contravention of the union's constitution.

September 24 — A petition of more than 586,000 names opposing the decriminalisation of homosexual acts is presented at Parliament. The petition campaign, supported by pentecostal churches and conservative groups, has caused division in the Christian church and the wider community.

October 18 — The first fuel production begins at Motunui in Taranaki. The $2 billion plant is the world's first synthetic petrol factory, making petrol from Maui gas. The hangover from Muldoon's 'Think Big' strategy is already in financial trouble because of low world oil prices.

October 30 — Canterbury farmers slaughter 2500 ewes in protest at the Labour government's agricultural policies. Their action is the result of the government decision to expose New Zealand to market forces, a policy of deregulation that will become known as Rogernomics after finance minister Roger Douglas.

October 31 — Keri Hulme becomes the first New Zealander to win the Booker

| | Prize for literature. The choice of her novel *the bone people*, published in 1984 by Spiral Collective having been turned down by major publishers, is not universally well received. |
|---|---|
| November 4 | French agents Alain Mafart and Dominique Prieur appear in an Auckland court in relation to the *Rainbow Warrior* incident, although at least 10 more agents have already fled the country. Mafart and Prieur plead guilty to charges of manslaughter and wilful damage, and on November 22 will be sentenced to 10 years' imprisonment. |
| November 20 | The Most Reverend Sir Paul Reeves assumes office as governor-general. He is the first clergyman, and the first man of Maori descent, to be appointed. |
| December 9 | The Treaty of Waitangi Amendment Act passes into law, giving the Waitangi Tribunal power to hear all grievances arising since 1840 instead of since 1975. |

## 1986

| | |
|---|---|
| February 16 | The Soviet cruise ship *Mikhail Lermontov* strikes rocks and sinks in the Marlborough Sounds. One crew member drowns. The Marlborough harbourmaster, who took the ship through a passage too shallow for the vessel, will later be found to be responsible. |
| February 23 | Queen Elizabeth II is struck by an egg flung by a protester at Ellerslie racecourse in Auckland. Later in the short tour she will also have bare buttocks flashed at her as a Maori insult. |
| April 17 | The bulk of the professional Cavaliers rugby team, many of them All Blacks, arrives in South Africa for a 'private' tour that is not sanctioned by the New Zealand Rugby Football Union. Although coach Colin Meads will be removed as an All Blacks selector as a result of his involvement, the rebel players will be suspended for only two international games. |
| July 7 | The United Nations secretary-general arbitrates an agreement between France and New Zealand that will allow the *Rainbow Warrior* conspirators to be released to do three years' |

military service on Hao atoll in the Pacific in return for $US7 million in compensation.

| | |
|---|---|
| July 9 | Fran Wilde's Homosexual Law Reform Bill passes its third reading in the House of Representatives. When the act comes into force in August, criminal sanctions against consensual male homosexual practices will be removed. |
| October 1 | The Goods and Services Tax Act, adding 10 per cent to the cost of most goods and services, comes into force. Within three years the rate will be raised to 12.5 per cent. |
| November 22 | John Paul II arrives on the first papal visit to New Zealand. On the three-day tour, the pope will draw smaller crowds than expected. |
| December 11 | A royal commission on the electoral system recommends the use of German-style mixed member proportional representation (MMP) in general elections. |
| December 14 | Chris Dickson and KZ-7 sail into the challenger semifinals of the America's Cup event in Fremantle. The 'plastic fantastic' yacht, the subject of rancorous protest, seems almost unbeatable after building a 32–1 win-loss record. |

# 1987

| | |
|---|---|
| January 1 | The Constitution Act 1986 comes into force, bringing together constitutional provisions already in place. |
| January 19 | In the America's Cup challenger final, Dennis Conner's *Stars and Stripes* team completes the defeat of New Zealand's KZ-7. |
| February 6 | The first five ordinary members of the Order of New Zealand receive their honours. This highest locally awarded honour will be restricted to 20 living members. |
| March 2 | An earthquake measuring 6.3 on the Richter scale strikes the Bay of Plenty. Edgecumbe, Whakatane and Kawerau are severely damaged and 35 people are seriously injured. |

| March 31 | The New Zealand Post Office has its last day of operation. The following day it will be split into NZ Post Ltd, Postbank Ltd and Telecommunications NZ Ltd. |
| April 1 | The State-Owned Enterprises Act 1986 takes effect. The aim is to increase efficiency and profitability by converting a number of government departments into corporations. |
| May 19 | An attempt to hijack an Air New Zealand jet is made at Nadi airport five days after Fiji's first military coup. Three flight crew are held hostage before the incident is resolved when the flight engineer hits the hijacker over the head with a bottle of whisky. |
| May 27 | Colin McCahon dies. He is recognised as New Zealand's most important modern artist. |
| June 8 | The New Zealand Nuclear Free Zone, Disarmament and Arms Control Act passes into law. The legislation implements various treaties on weapons of mass destruction and establishes the country as a nuclear and biological weapon-free zone. |
| June 19 | In a crime that shocks the nation, six-year-old Teresa Cormack is abducted from a street in Napier, raped and murdered. Her murderer will not be convicted until 15 years later. |
| June 20 | New Zealand defeats France 29–9 at Eden Park, Auckland, to win the inaugural Rugby World Cup. |
| June 29 | In a breakthrough judgment on the state-owned enterprises case, the Court of Appeal defines the principles of the Treaty of Waitangi, establishes the role of partnership, and requires the crown to safeguard Maori land claims in its legislation. |
| July 22 | The first tickets for Lotto are sold, with queues forming before outlets open. The first division prize of the inaugural draw will be nearly $360,000. |
| August 1 | Under the Maori Language Act, Maori becomes an official language, conferring the right to speak te reo in some legal proceedings. The act also establishes the Maori Language Commission. |

All Blacks captain David Kirk with the Rugby World Cup on June 20, 1987.

| August 28 | New Zealand wins the world netball championship in Glasgow, defeating Trinidad in the final 49–37. |
| September 30 | In its report on the Muriwhenua fisheries claim, the Waitangi Tribunal rules that the sea can be owned in the same way as land can be, opening the way for successful Maori challenges to the fishing quota system. |
| October 19 | The government agrees to sell New Zealand Steel to Equiticorp for $327 million. The government's asset sales programme will raise billions of dollars. |
| October 20 | A crash begins that will over two weeks wipe billions of dollars in value off New Zealand shares. Triggered by a sharp downturn in the US markets, the bust brings to a dramatic end an unprecedented New Zealand sharemarket boom and will result in dozens of publicly listed companies going into receivership. |
| December 2 | New Zealand's first heart transplant is performed at Green Lane Hospital, Auckland, with Brian Lindsay receiving the heart of an accident victim. The surgical team is led by Ken Graham. |

# 1988

| February 5 | NZ Post closes 432 post offices. State-owned enterprises minister Richard Prebble insists the closures will result in a better, more efficient service and that no one will be disadvantaged. |
| March 7 | Cyclone Bola strikes New Zealand. Floods devastate the East Coast, winds of up to 100 km/h destroy trees and tear off roofs, and landslips close roads. Three people die when their car is swept away by floodwaters. |
| July 1 | The government announces that it has agreed to the Waitangi Tribunal's recommendation that Bastion Point, Auckland, be returned to Maori ownership. |
| August 5 | The Cartwright Report is released to the public, confirming the |

failure of National Women's Hospital, Auckland, to adequately treat dozens of cervical cancer patients. The report on the 'unfortunate experiment' publicised by Sandra Coney and Phillida Bunkle in June 1987 will lead to sweeping changes in the health system.

| | |
|---|---|
| September 9 | New Zealand's second America's Cup challenge ends with a 0–2 defeat by Dennis Conner's *Stars and Stripes* catamaran. Michael Fay's 'rogue challenge' using the KZ-1 'big boat' has spent — and will continue to spend — much of its time and money in court. |
| November 12 | The inaugural bungy jump is made off the Kawarau bridge near Queenstown. Henry van Asch and A. J. Hackett's venture is the first permanent commercial bungy site in the world. |
| December 20 | The government announces the sale of Air New Zealand to a consortium led by Brierley Investments. Some of the shares will be sold on to the New Zealand public, while the government retains a small 'Kiwi share'. |

## 1989

| | |
|---|---|
| April 24 | The first school board elections are held. Reforms to the education system, outlined in the *Tomorrow's Schools* policy document of August 1988, will see more community and parent involvement in the running of schools. |
| May 1 | The New Labour Party is formed under the leadership of Jim Anderton, who has resigned from the Labour government over its New Right policy leap. |
| July 2 | Commercial-free Sunday television ends, with advertisements permitted from noon. The relaxation of regulations is part of a restructuring of broadcasting, opening it up to the free market. |
| July 22 | A New Zealand XV plays the California Grizzlies at Lancaster Park. The first national women's rugby team is not, however, recognised by the New Zealand Rugby Football Union. |

| August 8 | Geoffrey Palmer (Labour) assumes office as prime minister. He replaces David Lange, who has resigned after becoming disillusioned over the direction of Labour policy. The last straw has been a caucus decision to reinstate Roger Douglas, sacked by Lange in 1988, in the cabinet. |
| --- | --- |
| September 30 | The upturned *Rose-Noelle* breaks up on a reef just off Great Barrier Island. The trimaran, capsized by a huge wave off Hawke's Bay, has been drifting upside-down in the Pacific Ocean for 119 days but all four crew members have survived. For a while their unlikely story of survival will be doubted by some. |
| November 26 | TV3 goes to air for the first time. Within six months, the privately owned television station will be in receivership. |
| December 10 | Sunday shop trading begins. The event is something of a damp squib for many retailers, who are disappointed by the turnout. |
| December 20 | The Maori Fisheries Act passes into law, recognising the fishing rights accorded by the Treaty of Waitangi and conceding 10 per cent of the fishery to Maori. |
| December 20 | The Reserve Bank of New Zealand Act passes into law, establishing the Reserve Bank's role in maintaining price stability through monetary policy. |

# 1990

| January 1 | Lincoln College of the University of Canterbury becomes known as Lincoln University as part of wide-ranging tertiary education reforms. |
| --- | --- |
| January 24 | The Commonwealth Games begin in Auckland with a dramatic opening ceremony performance about New Zealand culture and history. A record 54 nations are competing in Auckland's second games. |
| February 6 | Sesquicentennial celebrations of the signing of the Treaty of Waitangi see 20 waka taua in the water at Waitangi — and |

| | Queen Elizabeth II struck by a protester's wet T-shirt. |
|---|---|
| June 14 | The government signs an agreement with Bell Atlantic and Ameritech to sell Telecom for $NZ4250 million, making it one of the first telecommunications companies in the world to be fully privatised. Some of the shares will be sold on to reduce foreign parties' holdings to less than 50 per cent. |
| June 29 | Penny Jamieson is consecrated as the bishop of Dunedin. She is the first woman in the world to head an Anglican diocese. |
| July 14 | Representatives of 37 iwi at Turangawaewae vote to form the National Maori Congress. The new organisation will seek to advance Maori causes and promote iwi tino rangatiratanga (self-determination). |
| August 13 | Five servicemen are rescued from a snow trench on Mt Ruapehu after two men trek for help in a blizzard. It is too late for six soldiers, however, who have already died. Three days later, a solo Japanese climber will walk down the mountain unharmed after spending five days waiting out the storm in a snow cave. |
| August 28 | The New Zealand Bill of Rights Act passes into law, protecting human rights and affirming the government's commitment to the International Covenant on Civil and Political Rights. |
| September 4 | Mike Moore (Labour) assumes office as prime minister, having ousted Geoffrey Palmer in advance of the general election. |
| November 2 | Jim Bolger assumes office as prime minister after National wins the election with a landslide. Ruth Richardson is also installed as the country's first woman minister of finance. |
| November 13 | At Aramoana, near Dunedin, David Gray begins a massacre that will see 13 of his neighbours shot dead, including children and a police officer. Gray will be killed by police gunfire the following day. |
| December 10 | Gary Ball and Rob Hall climb the 5140 m Vinson Massif, |

| | Antarctica, to become the first team to climb the seven tallest peaks of the seven continents in seven months. |
|---|---|
| December 12 | Former politician Dame Catherine Tizard assumes office as New Zealand's first female governor-general. |
| December 13 | Figures are released showing New Zealand has its highest ever total of registered unemployed and people in subsidised work: 202,054. |
| December 14 | Allan Hawkins, the founder of Equiticorp, is charged with six others in relation to a $440 million fraud. The collapse of the investment bank in 1989 has hit thousands of investors. |
| December 19 | In an attempt to balance the budget, the National government announces plans to slash benefits, cut subsidies on doctors' visits and treble the cost of prescriptions. |

# Index

Page numbers in **bold** indicate illustrations

**261**

boy scouts 138
*Boyd* 30, 31
Bracken, Thomas 106
Bradford, George 127
Brasch, Charles 190
Breathalyser 223
Bridge, Cyprian 67
bridges: Auckland Harbour Bridge 209–10, 224, 248; Grafton 141; Rakaia River 175
Brierley Investments 256
*Brilliant* 61
Bristow, Abraham 28
Britain, *see* Great Britain
*Britannia* (Captain Robert Turnbull) 25
*Britannia* (Captain William Raven) 22, 23–4
Britannia (Petone) 54, 55, 56, 57, 59, 63
*Britannia Spectator* 59
British Commonwealth 167, 191, 238
British Commonwealth Far East Reserve 202
British Consul 50, 51
British Empire Games 194
British Open golf championship 216
British Resident 45
*Britomart* 58
*Brothers* 35
Broughton, William 22
Brown, William 58, 70
Browne, Thomas Gore 79, 81, 83
Brown's Island (Motukorea) 58
Bruce, George 28, 29
Bruni d'Entrecasteaux, Antoine-Raymond-Joseph de 23
Brunner mine disaster 123
Brunner, Thomas 69, 70, 71
Bryce, John 110, 112
Brych, Milan 232, 237
Brydone, Thomas 111
Brynderwyn Hills 216
*Buchanan* 249
Buck, Sir Peter (Te Rangi Hiroa) 124, 147, 171, 200
budgets: 'Black Budget' 208
*Buffalo* 27, 56
Buller Gorge 70
Buller River 81
Bumby, John 50
Bumby, Mary 50
Bunbury, Thomas 56, 57, 63
bungy jumping 256
Bunkle, Phillida 256
Burgess, J.W. 174, 177
Burgess, Richard 95
Burton, Ormond 175–6
Busby, James 45, 46, 54, 177
buses 160, 193, 216
Butler, John 36, 37, 38, 39
Byrd, Richard 162
Byron, John 11

cabbage trees 9
Cable Bay, Nelson 106
cable cars, *see* trams – cable
Caddell, James 30
Cahill, David 97
*Calliope* 69
Cameron, Charles 86
Cameron, Duncan 86, 88, 89, 90, 91, 92, 93
Camp Waihi 96
Campaign Against Nuclear Warships 235
Campbell Island 30, 86
Campbell, John (architect) 143
Campbell, John Logan 58, 70, 129, 130
Campion, Richard and Edith 199
Canberra Pact 185
cancer: cervical cancer inquiry 255–6; Milan Brych investigation 232, 237
*Canterbury* (frigate) 245
Canterbury (New Zealand) Aviation Co. 150, 157
Canterbury (region) 69, 74, 77, 78–9, 96, 250. *See also* specific placenames
Canterbury Association 72, 73
Canterbury College, University of New Zealand 104
Canterbury Museum 102, 104
Canterbury Regiment 94
Canterbury Rifles 94
Canterbury Rugby Union 108
Canterbury University 104, 212, 257
Cape Brett (Rakaumangamanga) 13, 17
Cape Egmont 11, 45
Cape Kidnappers 12
Cape Maria van Diemen 11, 14, 152, 175
Cape Rodney–Okakari Point Marine Reserve 234
Cape Terawhiti 74
Cape Turnagain (Poroporo) 12, 15
capital punishment 62, 70, 95, 123, 155, 180, 195, 205, 213
capitals: Auckland 58; Russell 56, 58; Wellington 93
*Captain Hobson* 198
Cardigan Bay 223
*Carisbrooke Castle* 105
Carleton, Hugh 77
Carroll, James 121, 128, 129, 136
carless days 240
cars 125, 131, 135, 158, 232, 240. *See also* driving
Cartwright Report 256
*Castor* 68
Catholic Church, 49, 223, 252. *See also* missions – Catholic
Catholic–Protestant violence 109
Cavaliers rugby team 251
Cavanagh, James 26
Cawthron Institute 156
*Cecilia* 123

Tutaekuri River 124; Wellington 236
flour: first made in NZ 33; removal of subsidies
221
fluoridation 206
Folkes, Kenneth 181
food, *see* convenience foods; restaurants
Foodtown supermarket 208
football, association, *see* soccer
Forbes, George 165, 167
Forest Rangers 97–8, **98**
Forests Act 1921 157
forestry 157, 189. *See also* timber industry
Forsaith, Thomas 78
Foveaux Strait 29, 30, 57, 110
Fox, William 80, 84, 100, 104
France: colonial ambitions in NZ 44, 49;
colonies in Pacific 115; immigrants from
58; Marion du Fresne's officers claim NZ as
possession of 17; nuclear testing 229, 231,
250; *Rainbow Warrior* bombing 250, 251–2
franchise: male property owners 76, 77; Maori
77, 96; permanent residents 234; property
qualification lifted 111; twenty-year-olds
224; women 118, 120, 121, **121**. *See also*
elections
Frankton Junction 192
Franz Josef Glacier Hotel fire 202
Fraser, Peter 150, 177, 178, 181, 186
French Pass 41, **42**
Freyberg, Bernard Cyril Freyberg, Baron 176,
183, 189
Friendly Road radio station 170
Froebel kindergarten 116
Funcke, Henry 117
Furby, W.S. 107
Furneaux, Tobias 18, 19, 20
Fyfe, Thomas 122

Gabriels Gully 83, 84
*Galatea* 100
Gallaher, Dave 131
Gallipoli campaign 147, 148, **148**, 149
Galway, George Vere Arundell Monckton
Arundell, Viscount 170
Garrett, Mrs H.L. 211
gas, natural 209, 214, 221, 223
Gate Pa 90
*Gazelle* 77
Geering, Lloyd 221
General Assembly 76, 78
*General Gates* 36, 37
*General Grant* 95
*General Wellesley* 29
George V, King 141, 146
George VI, King 160, 173, 198
geothermal power 209
German Colonisation Company 64

Germany: immigrants from 48, 64; World War I
146, 148, 151, 152; World War II 175, 178,
183, 184, 186
Gilbert and Ellice Islands 159
Gilfillan family, murder of 70
Gillespie family, murder of 69
Gillies, John 217
Gilsemans, Isaac 10
Gipps, Sir George 50, 54
'Girls' War' 43
Gisborne 144
'God Defend New Zealand' 106, 177, 198, 229,
238
Glasgow, David, Earl of 120
Glasgow, John 227
Glen Afton mine tragedy 176
Glenbrook steel mill 223, 224
Gleneagles agreement 237
Glenelg, Charles Grant, Baron 50
Glenn, John 29
*Glory* 41
Glover, Denis 196
Gnatt, Poul 200
Godley, John Robert 72, 73
Gold, Charles 81, 82
gold: Buller River 81; Chinese miners 95;
Coromandel 76; Nelson 80; Otago 83, 85;
West Coast 91
Golden Bay (Taitapu) 10, 52, 80
Golden Kiwi lottery 214
golf 216
Gonneville, Binot de 16
goods and services tax 252
Gordon, Sir Arthur 110
*Gothic* 200
Gough, Peter 227
Gould, Philippa 205, 208
Gourmet restaurant 213
government: Crown colony, 59, 60, 63, 65,
68; New South Wales, under jurisdiction
of 50, 54, 59; provincial 76, 77, 78, 79,
106; responsible 69, 71, 76, 79, 80, 84;
war cabinet, World War I 148; war cabinet,
World War II 178, 186. *See also* Labour
governments; Liberal Government; loans
– government; local government; National
governments; Reform Government; United-
Reform Government
Government House 29, 62, 71, 136, 228, 247
*Governor Bligh* 31
*Governor Wynyard* 76
governors 60, 65, 68, 71, 77, 79, 84, 97, 104,
105, 106, 108, 110, 112, 116, 120, 124,
142, 144, 151. *See also* specific names
governors-general 106, 151, 153, 156, 158,
165, 170, 179, 189, 199, 206, 215, 222,
229, 237, 242, 251, 259. *See also* specific
names

**276**

**278**

Pompallier, Jean-Baptiste 49, 50
population 187, 198, 224
Poroporo (Cape Turnagain) 12, 15
Porritt, Sir Arthur 222, 224
Port Chalmers (Koputai) 66, 71, 111, 142
Port Cooper 49
Port Employers' Association 195
Port Hills 73, 97, 174, 217
Port Jackson 21
*Port Kembla* 151
Port Louis-Phillippe 57
Port Nicholson 46, 51–2, 54, 55, 56, 57, 60.
    *See also* Wellington
Port Underwood 57
Post Office 226, 228, 253
Post Office savings banks 96
postal services: first Auckland–San Francisco
    airmail flight 174; first franking machine
    133; first inland parcel post 115; first official
    airmail flight 154; first trans-Tasman airmail
    flight 169; first trunk airmail service 171; first
    unofficial airmail delivery 146; health stamps
    164; NZ-UK airmail 177; penny postage
    128; Pigeongrams 124; post offices 56, 255;
    postage stamps, first 79; six-days-a-week
    airmail service 156; stamp vending machine
    134
Postbank Ltd 253
Potatau Te Wherowhero 70, 80, 83
Potatu II, see Tawhiao
Potter, H.R. 151
Poverty Bay 12, 94, 99
*Powerful* 138
Powles, Sir Guy 215
Poynton, Catherine 49
Prebble, Richard 255
Preece, George 103
premiers: 79, 80, 84, 87, 91, 93, 100, 104,
    105, 106, 109, 111, 112, 113, 115, 117,
    120. *See also* prime ministers
Prendergast, Sir James 107
Presbyterian Church, 55, 221
*Press* 83, 170
price control 221, 239, 245
Prieur, Dominique 251–2
prime ministers 106, 120, 134, 135, 143, 154,
    159, 162, 165, 167, 170, 177, 206, 212,
    227, 229, 230, 233, 234, 249, 257, 258.
    *See also* premiers
printing 43, 46, 48, 55, 59
prisons 211, 214, 219
Privy Council 245
prohibition, see alcohol
Protestant-Catholic split 109
protests: aluminium smelter 242; anti-nuclear
    229, 231, 235, 247; Auckland University
    engineering students' haka 239–40; 'Kiwis
    Care' march 243; Maori land 234, 236, 238,

247; Springbok tour 243–4, **244**; Vietnam
    War 220, 226, 227, **228**; Waitangi Day 227.
    *See also* conservation campaign
Prouse, John 133
*Providence* 24
provinces, boundaries constituted 77
provincial government 76, 77, 78, 106
*Psyche* 138
public access to recreational land 120
Public Health Act 1900 127–8
public service 167
public works 102, 104
Puckey, William G. 44
Puhirake, Rawiri 90
Puhoi 86–7
*Pukaki* 194
Pukapuka 9
Pukehinahina 90
Pukekawa 226, 227
Pukekura 114
Puketakauere pa 83
Puketutu 67, **67**
pulp and paper industry 203, 216, 242, 243
*Punjaub* 104
Putiki Maori Church 63
*Pyramus* 47

Queen Charlotte Sound 14–5, 18, 19, 20, 21, 51
Queen Elizabeth II Arts Council 216
Queen's Theatre, Dunedin 106
Queent Street riot 249
Queenstown 107, 111
Quincey, Colin 237

Rabbit Nuisance Amendment Act 1947 191
Race Relations Conciliator 229, 240
radio: 1YA station 159, 209; 1ZB station opened
    173; Aunt Daisy 216; early broadcast 156;
    first global transmission 158; first radio
    programme 157; Friendly Road station 170;
    *It's in the Bag* show 201; live broadcast of NZ
    Opera Group 202; parliamentary broadcasts
    171; privately-owned 220–1, 226
Radio Hauraki 220–1, 226
Radio i 226
Raetihi 152
Raglan Golf Course 238
railways: Auckland-Onehunga 105; Bluff to
    Invercargill 96; Christchurch-Dunedin 107;
    Christchurch-Invercargill 108; collision
    at Rakaia 126; derailment at Hyde 183;
    derailment at Ongarue 157; derailment at
    Ratana 174; derailment at Seddon 191;
    derailment on Rimutaka incline 109, **109**;
    Dun Mountain Railway 84; Dunedin railway
    station 133; electrified 203; first steam

Wellington Airport 210
Wellington Battalion 148
Wellington Harbour 54, 68, 78
*Wellington Independent* 70
Wellington-Lyttelton centennial yacht race 195
Wellington Province 77, 81
Wellington Racing Club 160
*Wellington Spectator* 59
Wellington Trades Hall bombing 247
Wellington Volunteers 97
Wereroa pa 93
Wesleyan mission 38, 39, 40, 41, 50, 63
West Coast: exploration by Brunner 69, 71; gold 91; routes over the Alps to 80, 86, 89, 95
Western Samoa 156, 159, 189, 213, 214, 245–6
Westland Province 105
*Westmeath* 112
*Westmoreland* 38
Whahawhaha, Ropata 99
Whakarua-tapu 215
Whakatane 99, 211, 252
Whakatu 52
whaling: ocean 25, **26**; shore-based 43, 48, 72, 218; stations 44, 218
Whangaehu 152
Whangaehu River 200
Whangamata 211
Whanganui River 90, 140
Whangarei 217
Whangaroa 30, 31, 39, 40, 41
Whare Uta, Maungatautari 114
Wharekaka station 65
Wharepoaka 43
Wharetutu 44
wheat 31, 33
Whitaker, Frederick 87, 111
*Whitby* 60, 61
White Island 146
White, William 39
Whitehouse, Alfred 123, 125
Whitianga 211
Whitmore, George 98–9
*Wi Parata* v *The Bishop of Wellington* 107
Wigram, Sir Henry 150, 157
Wilde, Fran 252
Wilder, George 214
Wilding, Anthony 135–6
wildlife, exotic 85, 96
Wilkins, Maurice 215
*Will Watch* 60, 61
*William Bryan* 60
William, Prince 246
Williams, Henry 39, 44, 45, 48, 54, 56
Williams, Pixie 192
Williams, William 48
Williams, Yvette 109, 198, 201
Wilson, Robert 108
Wimbledon 136, 247

*Wimmera* 152
wine 213
wireless telegraphy 132, 135, 138, 139, 142, 158
Wireless Telegraphy Act 1903 132
*Wolf* 150, 151, 152
women: academic pioneers 103, 106, 118; cabinet members 190; equal pay 231; first Anglican bishop 258; first doctor 118; first factory inspector 122; first governor-general 259; first magistrate 234; first mayor 121; first minister of finance 258; first ordained minister 210;first police recruits 180; first to climb Aoraki/Mt Cook 142; first to swim Cook Strait 238; first women's union 116; franchise 118, 120, 121, **121**; jurors 182, 211; Legislative Council membership 189; Maori 193, 198; Members of Parliament 154, 169, 189, 190, 193; National Council of Women 123; unemployment 165, 169; World War II 179, **179**. *See also* feminism
Women's Army Auxiliary Corps 179
Women's Auxiliary Air Force 179, **179**
Women's Christian Temperance Union 118, 120
Women Jurors' Act 182
Women's Parliamentary Rights Act 1919 154
Women's Royal Naval Service 179
Woods, J.J. 106
wool 65, 80, 103, 194, 199. *See also* sheep farming
Workers' Compensation for Accidents Act 1900 128
Workers' Dwellings Act 1905 134
working hours: 40-hour week 172, 242; eight-hour working day 55
World Bank 213
World Cup (rugby) 253, **254**
World Cup (soccer) 245
World War I: anti-German violence 148; armistice 153; casualties 147, 148, 149, 150, 151, 154; conscription 150–1; declaration of war 146; Egypt 147, 149; Gallipoli 147, 148, **148**, 149; Middle East 149, 151; Samoa 146; Western Front 147, 149, 150, 151, 153
World War II: acknowledgement of burden carried by Britain 190; American soldiers in NZ 182, 183; anti-war protests 175–6; casualties 180, 185, 186, 189; conscription 178, 183; Crete 180; declaration of war 175; Egypt 176; Greece 179–80; Home Guard 178; Italy 184, 185, 186; Maori involvement 178, 182, 189; Middle East 182; mobilisation of manpower 181; North Africa 180, 181, 182, 183; Pacific 182, 183, 184, 185; VE Day 186; VJ Day 186; women's services 179, **179**
Worthington, Arthur 124